Environmental Impact Assessment for Developing Countries

This book is dedicated to Sonia P. Maltezou, who encouraged us to hold the Conference on which this book is based, as a token of true regard for a friend.

Environmental Impact Assessment for Developing Countries

Edited by

Asit K. Biswas
President, International Water Resources Association
President, International Society for Ecological Modelling
Vice-President, International Association for Clean Technology
Oxford, England

and

S. B. C. Agarwal
Head, Pollution Control Research Institute
Hardwar, India

Sponsored by

Pollution Control Research Institute, BHEL
United Nations Industrial Development Organisation
United Nations Environment Programme
International Society for Ecological Modelling
International Water Resources Association
International Association for Clean Technology

Butterworth-Heinemann Ltd
Linacre House, Jordan Hill, Oxford OX2 8DP

A member of the Reed Elsevier plc group

OXFORD LONDON BOSTON
MUNICH NEW DELHI SINGAPORE SYDNEY
TOKYO TORONTO WELLINGTON

First published 1992
Reprinted 1993
Paperback edition 1994

© PCRI, ISEM, IWRA, UNEP, UNIDO 1992

British Library Cataloguing in Publiction Data
Environmental Impact Assessment for
Developing Countries
  I. Biswas, Asit K
  II. Agarwala, S.B.C.
  333.709172

ISBN 0 7506 2139 7

Library of Congress Cataloguing in Publication Data
Environmental impact assessment for developing countries/edited by
  Asit K. Biswas and S.B.C. Agarwala

  p. cm.

  Includes bibliographical references and index.
  ISBN 0 7506 2139 7
  1. Environmental impact analysis — Developing countries — Congresses.
  I. Biswas, Asit K.   II. Agarwala, S.B.C.   III. Pollution Control
  Institute (Hardwar, India)   IV. International Conference on
  Environmental Impact Assessment (1991: New Delhi, India)
  TD194.68.D44E58 1992
  333.7'14'091724–dc20   92–3236
                                                       CIP

Typeset by MS Filmsetting Limited, Frome, Somerset
Printed and bound in Great Britain by Ipswich Book Company

Contents

Preface

This book is based on selected papers presented at an International Conference on Environment Impact Assessment, held at New Delhi, India. The Conference was organized by the Pollution Control Research Institute, Hardwar, India, with the support of the Government of India, through BHEL, United Nations Industrial Development Organization, United Nations Development Programme, United Nations Environment Programme, International Society for Ecological modelling, International Water Resources Association, and International Association for Clean Technology. Less than half of the papers presented were finally selected for publication in this volume, after rigorous peer review.

While environmental impact assessment is of comparatively recent origin, the importance of preservation of the environment and respect for nature have been underlying principles of many cultures of various developing countries. For example, a study of the ancient religious texts of India like *Vedas* and *Rigvedas* would clearly indicate the importance of love and respect for nature.

During the 1970s and 1980s the interest in and the awareness of environmental issues in developing countries increased significantly. The close interrelationship between environment and development came into sharper focus and became clearer than ever before. The current view from the South can be summed up as follows: *environment must not be ignored but development must not be impeded.* It is now generally accepted that environment and development are the two sides of the same coin.

The interest in environmental management in developing countries can be judged by the exponential growth of national environmental machineries. In 1972, during the time of the United Nations Conference on The Human Environment, held in Stockholm, there were only 11 national machineries, predominantly in the industrialized countries. A decade later, in 1981, the situation had changed dramatically, when 106 countries had such governmental machineries, the majority of which were in developing countries. Another decade later, in 1991 nearly all countries of the South have some form of governmental machineries to deal with various environmental issues. In one sense the situation is very similar as in the industrialized countries: these environmental machineries work more efficiently in some countries than in others, and their effectiveness even in one country often varies with time, depending on the people who are in power and the overall socio-political climate.

Formal environmental assessment as an integral part of environmental management is a comparatively new development for most developing countries. The required legislations and setting up of appropriate institutions were initiated mainly during the second half of the 1970s and in the 1980s. Most developing countries now require an environmental assessment of proposed development projects. However, it should be noted that whereas countries like the Philippines required environmental impact assessments of major projects in 1977, some important industrialized countries like the Federal Republic of Germany institutionalized similar requirements only about a decade later.

Many developing countries now have made EIA an integral component of the project clearance process. An analysis of the environmental assessment processes of all developing countries indicates that generally the Asian countries have been at the forefront of this type of environmental review. Many Asian developing countries like China, India, Indonesia, Malaysia, Pakistan, the Philippines, South Korea, Sri Lanka and Thailand have now carried out environmental assessments of new projects for some time. Two countries — Thailand and the Philippines — have now carried out several thousand environmental impact studies. According to my own personal estimate, over 11,500 EIA studies have now been completed in the Asian developing countries alone thus far. These countries have thus gained considerable experience with EIA studies of various types of project and their general use for rational environmental management.

An objective analysis of the quality of these EIA studies and their overall effectiveness indicates some very mixed results. Not only has the general effectiveness varied from one developing country to another, but also significant variations can often be observed within the same country.

There is no doubt that good environmental assessment has to be the heart of any sound environmental management process. However, environmental assessment methodologies used at present in developing countries leave much to be desired. Overall benefits have been somewhat sub-optimal.

There is an urgent need for an objective and reliable review of the current status of the effectiveness of using EIA in developing countries, methodologies used, their relative merits and constraints, main features of their implementation processes, and the institutional arrangements within which such assessments are carried out. The present emphasis on negative environmental impacts and general disregard of positive impacts must change. Environmental impacts must not have only negative connotations. The papers included in this book partly answer some of these issues, but clearly much more remains to be done.

On the basis of the papers presented during this Conference and my own experience as Senior Advisor to 16 developing countries and all important international development-oriented institutions, it is clear that a major problem has arisen due to the absence of proper monitoring and evaluation of the actual environmental impacts of projects. Undoubtedly, monitoring and evaluation are essential to ensure that compliance measures are properly carried out within the required timeframe. Equally, regular monitoring and evaluation would give a clear picture of the accuracies of environmental assessments, which can be used to further fine-tune the forecasting methods. Absence of proper monitoring and evaluation is now a major handicap for carrying out reliable environmental assessment.

If environmental assessments are properly carried out, the general result has often been measurable environmental benefits, which are cost-effective. Admittedly, many of our current assessment techniques are rather mediocre and significantly dependent on the limited experience and judgement of the analysts concerned in developing countries, but in my personal view, *in the final analysis, the issue is very definitely on the side of having an environmental assessment, even a mediocre one, rather than having no assessment at all.*

A major international conference can only be successfully held through the collective work of many people. There is no question that the success of the present one was primarily due to the hard work and dedication of S. B. C. Agarwala, A. K. Gupta, N. C. Trehan and other staff members of the Pollution control Research Institute. They were assisted by many other people, both from within and outside India. International organizations like UNIDO, UNDP and UNEP made a major contribution through their financial support of the participation costs of many foreign experts. UNIDO made a special contribution in terms of editing arrangements of this book, and UNEP assisted in its publication.

As the Chief Technical Advisor to the UNIDO-administered but UNDP-supported project which established Pollution Control Research Institute, it was indeed a great privilege to have been associated with the Institute as well as the Conference. I firmly believe that one of the main results of this Conference is the ready availability of the results of environmental impact assessment in developing countries. Such studies are not easy to find at present. This book will thus undoubtedly be an important addition to existing literature on this increasingly important subject. It should be of direct interest to anyone who would like additional information about environmental impact assessment for developing countries.

Asit K. Biswas
Senior Consultant to UNDP, UNEP and UNIDO

Part I

Overview and General Considerations

1

Environmental protection and development: how to achieve a balance?

N. C. Thanh and D. M. Tam

Many of the development projects in the past, and even as recently as in the 1970s, have been implemented with little environmental concern. This is mainly due to the fact that knowledge of environmental impacts and impact assessment technology was not fully developed at that time. As a result, a number of large-scale development projects have led to adverse impacts of a large magnitude. These adverse impacts have created strong feelings among people aware of environmental problems and have bred movements that promote environmental protection and protest against development. Although this is an encouraging sign, the arguments for environmental protection have too often been focused on adverse impacts but ignored greater positive benefits. The publication *The Careless Technology* (Farvar and Milton, 1972) has become a classic in the fight for environmental protection. It was followed by various works focusing on criticizing large-scale development projects, notably the recent comprehensive compilation by Goldsmith and Hildyard (1985).

On the other hand, it is inevitable that, in their zeal, authorities have often pushed forward their development efforts with little consideration of potential adverse impacts or of how to minimize these impacts. Thus, it has been frequently observed that in our history of development the same mistake was made many times over.

The entire complex situation has been reduced to the issue of development versus environment, whose acceptable answer is still a subject for debates. This chapter will attempt to clarify the situation, and to raise some relevant issues for further consideration and study.

Environmental impact in the developing countries context

One of the common arguments from those raising environmental awareness in development is that developing countries often suffer more from adverse impacts created by development projects than in similar undertakings in developed countries. The situation becomes worse if the technology from industrialized countries is used in developing countries without proper adaptation. Adverse environmental impacts from development projects, indeed, seem to have been more severe in developing countries. However, the history of development in industrialized countries also abounds with resulting adverse impacts. In the US, the Tennessee Valley scheme in its debut led to violent outbreaks of malaria. The massive James Bay Project in Canada caused utter disruption in the socio-cultural structure of the native Indians. The Dust Bowl could be considered as an adverse impact from improper agricultural and soil conservation practices. These impacts created initial problems at a magnitude as in similar projects in developing countries. However, developed countries, thanks to their rich resources (including human and material), have been able to cope with those environmental disasters more effectively.

On the other hand, faced with so many top priorities and constraints, developing countries cannot cope with normal day-to-day difficulties, let alone with sudden adverse impacts caused by development. For instance, due to the improper resettlement process in hydropower projects in at least two African countries, the resettled people could not cultivate sufficient food for their own requirement. In each case, international aid agencies had to rush in relief to prevent a major food shortage. Even so, these incidences have become big news. The same mistake in resettlement could have occurred in any developed country, but it would have been dealt with more effectively, and so the incidence would have been soon all forgotten.

It is true that developing countries cannot afford to make severe mistakes. Nevertheless, they should have a chance to try and learn. In this regard, it is true the technology transferred from industrialized countries has sometimes not worked as well as expected. Due to specific climatic, sociocultural and economic conditions which are interlinked in complex mechanisms, development in developing countries takes a tortuous, difficult road. However, there are numerous factors that contribute to the fate of Western technology in the developing country environment. For one thing, most developing countries are in the tropics, and the special characteristics of the tropical ecosystem make a considerable difference. The development of tropical ecology as a unique branch of science has been relatively fast in the last few decades, and this helps us know more and more about the tropics. The treatise by Ewusie (1980) could be cited as an example.

But considering environmental impact in the physical and biological context – such as tropical forests, tropical wildlife, the mangroves, the corals – is not adequate. The human factor – humans themselves, their behaviours, structures – also needs to be considered. We are all aware, for example, that tropical rain forests are very rich in species diversity and have high turn-over rates of materials. Once this species diversity is altered, the delicate balance of the forest will be thoroughly altered. The high turn-over of chemicals means that, in contrast to temperate forests, most nutrients are locked in the luxurious vegetation but exist in small quantities in the soil. Under these conditions, the slash-and-burn cultivation technique can create extensive damage to this kind of ecosystem, perhaps more extensive than if the same technique is applied in temperate forests. The natural tendency, then, is to condemn slash-and-burn agriculture and to introduce modern sedentary agriculture using fertilizers, pesticides and improved crop varieties. However, resettling the moving subsistence agriculturists and teaching them modern agricultural techniques is not a satisfactory solution if we ignore the sociocultural characters of these people, such as the way they live together in close knits, their dietary habits, the crop varieties they cultivate, their disease resistance and susceptibility, etc. Ignoring these factors may cause utter disruption to the life of these people. Meanwhile, the state of the environment is no better as the single problem in forest conservation has now become the numerous problems of chemical contamination, eutrophication, soil alkalization, disease propagation ... due to improper introduction of modern technology and lifestyle to the ignorant people. Once these problems become apparent, we may find out – too late – that it is better not to have any interventions at all than to have inappropriate interventions.

The complexity of the interrelationships between humans and their environment is such that many facets are still not fully understood and appreciated. While more knowledge is needed about this complexity, we can look at the past and draw some lessons.

Development: the lessons learned

It is undeniable that development projects, particularly large-scale ones, may create adverse impacts. But essentially what do we know about the whys and hows of these impacts? We can extract some lessons learned from actual cases happening in the past which indicate what we know, or what we do not know, about development and impact.

The what and the why

In the search for knowledge about environmental impact of development, we often gather the bare facts but not the logic or mechanism behind them. For example, surveys on the Nam Pong Reservoir in Thailand as a part of the post-mortem assessment of this project indicated that impoundment had severe impact on catfish but favoured murrels (Chatarupavanich, 1979). However, the reason for this change in species diversity is not explained. This is quite unfortunate since, suppose we carry out ten similar studies in ten different projects and from one study we learn that species A is adversely affected and species B thrives, then from another study we find that species C is dying and species D is propagating, and so on ..., we still cannot learn anything from these studies! We still do not know how to promote the species we prefer and suppress the species we do not want. With such uncertainty, environmental impact assessment indeed still has a long way to go.

The cause-and-effect relationships

As mentioned above, adverse impacts occur often as a result of complex processes that have not been fully understood. In many cases, the causal linkages cannot be clearly seen. Environmental impact assessment and especially prediction is still an art, not a science. Among the adverse impacts caused by the project, it is difficult or even impossible to determine what extent or portion of the impact is caused by the project *per se*. For instance, it has often been claimed that water development projects have increased the number of cases of water-borne diseases such as schistosomiasis. While it is true that the incidence rate of these diseases increased after the completion of the project, the spread of these diseases has resulted from a number of factors, of which the project contributed only some. These factors include, for example: (1) a large number of labourers migrating to the construction site from far-away places, bringing with them diseases that do not exist at the site at first; or (2) subsequent spin-off development at the project region, attracting outside settlers and tourists; or (3) better transport which induces more people to come into contact with the natural water bodies which still have the same level of pathogenic agents as before.

More research is necessary to define the cause-and-effect relationships between interventions and impacts, so that sufficient knowledge will be put to good use in balancing environment and development. Current data and information need to be critically reviewed rather than perfunctorily accepted.

Data reliability

With regard to data and information, we tend to rely on what was said before, without assessing its reliability or validity. For example, it has been repeatedly quoted that the number of schistosomiasis victims all over the world is 200 million. Reviewing a limited literature, the authors found this figure from Obeng (1978), Biswas (1982), and Milligan and Thomas (1986) who quoted Platt (1974). Faced with the same figure first found in 1974 and quoted in 1978, 1982 and 1986, we cannot help but put some questions: (1) what is the very origin of this figure, in what study, conducted by whom and by what methodology?; (2) each time when the figure was quoted was there any update study which found the figure to be unchanged, or the same figure was simply quoted from the previous source?

Of course the authors of this chapter (who also have the same habit of quoting without question!) do not mean to criticize our colleagues. We raise this fact simply to stress that, indeed, we still know quite little about what we have achieved in the past, and where we are standing now. As long as this state remains, it is still difficult to learn from the past and plan for the future.

Sociocultural impacts

Among adverse impacts that have been observed, those on sociocultural systems are usually the most severe. In many cases, the entire social structures have been disrupted, causing extensive trauma to the local people whose life has been irreversibly altered. Again, this type of impact also occurred in industrialized countries. We have seen that the large hydropower projects in Canada caused considerable hardship to the native Indians. Many of the hydropower projects in Africa have also caused severe disruption to native people, who could not adapt to modern life once uprooted from their traditional environment.

These cases indicate that while engineers can build huge and solid physical structures under extremely difficult conditions, tap large amounts of natural resources and dominate natural powers, engineering sociology seems to lag behind. Humans have learned substantially about the environment around them, but they have yet to know much about their brethren! In the past, emphasis in project planning was biased towards physical hard figures. Gradually sociocultural study was introduced into the planning, but the findings were usually expressed in numerical terms. Now the situation is improving. International agencies, such as the World Bank, have insisted that the relocated people should be no worse off, and preferably better off, with the project. All resettlement costs, such as employment creation and compensation expenses, have to be incorporated in project analysis. Detailed resettlement plans are essential before any project is to be appraised for assistance by the World Bank. While headquarters of agencies have good intentions, it may take time for local project personnel seriously to adopt the new policy direction.

The trade-off

Adverse impact should be compared with benefits, and this is where trade-offs exist. Take an example from a hydropower scheme. This project will improve the agronomy (and hence nutrition) and develop the industry (and hence export earnings), while it will reduce the area of virgin forests and wildlife. The key question is, in the long term in which way the country will be better off: with the improved agronomy and industry but with a damaged environment?, or with the subsistent agronomy and outdated industry but with a preserved wild ecosystem? It is the ultimate fate of the nation as a whole that counts, not the present or near-future conditions of a certain sector of the economy, a certain region of the country, or a certain group of the population. Evaluating the trade-offs is a delicate issue and consensus is seldom achieved. In this regard, case studies from elsewhere can be helpful. Some examples can be found in Goodland (1986).

The compensation

As discussed above, adverse impacts may occur for some sectors of the economy or regions of the country while benefits are brought about to other sectors/regions, and the total result for the entire economy is usually beneficial. Much has been said about the loss of sardine in the Mediterranean as a result of the High Aswan Dam, but the gain in fisheries in the newly-created reservoir has been many times over the sardine loss. The High Aswan Dam has doubled Egypt's electricity generating capacity, helped prevent disastrous floods, improved river navigation, created a vast potential fishery in the reservoir that has more than compensated for the sardine loss in the Mediterranean, and attracted more tourism. While the total construction cost of the dam (including subsidiary projects and electric power lines) was Egyptian sterling 450 million, the annual return on full operation was 225 million: 140 million from agricultural production, 100 million from hydropower, 10 million from flood protection, and 5 million from navigation. In any economic sense, the dam is a good investment indeed. Thus, it is not wise to lament on adverse effects while overlooking the real purposes of, and accomplishment in, development.

Are we too negative?

In many environmental impact assessment studies, more attention has been given to adverse impacts and their remedial measures rather than to a balance analysis between adverse impacts and benefits. So much so that the neutral term 'impact' is now often used — and understood — as 'adverse impact'! To be fair, this situation is understandable since adverse impacts are more conspicuous and can make big news while benefits tend to happen more silently. While we have often heard, in clear numerical terms, about the increase in the cases of water-borne diseases as a result of water development projects, we have seldom been informed about the improvement in nutrition of the local people as a result of increased food production, about the fact that more and fresher farm products are delivered to the urban markets as the result of improved transport, or little about the increase in school attendance as a result of reduced child labour at the home. These benefits are difficult to measure and even harder to see.

Similarly, while we have known about earth tremors or downstream fishery losses as possible consequences of large reservoirs, we have heard little about spin-off development achievements such as community development, hygiene education, or illiteracy eradication. While an entire specific agency is blamed for some obvious mishaps, many of their field workers do not get credit for what they accomplish in obscurity.

It is high time we asked ourselves if we have made a fair evaluation between improvement of poverty and backwardness on the one hand and the protection of our environment on the other.

Toward a balance between sustained development and environmental protection

Combining the lessons learned, it could be concluded that criticisms towards past and planned development projects, while usefully creating awareness among the general populace as well as in policy-makers, have often become unduly harsh and may even impede development.

Meanwhile, more and more lodging, food, water and other commodities have to be provided to *each* person in the ever-increasing population. This means that the total commodities and services to be provided will have to be increased at a rate much faster than the population growth rate. Thus, the development process cannot even be slowed down; it should be accelerated to satisfy various human needs. Governmental and international agencies have been hard pressed to push their projects to the implementation phase in order to achieve results as early as possible at an economic cost as low as possible. This has caused them to play down the importance of environmental protection. The common attitude once was to develop first and deal with impacts later. Of course, this is not justifiable. There are signs indicating that this situation is being rectified.

A balance between environmental protection and sustained development should be sought so that the environment is protected while the development pace is ensured. In order to do this, it is necessary to re-assess the common arguments of both 'environment' and 'development' camps. The following principles are outlined to achieve this balance.

Sound awareness towards environment and development

It is necessary to create rational and sensible environmental awareness in all people concerned: environmentalists, engineers, planners, politicians, and the general public. This awareness should be based on the consensus that the environment must be protected, and the development process must be carried on. Public education and participation is necessary to create a healthy atmosphere for the debates on the pros and cons of a development project.

More environmental awareness should be raised among development authorities. In many cases in the past, potential adverse impacts had been forewarned – in vain, and recommendations made for mitigation measures – without follow-up. Before the construction of one large dam in Africa, the planners had been aware of potential public health problems and prepared an *'exceptionally detailed and excellent study'* which *'should be considered as a classic model for the planner'* (Donaldson, 1978). Nevertheless, the recommendations in this study were not fully implemented, leading to costly damages and costly remedial measures. Warnings have not been heeded with various reasons: time is short, resources are limited, qualified personnel is lacking ... But the usual basic reason behind all of this has been that project personnel have not been fully aware of potential impacts, and have not seen the need for those mitigation measures. What they really have had in mind has been the 'gross benefits', not the 'net benefits' (being 'gross benefits' minus adverse impacts). There are 'hidden costs' in these impacts that seldom show up in engineer's proposals or economist's balance sheets. For example, 100 000 people evacuated from Lake Nasser have become more dependent on the government since their economic self-sufficiency has decreased (Lee, 1985). As gross benefits have been predetermined, we have to maximize the net benefits of the project by minimizing the adverse impacts.

Likewise, 'development awareness' should be raised among environmentalists. Development is inherently difficult. And yet, the issue has been over-simplified: if there are potential adverse impacts, then the project should be scrapped! While no alternative is offered, there is no clear suggestion on how the vicious cycle of poverty can be broken, how the nutritional status of the people increased, how to earn more foreign exchange for industrialization, etc.

Public participation

In the debates concerning the pros and cons of a specific large-scale development project, there are often two extreme sides: the development authorities as a defender, and a group of environmentalists as an accuser. The so-called victims of the project (e.g. the native people to be resettled elsewhere as their land will be flooded by a new hydropower reservoir) and the beneficiaries (e.g. the city people who will enjoy inexpensive electricity) are largely not involved. Had they been, the first group would have expressed their wish on how they want their new life to be, and the second would have requested that the project be implemented perhaps with some modifications. Had the environmentalists been involved in the development policy-making process and presented with 'inside' hard facts, they would realize that, in fact, the matter of whether to go ahead with the project or to stop it is not that simple.

Especially the roles of women should be enhanced. Women play key roles in home economics (including activities to generate home income such as animal husbandry, vegetable gardening, crafts making), hygiene education for their children, and home financial planning. Women suffer first from hardship in water collection, disposal of wastewater, nightsoil and refuse, and malnutrition (while their husbands and children have more privilege in sharing the limited amount of food available to the family). Development projects should be planned and implemented with a view toward enhancing women's status and privileges while not creating more burdens for them.

Interdisciplinry teamwork

The above observation indicates that in our modern but complex times, an endeavour in development requires teamwork from people of various disciplines: planners, administrators and managers, engineers, financial analysts, economists, and sociologists.

In fact, it is now generally recognized that 'hardware' specialists alone cannot bring about sustained development. They should be assisted by 'software' colleagues; those working in the fields of community development, public information, women-in-development, institutional strengthening, and other sociocultural aspects. Specialized software fields of expertise such as social agronomy, social forestry, social water, etc., should be developed in parallel with other capabilities.

Compromising attitude

In the debates on the planned project, besides studying the potential adverse impacts if the project is implemented, possible hardship or problems if the project is rejected should also be considered. Inasmuch as we have to preserve our environment, we likewise have to continually improve our standards of living. Usually a compromise, but not a fanatic attitude, is required.

Target definition

The expected benefits and intended beneficiaries of development projects should be clearly defined and agreed upon from the start. Failing this, we will witness unwanted results deviating far from what we intend. As a specific example, in a hydropower project in one Southeast Asian country the people living around the newly-created reservoir did not benefit from the project to any appreciable extent. While it has been taken for granted that the nutritional status of the people in the dam and irrigation areas will be improved due to the increase in food production, in practice this may not materialize. The reasons for the lack of improvement in the nutritional status of the beneficiary people include: (1) increase in endemic diseases if the living and eating habits do not change; (2) without radical changes in dietary habits the people may have more money but use this money for purposes other than to buy more food; and (3) increased food production does not mean increased income earning for the local people, but instead the middlemen are those who benefit (Harinasuta, 1975).

This case suggests that contingency measures should be planned, to be taken if the results differ from initial expectations and intentions.

Equitable distribution of benefits

In almost every hydropower project, city dwellers hundreds of kilometres away enjoy inexpensive electricity while people at the site have their social life utterly disrupted, their health threatened by new diseases, and their means of living destroyed. This unequal distribution is a cause for dissent from the disadvantaged and for strong protest from the sympathetic people fighting against the project. While development projects aim toward the majority, they should not cause excessive damage to the minority, the underprivileged, or the politically weak. While benefit maximization is the norm, equitable benefit distribution is equally important. In this regard, environmental movements, on behalf of those who lack economic and political power and those cannot speak for themselves, are laudable.

Constant re-assessment of the development process

Experience has indicated that adverse impacts could, indeed, have been prevented or minimized using available technology and proper management techniques. On the other hand, new impacts may develop with a change in development policy. One example will clarify this fact. The spread of guinea worm has had an adverse impact on a number of water-development projects. However, in Ghana the disease was once reduced largely as a result of a major borehole-handpump project which encouraged the use of water collected from protected wells. The situation changed when the authorities introduced tariffs as a means of cost recovery. This tariff scheme forced villagers to revert to their traditional contaminated water sources. Guinea worm, again, has spread throughout the Upper Region of Ghana.

Once again, this example shows that technology is not enough. It depends on how the technology is used, and how the development process is planned and managed.

Project evaluation

Development projects in the last two or three decades offer rich lessons from which we can learn. It is also desirable that we facilitate this learning process for those who will take up the work based on our successes and failures. Project evaluation should be an integral part in the project cycle. Unfortunately, many project evaluations in the past have not yielded meaningful results due to the lack of suitable baseline data. Collection and analysis of baseline data during the preparatory phase of the project is vital for subsequent evaluation. International development agencies have now realized the importance of project evaluation, and have prepared methodology for this purpose. For example, see CIDA (1985). As a rule of thumb, approximately 5 per cent of the total project should be allocated for project evaluation.

Environmental auditing

As a deviation from project evaluation but with the same goal, the concept of environmental auditing could be introduced for environmental protection in development projects. In this context, environmental auditing may be understood as a systematic process of determining whether the interventions of the project are in compliance with regulatory requirements and with the national policies and standards for environmental management. Auditing is a methodical examination involving analyses, tests and confirmations of the procedures and practices in place at the project area. As financial auditing is to protect the investors and the companies in general by ascertaining that proper procedures are applied to all transactions, environmental auditing is to assure the authorities and the public that all measures have been taken to protect the environment, the public and the project staff against all short-term and long-term hazards.

Environmental auditing could well be the only tool to help identify critical factors such as:

- lack of awareness and/or understanding of environmental regulations;
- inadequately designed, poorly maintained and protected facilities and equipment;
- the lack of authority and responsibility delineation in environmental matters; and
- external forces (such as earthquakes, floods, fires, sabotage ...) which may affect the project integrity.

Conclusion

Development is complex. This paper cannot discuss in-depth all relevant issues. Worse, there may be more questions than answers. As many of the issues raised have not reached consensus, each of the points discussed here could well become a controversy. Debates are still raging on the how-to in achieving both development and environmental protection at the same time. These debates have often involved much emotion rather than reasoning. For example, a question of *'Who is more important, man or monkey?'* arose during one debate on a dam proposal in India. The issue should be reviewed from all viewpoints with rationale, so that the environment will not be ignored, and development will not be impeded.

Observing the current trends, it is encouraging to note that governmental agencies have lately taken more serious consideration towards environmental protection in development. All have learned hard lessons, and have not tried to repeat the same mistakes. They should be encouraged and assisted in this endeavour.

Acknowledgements

We thank our friend, Dr Asit K. Biswas, who contributed some ideas discussed in this paper. While Dr Biswas can share any appreciation, the authors are solely responsible for the contents presented in this paper. The ideas expressed herein do not necessarily reflect the views of the authors' affiliations.

References

Biswas, A. K. (1982) Environment and sustainable water development. In *Water for Human Consumption — Man and his Environment.* Tycooly International Publishing, Dublin.

Chatarupavanich, V. (1979) Nam Pong 'post-mortem' environmental analysis. In *Proceedings of National Seminar on Environmental Impact Statement — Guidelines for Water Resources Development*, Office of the National Environment Board, Bangkok, Thailand.

CIDA (1985) *A Practical Guide for Conducting Project Evaluations*, Canadian International Development Agency, Hull, Canada.

Donaldson, D. (1978) Health issues in developing country projects. In *Environmental Impacts of International Civil Engineering Projects and Practices* (eds C. G. Gunnerson and J. M. Kalbermatten), American Society of Civil Engineers, New York.

Ewusie, J. Y. (1980) *Elements of Tropical Ecology*, Heinemann Educational Books, London.

Farvar, M. T. and Milton, J. P. (eds) (1972) *The Careless Technology*, The Natural History Press/Garden City, New York.

Goldsmith, E. and Hildyard, N. (1985) *The Social and Environmental Effects of Large Dams*, Wadebridge Ecological Centre, UK.

Goodland, R. (1986) Hydro and the environment: Evaluating the tradeoffs. *International Water Power and Dam Construction*, **38**(11), 25–33.

Harinasuta, C. (1975) Ubolratana Dam Complex, Thailand. In *Man-made Lakes and Human Health* (Eds N. F. Stanley and M. P. Alpers), Academic Press, New York.

Lee, J. A. (1985) *The Environment, Public Health and Human Ecology — Considerations for Economic Development*, Johns Hopkins University Press, Baltimore, Maryland, USA.

Milligan, P. and Thomas, M. P. (1986) Relationship between development and disease. *The Environmentalist*, 6(2), 129–140.

Obeng, L. (1978) Starvation or bilharzia? — a rural development dilemma. *Water Supply and Management*, 2(4), 343–350.

Platt, J. (1974) *Medical Care and Society*, 9th CIOMS Conference, Rio de Janeiro.

2
Environmental impact assessment in Asia: Lessons from the past decade
G. Werner

Environmental protection is a relatively new issue for most developing countries. Their pertinent legislations and institutional set-ups stem from the late seventies or early eighties, while industrialized countries have a longer tradition, especially in the field of pollution control. Environmental impact assessment (EIA), however, is a new instrument for both developed and developing countries. Interestingly, while the Philippines required EIA for certain types of projects since 1977, Germany has just started to institutionalize the use of EIA.

Many developing countries in Asia have EIA regulations and gained experience with this approach. For example China, India, Indonesia, Malaysia, Pakistan, the Philippines, the Republic of Korea, Sri Lanka and Thailand have legal provisions for government agencies to require EIA approval of specific types of projects. Thailand and the Philippines have processed several thousands of Impact Documents. Over 10 000 EIA documents are likely to have been produced in Asian developing countries. This indicates the extent of experience that some developing countries have gained with EIA.

Most experts from international institutions (e.g. UNEP, World Bank, etc.), national environmental agencies as well as the academics, agree that EIA still needs promotion and improvement. It is now possible to make recommendations based on the experience so far gained in the Asian countries. This paper summarizes practical experiences gained with EIA in selected Asian developing countries in order that appropriate recommendations can be made. The discussion is focused on issues rarely dealt with in scientific publications but is undoubtedly of considerable practical significance.

EIA in developing countries of Asia – present status

The EIA procedure used at present is more or less standardized and consists of the basic steps of screening, initial environmental examination

(IEE), scoping, impact statement preparation, review and final decision, monitoring and auditing. Most countries review projects based on their potential environmental impact. The definitions used are however often somewhat general. Typical formulations are 'major industrial projects' or 'large reservoirs'. Only two countries, Thailand and the Philippines, have quantitative technical specifications which are part of the regulations. Malaysia, India and Indonesia are currently in the process of preparing such project specifications. Questionnaires or checklists are additionally employed for screening purposes.

Initial environmental examination, called preliminary assessment in Malaysia and project description in the Philippines, is carried out in order to determine the need and desirability of an impact study and to identify the relevant issues to be covered by the assessment report. Formalized outlines, matrices or checklists are provided by the environmental agencies.

All countries consider the full-scale impact assessment. This may be called environmental impact statement, impact study or detailed assessment report, and can be considered to be the heart of the EIA process. The contents of an impact statement should cover the following topics:

- description of the project, focusing on possible sources of environmental impacts;
- description of the environmental situation before the implementation of the project;
- analysis and prediction of environmental impacts resulting from the project;
- comparison/evaluation of environmental conditions with or without the project (eventual project alternatives); and
- outlining of mitigation measures needed to minimize adverse impacts.

The formal responsibility for the preparation of the impact statement usually lies with the project proponent, but the actual work is mostly carried out by consultants.

On the basis of the reviews carried out for various Asian countries, it can be said that mitigation measures and their implementation, environmental monitoring and compliance control need to be strengthened. Most countries do not have specific regulations to monitor and control the extent of implementation of the proposed remedial measures. Indonesia and Sri Lanka require an environmental management plan. Only Thailand carries out post-project appraisal on a regular basis. Specific regulations, however, do not exist.

A problem still unresolved is proper co-ordination with other concerned ministries, especially when their co-operation is needed to implement mitigation measures, which are their responsibility. Existing provisions only stipulate responsibilities of the project proponent in this area.

Legislation and administration

Most Asian countries have enacted general environmental legislations only recently. These framework legislations state the right of every person to a good and healthy environment and stress the need to harmonize development and environment. Regulatory functions lie with environmental agencies, either as a department or a ministry (India, Indonesia, Malaysia, Sri Lanka, Bangladesh and Nepal) or a central environmental agency (the Philippines, Thailand, China). Most of the organizations responsible for EIA are weak in terms of available manpower, budget and resources.

EIA techniques

Various guidelines, models and methods have been developed to make the EIA process more effective. The main focus was directed at the development of methods for impact identification and evaluation. Formalized outlines, questionnaires, checklists and matrices have been developed and put into use for screening, IEE and scoping. Manuals, handbooks and sectoral guidelines assist the preparation of impact statements. In addition, supportive information systems such as directories, reference materials and data banks, where available, are helpful.

Practical guidelines to assist the project proponent to identify and select adequate mitigation measures and to implement an environmental management plan are still lacking. Existing recommendations are sometimes too general ('careful planning required') or limited to a list of environmental standards. Guidelines for compliance monitoring, for the most part, are non-existent.

Some problems and overlooked issues

Most developing countries now recognize the need to promote and strengthen EIA processes. The following discussion attempts to draw attention to sometimes overlooked or underestimated problems and issues. This is not intended to provide a complete list of problems that need to be resolved but to reflect the author's practical experience with EIA in various Asian countries.

EIA – means or an end?

The practical use of EIA in many developing countries leads to the impression that EIA is often considered to be an end rather than means to ensure better environmental protection. Endorsement of the impact statement often seems to be the final activity. In the vast majority of cases, only very limited sections of the statement deal with environmental management. Research has concentrated on impact identification and evaluation. Legal provisions are incomplete. Compliance monitoring at best is weak and no national environmental agency or research institution has ever tried to quantify the contribution of EIA to enhance environmental quality or to reduce pollution. It is thus impossible to evaluate the usefulness of EIA compared with other environmental policy instruments such as standards, regulations, incentives, etc. The issue raised might be related to a second problem.

EIA – planning tool or decision-making instrument?

EIA can be used for two principal functions:

1 as a decision-making instrument to decide upon acceptability of a project based on its environmental costs, and
2 as a planning tool to minimize adverse impacts caused by a project (assuming that the project will be approved).

Practical experiences from Thailand and the Philippines, the two countries having the longest EIA experience in Asia, show that out of several thousand impact statements processed during the past decade, *not a single project* was denied clearance due to environmental reasons. In other words, those countries use EIA as a planning tool.

The consequence of this state of affairs is obvious: not impact evaluation but environmental management should be the heart of the EIA process. Only Indonesia and Sri Lanka explicitly require such an environmental management plan. These observations indicate that EIA is still considered a decision-making instrument. The implications for effectiveness and efficiency are obvious.

Some countries require EIA even for small projects with rather minor environmental impacts (e.g. sawmills or sand and gravel mining projects in the Philippines). The usefulness of EIA for such projects is somewhat questionable since regulations might be more appropriate to ensure their environmental appropriateness and acceptability. The issues raised show the need to clarify the role of EIA as an environmental policy instrument and to readjust this tool accordingly.

Lack of integration into the project cycle

Experience indicates that impact assessment processes are initiated only after project preparation is near completion. The co-ordination of the EIA procedure and the project cycle is still weak. Environmentalists do not communicate with the project engineers who for the most part are not aware of the environmental consequences of their work. Integration of EIA into project planning should maximize its effectiveness and also minimize delays in project implementation.

Lack of resources and information

In contrast to developed countries, availability of resources and background data in developing countries is limited. The EIA Group of the Philippines, for example, responsible for processing hundreds of EIA documents annually, had only a staff of five experts in 1985/86. Environmental quality monitoring (air, water, natural resources, etc.) is still in its infancy. The need for support, however, has been recognized by many donor agencies and accordingly programmes and projects are being initiated.

Conclusions and recommendations

On the basis of the analysis carried out, the following conclusions and recommendations can be made.

1 All concerned environmental agencies should clarify their perception of EIA as an environmental policy instrument. If EIA is considered to be a planning tool for individual, project-specific mitigation measures, then the EIA procedures should be adjusted accordingly. This would require consideration of the following factors.
   - The environmental management plan must be the heart of the EIA procedure. Impact identification, impact assessment, etc., have to serve the purpose of environmental management. Recommended outlines and guidelines have to be adjusted accordingly. Emphasis on environmental management should be reflected in the project documents.
   - Compliance monitoring and project auditing should be institutionalized and carried out on a regular basis.
   - Close co-ordination of EIA with project cycle should be institutionalized. In the long run, EIA should be considered to be an integrated part of the pertinent project documents (pre-feasibility study, feasibility study, engineering report).
2 The legal provisions should be adjusted and expanded accordingly. For certain project types, it might be necessary to regulate responsibilities and involvement of other concerned ministries.
3 A sawmill has only minor impacts compared with a large reservoir. Environmental agencies requiring EIA even for small projects should

evaluate the usefulness of EIA compared with other instruments. Regulations might eventually prove more effective and less costly.

4 The lack of manpower and resources in most developing countries calls for flexible and innovative solutions. Biological monitoring of environmental quality (air, water), for example, could play an important role in the future.

Part II

Environmental Impact Analyses

3

Air pollution impact assessment of chemical plants in Israel

Michael Graber

Regulations in Israel requiring the preparation of environmental impact assessments (EIAs) for certain new development projects became effective in July 1982.

These regulations, issued under the authority of the Planning and Building Law (1965), state that planning agencies (i.e., the National Planning Council, or the Regional and Local Planning Committees) shall not review certain new project plans and shall not issue them a building permit unless an EIA has been prepared and is attached to the project plan submitted to the planning agency.

Preparation of an EIA is mandatory for any of the following types of projects, if in the opinion of the planning agency it will have a significant impact on its environment:

1 Electric generation power plants; airports; seaports; and hazardous waste disposal sites.
2 Helipads; jetties; national lines of water supply; dams and reservoirs; wastewater treatment plants; mines; and quarries.
3 Any industrial plant located outside an area assigned to industrial activities or, any industrial plant the siting, scope or production process of which, in the opinion of the planning agency reviewing the project plan, is likely to cause a significant environmental impact beyond the local neighbourhood.
4 In addition, any member of the planning agency reviewing the project plan may require at any stage of the review that an EIA is submitted by the project proponent for the review of the planning agency.

The EIA submitted to the planning agency should cover the following topics:

1 An environmental description of the existing site(s) of the proposed project within the area that, in the opinion of the planning agency, might be adversely influenced by the project.
2 Justification for choosing the preferred site for the project.
3 Description of the new activities to be carried out as part of the proposed project.

4   Description and assessment of the anticipated or forecasted impact on the environment as result of the new activities, as well as a description of the measures to be taken by the project proponent to prevent or minimize adverse impacts.
5   Findings and proposals for specific instructions, to be included in the building permit.

The EIA should be prepared along guidelines issued by the planning agency. In practice, the guidelines are being prepared by the Director of the Israel Environmental Protection Service (IEPS), who acts also as the environmental adviser to the National Planning Committee.

Since 1982, more than 50 EIAs dealing with various development projects have been submitted to, reviewed and approved by the planning agencies in Israel. The first EIA (the coal-fired power plant near Ceasarea — a historic centre dating from the Roman era) was actually approved before the EIA regulations were promulgated. A description of the Israeli experience with EIAs has been presented in a report on the Ceasarea EIA prepared for UNEP (Etzion, *et al.*, 1986) and by Marinov and Jernelov (1987). It is worthwhile to note the similarity between the EIA system practised in Israel and the EIA system recommended by Biswas and Geping (1987, Chapter 7).

EIAs were also required for new installations to be added to existing chemical plants situated in the Ramat Hovav Industrial Complex near Be'er-Sheva. The guidelines issued by the IEPS for the preparation of the air quality section of these EIAs required information regarding emission inventory, air quality assessment and industrial hazard assessment. These subjects will be dealt with in detail in the following sections.

Plant emission inventory

The objective of a plant emission inventory (namely, an inventory of all the pollutants and toxic substances emitted from a given plant into the atmosphere) is to supply information regarding the types of airborne substances emitted by the plant, the types of emission sources and their location inside the plant, the strength of these sources (in terms of quantities of pollution emitted as well as emission rates), expressed both as a function of the production rate and of the efficiency of the equipment installed to control those emissions.

It should be noted that through the EIA process project proponents are encouraged to adopt plant designs which are based on clean technologies which both reduce industry's emissions of pollutants into the atmosphere as well as use less energy (UNEP, 1982).

The information obtained from emission inventories is essential to air quality management. It serves, for example, as input data for mathematical dispersion models and in the investigation of the efficiencies of the measures chosen to control airborne emissions.

Types of substances emitted into the atmosphere

An emission inventory should identify and list the different types of pollutants (including odorous and toxic substances, as well as fuel burning products such as SO_2, NO_x, CO, and particulate matter) emitted into the atmosphere from all the sources of the plant, including fugitive emissions, under both normal operating conditions and during chemical incidents.

Information on the installations and facilities in the plant

In this section of the EIA, a description should be given of the installations and facilities of the plant, the production processes that are of relevance to airborne emissions, as well as the equipment installed to control air pollution emissions.

A summary listing all the installations and facilities of the plant emitting airborne pollutants (through stacks, vents, or fugitive emissions) under normal operating conditions should be provided. This summary should also list, for each type of pollutant and for every installation, the quantities of pollutant emitted and rates of emission, the airflow through the stacks and vents emitting airborne pollutants (under standard temperature and pressure conditions), as well as the typical control efficiency of the equipment installed in that installation.

A process flow chart of the plant's production should be provided, as well as maps detailing the location of the installations inside the plant and the plant's location *vis-à-vis* its neighbourhood.

Fuel and raw materials

In this section, a material inventory (a list of the main types and quantities used) of raw materials (including fuel), intermediate and end products, which have a potential impact on the air quality should be provided. The annual consumption and production rates of these substances in the plant should be specified, as well as those for shorter periods of time (monthly, weekly, daily, and per hour for continuous processes, and monthly, weekly, daily, and per batch for batch processes). Emphasis should be given to toxic and volatile substances used in large quantities, as described later and in Table 3.2.

For fuels, details should be given as to the type of the fuels (gas, oil, coal, or other), as well as to its sulphur, ash and trace metals contents. The asphaltene content of oil, if available, is of interest since fuels with a high asphaltene content (usually low-grade and sulphur-rich fuels) are extremely difficult to burn cleanly and cause large quantities of black soot emissions.

Emission rates of airborne pollutants

In this section, data should be presented on the emission rates of airborne pollutants from the various sources in the plant (such as its production facilities, storage areas, the sewage treatment plant, sludge drying ponds, etc.) under normal operating conditions (i.e., not involving accidents), including the unavoidable small leaks.

These airborne emission rates should be based as much as possible on field measurements and on stack samplings. However, in the absence of measured data, estimates can be based on emission factors such as those published by the USEPA (1985), or by the Dutch Ministry of Housing, Physical Planning and Environment (MHPPE, 1983). For these estimates the data required on the consumption rates of raw materials and fuel, as well as on the gasflows, are essential.

To evaluate the pollution emission rates from the individual installations, they should be compared with relevant emission standards. In the absence of suitable emission standards, they can be compared with the applicable Performance Standards for New Stationary Sources, published in the United States by the Environmental Protection Agency (USEPA, 40 CFR 60). In these standards permissible emission rates have been established for installations of close to 60 different types of industry.

Adding the emission rates of a given pollutant from all the installations of the plant, one obtains the total emission rate of the plant, which is sometimes referred to as the plant's 'bubble' emission rate (Borowsky and Ellis, 1987). It should be noted that in the bubble approach total emission rates of the plant are controlled rather than the emission rates of the individual installations, thus providing the plant's management more flexibility in complying with the emission limitations.

Air quality assessment

Air quality in the vicinity of the proposed plant can be forecasted by using air pollution dispersion models, in which a given pollutant concentration field is calculated, for a given configuration of emission rates and meteorological conditions (see, for example, Turner, 1970; Hanna *et al.*, 1982). Considerations should also be given to the possibility of chemical transformations and to the long-range transport of pollutants in the atmosphere (Schroeder and Lane, 1988).

The input data necessary for the models includes the pollution emission rates and atmospheric stability data such as wind speed and direction, depth of the mixed layer and the change of temperature with height above ground level.

Air quality monitoring data obtained from field measurements are required to establish the levels of the background pollutant concentrations and also, to verify the results obtained by the air pollution dispersion models.

Ambient monitoring of airborne pollutants such as SO_2, NO_x, CO (which are typically fuel burning products) and particulate matter is by now well established, as is the monitoring of atmsopheric stability parameters. Instruments and equipment for monitoring these pollutants and atmospheric stability parameters are quite standardized and commercially available.

On the other hand, methods for monitoring ambient airborne chemicals (toxic or odorous) are generally not standardized and for many substances monitoring instruments are not available as 'off-the-shelf' equipment (Jayanty and Hochheiser, 1988). Thus, in the vicinity of chemical industry complexes, specially designed surveys might be necessary to establish their background pollution levels (Swallow *et al.*, 1988).

To evaluate the ambient air quality in the vicinity of the proposed plant ('ambient' is defined here as the area outside the fenceline of the plant), the pollutant concentrations calculated from the air quality dispersion model should be compared with ambient air quality standards but if not applicable, to the guidelines for ambient air quality published by the World Health Organization (WHO, 1987), or the levels of concern (LOC) specified by the USEPA (USEPA/FEMA/DOT, 1987). Concentrations of odorous chemicals should be compared with odour threshold limits (NAS, 1979). For certain toxic chemicals, fractions of the immediate danger for life and health (IDLH) levels, threshold limit values (TLVs), median lethal concentrations (LC_{50}), or doses (LD_{50}), may serve as guidelines for establishing the acceptable ambient levels of pollution (USEPA/FEMA/DOT, 1987).

Chemical incident hazard assessment

In the section of the EIA dealing with air quality, special interest should be focused on potential incidents in chemical plants that might lead to the exposure of human populations living in the area surrounding the plant to high concentrations of airborne toxic substances. It should be noted that the most frequently occurring accidents in the chemical industry involve releases into the air of HCl, NH_3 or Cl_2 (Cutter, 1987). However, since airborne releases of other acutely lethal substances, while infrequent, can be catastrophic (such as, for example, the methylisocyanate release at Bhopal, or the dioxin release at Seveso), special considerations are required in plants using hazardous chemicals, such as: installation and maintenance of control equipment (USEPA, 1986) and alert systems, preparation of response plans (NRT, 1987; USDOT, 1987) and emergency evacuation etc. However, through the EIA, project proponents are encouraged to adopt plant designs which are 'inherently safe' (Kletz, 1985), i.e., the inventories of toxic substances are kept to a minimum (World Bank, 1985), rather than to rely on sophisticated and expensive control equipment and on emergency response procedures.

Guidelines as to how to carry out hazard assessment in the chemical industry have been published by UNEP (1982), the World Bank (1985) and the International Labor Organization (ILO), 1988).

Recently, official guidelines have been published in the United States as to how to perform hazard assessment for releases from chemical plants of what is termed 'extremely hazardous (airborne) substances' (EHSs) (NRT, 1987; USEPA/FEMA/USDOT, 1987). USEPA identified, out of more than 60 000 chemicals used in commerce, a list of about 400 chemicals which were termed EHSs on the basis of their acute toxicity data (for the criteria of toxicity, see Table 3.1). The list of 400 EHSs includes also 24 substances, based on both the criterion of toxicity and on high production capacity (Table 3.2).

Table 3.1   *Criteria to identify extremely hazardous substances (EHSs) and other hazardous substances produced in large quantities (OHSs) that may present severe health hazards to humans during a chemical accident or other emergency (USEPA/FEMA/DOT, 1987)*

Rate of exposure*	Acute toxicity measure†	Value	
		EHSs	OHSs
Inhalation	Median lethal concentration in air (LC_{50})	Less than or equal to 0.5 mg/l of air for exposure times of 8 h or less	Less than or equal to 2.0 mg/l of air for exposure times of 8 h or less
Dermal	Median lethal dose (LD_{50})	Less than or equal to 50 mg/kg body weight	Less than or equal to 400 mg/kg body weight
Oral	Median lethal dose (LD_{50})	Less than or equal to 25 mg/kg body weight	Less than or equal to 200 mg/kg body weight

* The route by which the test animals absorbed the chemical, i.e., by breathing it in air (inhalation), by absorbing it through the skin (dermal), or by ingestion (oral).
† LC_{50}: The concentration of the chemical in air at which 50 per cent of the test animals died; LD_{50}: The dose that killed 50 per cent of the test animals. In the absence of LC_{50} or LD_{50} data, LCLO or LDLO data should be used; LCLO: Lethal concentration low, the lowest concentration in air at which any test animals died; LDLO: Lethal dose low, the lowest dose at which any test animals died.

Table 3.2 *The US Environmental Protection Agency list of extremely hazardous substances (EHSs) produced in large quantities (names, chemical abstracts registration number – CAS No, and United Nations Identification Number – UN No), and their corresponding levels of concern (LOC) (USEPA/FEMA/ DOT, 1987)*

	Substance name	CAS No.	UN No.	LOC (mg/ m³)
1	Acrylamide	79-06-1	2074	111
2	Acrylonitrile	107-13-1	1093	111
3	Adiponitrite	111-69-3	2205	17
4	Ammonia	7664-41-7	1005	35
5	Aniline	62-53-3	1547	38
6	Bromine	7726-95-6	1744	6.5
7	Carbon disulphide	75-15-0	1131	160
8	Chlorine	7782-50-5	1017	7.3
9	Chloroform	67-66-3	1888	490
10	Cyclohexylamine	108-91-8	2357	160
11	Epichlorohydrin	106-89-8	2023	38
12	Ethylene oxide	75-21-8	1952	140
13	Formaldehyde	50-00-0	1198/2209	12
14	Hydrogen chloride (gas)	7647-01-0	1050	15
15	Hydrogen peroxide (>52%)	7722-84-1	2015	10
16	Hydrogen sulphide	7783-06-4	1053	42
17	Hydroquinone	123-31-9	2662	20
18	Methyl bromide	74-83-9	1062	780
19	Nitrobenzene	98-95-3	1662	100
20	Phosgene	75-44-5	107	0.8
21	Propylene oxide	75-56-7	1280	480
22	Sulphur dioxide	7446-09-5	1079	26
23	Tetramethyl lead	75-74-1	1649	4
24	Vinyl acetate monomer	105-05-4	1301	54

Hazard assessment in the United States involves the three following steps, hazard identification, vulnerability analysis and risk analysis:

1   Hazard identification: This is a process of collecting information on the chemical identity of the EHSs and other information as outlined earlier. A detailed description of the nature of the hazard is required, such as the conditions of manufacture, storage, processing and use, as well as transportation routes and potential hazards associated with spills and releases. This information is intended for the use of the various emergency planners (fire and rescue services, police, health and environmental protection departments) and also in the next following two steps.

2   Vulnerability analysis: An estimation of the vulnerable zone around the plant for each EHS reported, and the conditions and assumptions that were used to estimate each vulnerable zone should be presented. The following information is required for vulnerability analysis:
   ● the population in terms of numbers and types (permanent residents, high density transient populations such as workers or spectators in a stadium, and sensitive populations in hospitals, schools, nursing homes, etc.), and essential service facilities, emergency response centres and communication facilities;
   ● atmospheric dispersion conditions (see Section 3);
   ● the topography in the area surrounding the plant;
   ● the levels of concern (LOCs) of the EHSs under discussion.
   Estimates of the quantities and rates of release of the EHSs into the air are required. For these estimates, scenarios of specific probable chemical incidents have to be devised.

3   Risk analysis: The information obtained from risk analysis should enable emergency planners to focus on the greatest potential risks. It should provide a measure of:
   ● the likelihood of the occurrence of various possible hazardous events (such as a release of a chemical substance);
   ● the severity of the consequences of such a release.
   A review of the historical records of hazardous material releases in similar chemical plants in other places can be helpful for this type of risk analysis.

One of the problems related to performing risk assessments is the lack of guidelines regarding the risk from chemical industries that can be considered as acceptable. There seems to be a consensus that a risk of 10^{-6} (a chance of one in a million of an incident to occur) is low enough to be accepted, in the sense that nothing is done to avoid or reduce such risks. It should be noted that 10^{-6} is the average risk imposed on us by natural phenomena, over which man has no control and as such could be considered the 'background' risk (UNEP, 1982). also, Travis et al. (1987) indicate that for exposure to carcinogenic chemicals, a lifetime individual risk (defined as the probability for an individual of contracting cancer following the exposure to the maximum modelled or measured concentration of a carcinogen during a 70-year lifetime) of 10^{-6} is considered to be low, and thus constitutes perhaps what is termed an 'acceptable risk'. On the other hand, a proposal for an industrial activity involving a risk of 10^{-3} is certain to be unaccepted by the public (UNEP, 1982), whereas for other types of human activities this level of risk does seem to be acceptable (Wilson and Crouch, 1987).

As yet there is no consensus as to how much above the background risk (10^{-6}) can be regarded as acceptable for a chemical incident and can thus be used as the criterion of what is permissible in the risk analysis.

The situation is further complicated because different groups of people rank the risks from a given list of human activities in a different way (Slovic, 1987).

In addition, undertaking a complete analysis of all hazards from all sources of the plant may not be feasible or practical for given resources and time constraints. Moreover, as specified in the US guidelines (NRT, 1987), in many cases an elaborate risk analysis may not be necessary and a limited hazards analysis that includes only identification of the nature and location of the hazards to the community may be sufficient. This is particularly so if the hazards identification indicates, obviously only in a qualitative manner, that the risk is not unusually high (e.g., for cases where the quantities of EHSs involved or their LOCs are small).

In Israel, chemical incident hazard analysis is still in its first stages. Only a few chemical plants located in the Ramat-Hovav area and in Ashdod have been analysed regarding their potential chemical hazards. Specific chemical incidents (scenarios) were defined for these analyses, and the output of these studies was used mainly to assist land-use planning, in determining what type of activities should be permitted in the zone around the plants. In this respect these studies can be looked upon as limited hazards analyses which cover only the phases of the hazards identification and vulnerability analysis.

References

Berry, J. C. (1986) Process emissions and their control, part II. In *Air Pollution*, 3rd edn, vol. 7 (supplements) (ed. A. C. Stern), Academic Press, Orlando, pp. 395–508.

Biswas, A. K. and Geping, Q. (1987), *Environmental Impact Assessment for Developing Countries*, Tycooly International, London, 232 pp.

Borowsky, A. R. and Ellis, H. H. (1987), Summary of the final federal emissions trading policy statement. *Journal Air Pollution Control Association*, **37**(7), 798–800.

Cutter, S. L. (1987), Airborne toxic releases. *Environment*, **29**(6), 12–31.

Etzion, R., Graber, M., Cohen, Y, and Brovender S. (1986), *An Historic Center and a New Power Plant: Can they Coexist in a Neighbouring Environment – The Application of the Israeli Environmental Impact Statement System*. Prepared within the framework of the United Nations Environment Programme (UNEP) for the Priority Action Plan (PAP), Regional Activity Center (RAC), Split, Yugoslavia, 59 pp.

Hanna, S. R., Briggs, G. A., and Hosker, R. P. (1982) *Handbook on Atmospheric Diffusion*, Report No. DOE/TIC-11223, Department of Energy, Washington D.C.

ILO (1988) *Major Hazard Control – A Practical Manual*, International Labor Organization (ILO), Geneve, 296 pp.

Jayanty, R. K. M. and Hochheiser, S. (1988), Summary of the EPA/APCA

International Symposium on Measurement of Toxic and Related Air Pollutants. *Journal Air Pollution Control Association*, **38**(10), 1259–1265.

Kletz, T. A. (1985), *Cheaper Safer Plants (Notes on Inherently Safer Plants)*, 2nd Edition, The UK Institute of Chemical Engineers, Rugby, England, 118 pp.

Marinov, U. and Jernelov, A. (1987), Environmental Impact Assessment – A Practical Approach. Prepared within the Framework of UNEP. *Israel Environment Bulletin* (Jerusalem), **11**(1) 15–24.

MHPPE (1983), *Handbook of Emission Factors*, Part 2, Prepared by TNO for the Dutch Ministry of Housing, Physical Planning and Environment, The Hague, 569 pp.

NAS (1979) *Odors from Stationary and Mobile Source*, A Committee Report (Chairman A. Turk), National Research Council, National Academy of Sciences (NAS), Washington D.C., 491 pp.

NRT (1987) *Hazardous Materials Emergency Planning Guide*, Report No NRT-1, Prepared by ICF Inc. for the National Response Team (NRT) to comply with the requirements of Sec. 303(f), Title III of SARA, Washington D.C., 72. pp.

Schroeder, N. H. and Lane D. A. (1988), The fate of toxic airborne pollutants *Environmental Science and Technology* **22**(3), 240–270.

Slovic, P. (1987), 'Perception of risk. *Science*, **236**(4799), 280–285.

Swallow, K. C., Shifrin N. S. and Doherty, P. J. (1988), Hazardous organic compound analysis. *Environmental Science and Technology*, **22**(2), 136–142

Travis, C. C., Richter, S. A., Crouch., E. A. C., Wilson, R. and Klema, E. D. (1987) Cancer Risk Management. *Environmental Science and Technology*, **21**(5), 415–420.

Turner D. B. (1970) *Workbook of Atmospheric Dispersion Estimates* (Revised), Document No AP-26, US Environmental Protection Agency, RTP, NC, 84 pp.

UNEP (1982) *Guidelines on Risk Management and Accident Prevention in the Chemical Industry*, United Nations Environment Programme (UNEP), Nairobi, 52 pp.

UNEP (1987), *The State of the World Environment in 1987*, Document UNEP/CG.14/6, United Nations Environment Programme (UNEP), Nairobi, 76 pp.

USDOT (1987) *Emergency Response Guidebook, 1987 – Guidebook for Initial Response to Hazardous Materials Incidents*, Document No DOT-P-5800.4, US Department of Transportation (USDOT), Washington D.C.

USEPA (1985), *Compilation of Air Pollutants Emission Factors* (4th Edn), Document No AP-42, US Environmental Protection Agency (USEPA), RTP, NC.

USEPA (1986) *Handbook – Control Technologies for Hazardous Air Pollutants*, Report No EPA/625/6-86-014, US Environmental Protection Agency (USEPA), RTP, NC, 176 pp.

USEPA/FEMA/USDOT (1987) *Technical Guidance for Hazard Analysis – Emergency Planning for Extremely Hazardous Substances (EHSs)*, US

Environmental Protection Agency (USEPA) Federal Emergency Management Agency (FEMA), US Department of Transportation (USDOT), Washington D.C.

WHO (1987) *Air Quality Guidelines for Europe*, WHO Regional Publications, European Series No 23, World Health Organization (WHO), Copenhagen, 426 pp.

Wilson, R., and Crouch, E. A. C. (1987), Risk assessment and comparisons – an introduction. *Science*, **236**(4799), 267–270.

World Bank (1985) *Manual of Industrial Hazard Assessment Techniques*, prepared by Technica Ltd. in co-operation with the World Bank, Washington D. C., 99 pp.

4
Environmental impact assessment of an opencast coal mining project
A. V. Chiplunkar

The Government of India has accorded high priority for the protection and restoration of environment in mining areas. It has been made obligatory to submit environment management plans (EMP) for proposed mining projects. The Department of Environment, Forests and Wildlife, Government of India has issued guidelines for preparation of EMP and involves the following aspects:

1 description of project activities including their environmental implications;
2 collection of baseline data of environmental setting around the project;
3 anticipated environmental impacts due to proposed project;
4 Environment Management Plan including proposed safeguards to control adverse impacts, implementation and monitoring schedule.

This chapter briefly reviews various aspects of the EMP for an opencast coal mining project in order to bring out the adverse impacts of the project and discusses the environment protection measures proposed along with the costs. A case study has been selected on the basis of a study undertaken for Karo Phase I Opencast Project in East Bokaro Coalfields.

Case study details

Project

Karo Phase I Opencast Project (OCP) is part of East Bokaro Coalfields in Bihar to be developed by Central Coalfields Ltd. (Figure 4.1). It is planned to produce coal at 1.5 million tonnes per year (MTY) to meet the coal requirements of Tenughat Thermal Power Station Phase II (2×210 MW). The site is located about 40 km south-west of Dhanbad.

Reserves and overburden

The mineable reserves of coal have been estimated as 70.91 million tonnes

(MT). At a rated capacity of 1.5 MTY, the life of the project is about 50 years. The average stripping ratio is 0.63 m³ overburden per tonne of coal, due to which 44.33 million m³ overburden will be generated during the project life.

Mining activities

The selected method for mining is the 'shovel and dumper system'. The heavy earth moving machinery (HEMM) mainly comprises 3.8 m³ electric hydraulic shovels, 5.0 m³, electric rope shovels, 35 T dumpers and 320–410 HP dozers. The activities involved are as follows:

1   drilling and blasting
2   removal of coal and overburden
3   sizing of coal in coal handling plant (CHP)
4   disposal of overburden
5   transportation of clean coal.

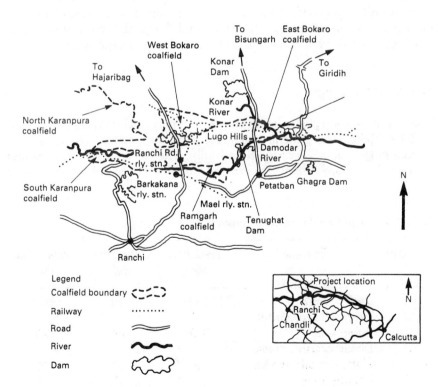

Figure 4.1   *Project location*

Land requirement

The land requirement for the project is given in Table 4.1. As indicated therein the project requires 302 ha forest land.

Water requirement

The water requirements of the project in million litres per day (MLD) are as under:

1	Potable water demand (schools, residents, canteens etc.)	0.37 MLD
2	Industrial water demand (washing HEMM, dust suppression, fire fighting etc.)	0.27 MLD
	Total	0.64 MLD

Services

The total manpower to be deployed for the project is 660 of which 363 persons will be provided housing. The infrastructure and support services include service buildings, rest house, school, hospital, bank, water supply, sewerage, transport and communication facilities, electricity etc.

Environmental setting

The proposed project site lies in the eastern part of Chota Nagpur plateau of Bihar State. The general topography of the project area as well as surrounding area is very rough and hilly. The average elevation ranges between 243 m and 335 m. The forest land which covers the large project

Table 4.1   *Land requirements of project*

Sr. No.	Purpose	Forest land (ha)	Other land (ha)	Total land (ha)
1.	Quarry area	118	22	140
2.	External overburden dump area	123	11	134
3.	Infrastructure, roads, CHP, substation etc.	61	15	76
4.	Colony area	-	12	12
	TOTAL	302	60	362

area and also the surrounding area is of a dry deciduous type. However recent Landsat imagery indicates absence of vegetative growth though the land is designated as forest land.

The project site is surrounded by existing coalfields, the impact of which already exists in the baseline environmental quality generated for this project.

The river Damodar flowing to the south is the main receiving water body for all liquid wastes joining it through drains. Its quality, as measured at more than nine locations over a distance of more than 6 km, largely conforms to Class 'A' waters as per IS:2296 viz. drinking water source after disinfection only.

The climatological conditions are similar to Dhanbad. Hence Indian Meteorological Department (IMD) data for Dhanbad was used in addition to that generated in East Bokaro Coalfield area.

The ambient air quality is characterized by high suspended particulate matter (SPM) above 200 $\mu g/m^3$ (200–570 $\mu g/m^3$), significant presence of oxides of nitrogen in a range 40–70 $\mu g/m^3$ and very low concentrations of SO_2 (less than 5 $\mu g/m^3$).

The socio-economic profile indicates very rapid growth of population (79 per cent per decade during 1970–80) due to availability of better employment opportunities, higher literacy rate (45–75 per cent), improved transport and communication means but lack of adequate facilities for water supply (especially in summer) and sewerage.

Environment impact assessment

An EIA study was done for premining phase and operational phase. The impacting actions and environmental parameters affected are depicted in Figure 4.2. The evaluation of environmental impact has been done by the 'Matrix Method' and is presented in Table 4.5 at the end of this section.

Impact on air quality

The activities contributing to air pollution are blasting and drilling, operation of petrol and diesel driven HEMM, transportation of coal and overburden, screening and crushing activty in CHP and overburden dumps.

The predicted pollutant concentrations at the proposed project site without mitigation measures are given in Table 4.2.

Thus the major impact on air quality will be due to generation of dust affecting SPM and dustfall rate significantly within the project area. Its impact on surrounding ambient air quality will be limited due to criss crossing of hills which will arrest free flow.

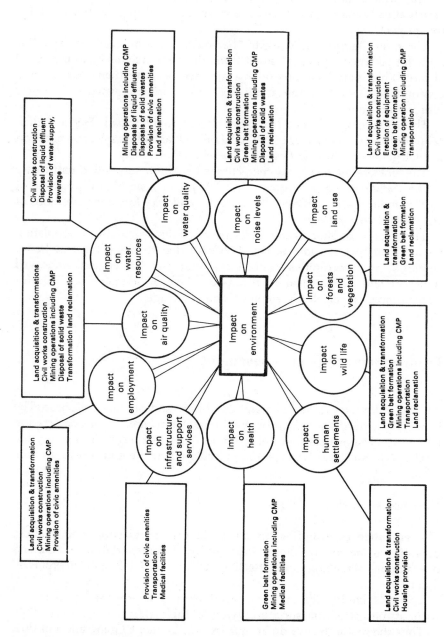

Figure 4.2   Summary of environmental impacts of Karo-I OCP

Impact on water resources

The withdrawal of 0.64 MDL from Damodar river will not have any impact. The mine water pumping however is significant in quantity. In summer it is expected to be 10–15 MLD. while in monsoon, due to accumulated surface run-off in excavated pits, it is expected to be about 215 MLD. This is let off into drains.

The scarcity of water in summer is experienced in surrounding villages. But as the project is on hilly terrain with villages at foot hills, the impact is reduced compared with a situation when the terrain is flat.

Impact on water quality

The two major sources for effluent are mine water and, domestic and service effluents.

The mine water is proposed to be discharged into Karo drain (joining Damodar river) after settling in the drain itself by construction of bunds, to reduce suspended solids.

The domestic effluent will be treated by trickling filters to limits specified by IS:4764 and let off. The quantity (0.3 MLD) compared with the mine water is negligible.

The existing quality of Damodar river will therefore not be affected as the discharges will be within specified limits for discharge of effluents into inland surface water. Table 4.3 presents the existing quality of river, effluent quality and the standards.

No appreciable impact is envisaged on the water quality of the receiving body.

Table 4.2　*Predicted air quality at proposed project site*

Sr. No.	Location	SPM ($\mu g/m^3$)	NO_x ($\mu g/m^3$)	SO_2 ($\mu g/m^3$)	Dust fall ($\mu g/m^2$) day
1.	Opencast mining operations area	200–500	25–65	Up to 2.0	400–2000
2.	Movement of HEMM, dumping area	200–500*	40–65	Up to 2.0	Up to 2000
3.	Residential colony	50–400	40–65	Up to 1.5	200–2000
4.	Baseline area at Chalkari village	318	44	2.3	1245

*May exceed 500 at times up to 600.

Table 4.3   *Water quality of effluent and Damodar river*

Sr. No.	Parameter (mg/l)	Class 'A' water (IS-2296)	Damodar river	Mine water before treatment*	Discharge limits IS-2490
1.	pH	6.5–8.5	6.8–7.4	5.2	5.5–9.0
2.	Temp (deg.C)	NS	30–37	31	40
3.	TDS	500	80–260	240	2100
4.	TSS	NS	35–770	410	100
5.	BOD	2	0.5–7.2	6	30
6.	COD⁵	NS	33–1161	63	250
7.	Oil and grease	0.01	BDL	BDL	NS
8.	Chlorides (Cl)	250	28–48	20	1000
9.	Nitrates (N)	20	BDL–8.4	2.1	NS
10.	Sulphates (SO$_4$)	400	28–132	122	1000
11.	Phosphates (PO$_4$)	NS	0.18–0.72	0.24	5
12.	Kjeldhal N	NS	0.2–1.0	0.2	100
13.	Fluorides (F)	1.5	0.3–0.7	-	-
14.	Iron (FE)	0.30	0.1–0.9	0.37	NS
15.	Particle size of TSS (micron)	NS	200–425	Up to 300	850

NS, Not specified; BDL, Below detectable limits; *, Based on adjoining Karo Special Project.

Impact on noise levels

Various measurements at noise generating activity locations for estimating the background noise level, equivalent noise level exposure for 30 min exposure and peak noise levels were taken for similar existing projects.

Table 4.4 summarizes the anticipated levels and permissible exposure limits.

Considering that permissible continuous exposure in the industrial area varies between 90 dBa for 8 h to 108 dBa for 7.5 min, and not more than 65 dBa for 8 h per day in the residential zone, the impact on noise levels is significant.

Table 4.4   *Anticipated noise levels (dBA)*

Sr. No.	Zone	Background	Equivalent	Peak
1.	Industrial activity zone	53–57	74–99	99–149
2.	Project administration office	41–58	41–75	94–109
3.	Residential colony at site	46–51	68	101–105
4.	Village near mining project	44	65	102

65 dBA for 8 h per day in the residential zone, the impact on noise levels is significant.

Impact on land use

The major impact on existing land use during the pre-project stage is the deforestation of 283 ha of forest land (19 ha in the safety zone will not be removed).

The major post-mining impact on land use is the creation of an external overburden dump on 134 ha, creation of a void of 24.8 million m³ covering an area of 47 ha in the quarry area, and creation of civil structures etc. This will be the single and most adverse impact. Not only is the land deforested but it is further made unfit for any positive use in the absence of stabilization and reclamation measures.

Impact on forests, vegetation and wildlife

Loss of vegetative cover results in increased soil erosion, degradation of soil quality, reduction of moisture retention capacity, removal of moderating effect on climate and brings about a change in local ecology.

The loss of habitat has a significant adverse impact on population and density of fauna.

Impact on human settlements

The provision of housing to 55 per cent of staff is beneficial as it eases the strain on surrounding areas. But there will be a significant impact due to the migration of experienced people which is increasing at 79 per cent per decade due to increased employment opportunities.

There will be negligible displacement of families as over 83 per cent of the land is forest-land. Acquisition of private tenancy land is almost negligible as the balance is mostly government land.

Impact on health

The major impact will be on the health of mine workers who will be exposed to noise and dust pollution resulting in gradual but permanent health deterioration. Present experience indicates the prevalence of nystagmus, pneumoconiosis and hearing losses to be common.

Impact on infrastructure and support services

There will be an appreciable beneficial impact on roads, transport and communication facilities, power, civic amenities like water supply and sewerage, medical services, educational facilities, markets and recreation.

Impact on employment

The proposed project will have a significant impact in providing employment opportunities. Present trends indicate that more than 50 per cent of the work-force is engaged in mining and allied activities.

Environmental impact without control measures

The environmental impact of the project during the premining and operational phase of the project has been assessed by the Matrix Method as depicted in Table 4.5. The criteria adopted for quantitative evaluation of impact is as follows:

Severity criteria	*Impact score*
No impact	0
No appreciable impact	1
Significant impact – slight or short term effect	2
Major impact – occasional irreversible effect	3
High impact – irreversible or long term effect	4
Permanent impact	5

The importance value attached to each environmental parameter is based on the priority assigned by the Department of Environment, Forests and Wildlife, Government of India to various environmental problems. The total impact score has been assessed as follows:

Up to − 1000:	No appreciable impact on environment.
− 1000 to − 2000:	Appreciable but reversible impact, mitigation measures important.
− 2000 to − 3000:	Significant impact mostly reversible after a short period, mitigation measures crucial.
− 3000 to − 4000:	Major impact which is mostly irreversible, site selection to be reconsidered.
− 4000 and above:	Permanent irreversible impact, alternative site to be considered.

Accordingly the impact score without control measures is − 2900 indicating that the mitigation measures are crucial to reduce the adverse impact.

Mitigation measures in proposed EMP

Considering the impacts described in the earlier section, the significant adverse impacts requiring mitigation are for reclamation of land; measures

Table 4.5   *Environmental impact matrix without control measures*

Sr. No.	Environmental parameters	Importance value	Premining phase				Operational phase							Impact score
			Land acquisition and transformation	Civil works construction	Erection of mechanical and mining equipment	Green belt formation	Mining operations incl. CHP	Disposal of liquid effluents	Disposal of solid wastes on land for reclamation	Housing provision	Provision of WSS electricity and other civic amenities	Transportation	Medical facilities	
1.	Air quality	100	−1	−1			−2		−2			−1		−70
2.	Water resources	75		−1				−1			−1			−22
3.	Water quality	100					−1	−2	−1		−1			−50
4.	Noise and vibration	75	−1	−1	−1	+1	−2		−1			−1		−45
5.	Land use	150	−3	−1		+1	−2		−1					−90
6.	Forests and vegetation	150	−4			+1								−45
7.	Wildlife	50	−2			+1	−1					−1		−15
8.	Human settlements	75	−1	+1						+1				+75
9.	Health	100				+1	−3						+1	−100
10.	Infrastructure and support services	50									+2	+1	+2	+250
11.	Employment	50	+1	+1			+2				+1			+250
12.	Places of tourist/archaeological importance	25												0
	TOTAL	1000	−1350	−275	−75	+525	−1000	−275	−525	+75	−75	−175	+200	−2900

+ Sign shows beneficial impact; − Sign shows adverse impact

to control air, water and noise pollution; and provisions for compensatory afforestation and human rehabilitation. The environmental impact after implementation of mitigation measures is presented in Table 4.6 at the end of the section.

Mitigation measures for solid waste disposal and land reclamation

These are divided into two aspects as under:

Compensatory afforestation
When forest-lands are used for non-forest purposes, as per the norms of Ministry of Environment and Forests, Government of India, compensatory afforestation required to be done is as follows;

1   where non-forest lands are available, compensatory afforestation be raised over an area equivalent to the diverted area;
2   where non-forest lands are not available it should be raised over degraded forests twice in extent to the area being diverted.

Accordingly, provision for compensatory afforestation on 283 ha of non-forest land has been proposed.

Land reclamation
The stabilization of external dump and internal dump in the quarry area is proposed to be done by stage-wise vegetative plantation on these areas. Reclamation schemes at 5-year intervals has been prepared. In addition, vegetative plantation is also proposed to be done along haul roads and colony.

The scheme for reclamation of land also includes the major machinery required for dumping and levelling the solid waste being disposed.

Mitigation measures for air pollution control

The proposed measures address themselves towards arresting the generation and spread of dust. These mainly include

- Water spraying on surface at blasting site before drilling, loading and unloading operations, haul road, CHP and dumps
- Provision of tarred haul roads
- Development of green belt along roads, around service buildings and residential area
- Stabilization of overburden dumps
- Other preventive measures

Mitigation measures for water resources management

Though there are no significant impacts identified on water resources availability, it is proposed to recycle the mine water for water spraying

Table 4.6   Environmental impact matrix with control measures

Sr. No.	Environmental parameters	Importance value	Premining phase — Land acquisition and transformation	Civil works construction	Erection of mechanical and mining equipment	Green belt formation	Operational phase — Mining operations incl. CHP	Disposal of liquid effluents	Disposal of solid wastes on land for reclamation	Housing provision	Provision of WS,S electricity and other civic amenities	Transportation	Medical facilities	Land reclamation	Impact score
1.	Air quality	100	−1	−1		+1	−1		−1			−1		+1	−300
2.	Water resources	75		−1				−1			−1				−225
3.	Water quality	100						−1	−1					+1	−100
4.	Noise and vibration	75	−1	−1	−1	+1	−1		−1			−1			−375
5.	Land use	150	−3	−1		+1	−1		+1					+2	−150
6.	Forests and vegetation	150	−4			+1								+4	+150
7.	Wildlife	50	−2			+1	−1					−1		+1	−100
8.	Human settlements	75	−1	+1						+1					
9.	Health	100				+1	−1						+1		
10.	Infrastructure and support services	50									+2				
11.	Employment	50	+1	+1			+2				+1	+1	+2		
12.	Places of tourist/archaeological importance	25													
	TOTAL	1000	−1350	−275	−75	+625	−375	−175	−125	+75	+75	−175	+200	+1150	

+ Sign shows beneficial impact; − Sign shows adverse impact

and application to land for watering vegetation as it conforms to the limits for this purpose.

Similarly industrial wastewater is proposed to be recycled after oil and grease removal, sedimentation etc. for vehicle washing.

As regards water pollution control it is proposed that:

- Mine water be settled before discharge into drains and bunds be constructed along the drains for further sedimentation
- Domestic and service building effluent be collected and biological treatment be given by means of extended aeration. This will ensure that effluent after treatment conforms to IS-4764 (BOD_s and TSS limits of 20 mg/l and 30 mg/l respectively)
- Vegetative plantation be grown on overburden dumps to prevent excessive suspended solids in surface run-off from these areas after stabilization.

Mitigation measures for noise pollution control

The nature of mining activity itself is such that noise generation cannot be eliminated. Hence the control measures address themselves to preventive measures as under:

- use of noise absorbent paddings in fixed plant installations
- use of silencers/mufflers in HEMM
- Use of ear-muffs by employees to reduce noise level exposure
- plantation of green-belt to create barriers between source and receiver
- location of residential colony away from noise generating sources.

Rehabilitation of displaced persons

The provisions required for this purpose include the following:

- compensation of land to be acquired
- development of alternate land for rehabilitation
- provision for shifting
- compensation in lieu of earnings
- provision of infrastructure and facilities such as roads, wells, water supply and sewerage, school etc.

The Department of Coal, Government of India has given certain guidelines for rehabilition of displaced persons as under:

1 Compensation to be paid for house and land acquired from each family.
2 House site 0.02 ha of developed plot to be given to each family.
3 Shifting allowance of Rs. 2000 to be paid per family.
4 Civic facilities to be provided in the rehabilitation colony will include water supply, power, roads and sanitary arrangements.

5   For employment, displaced persons to be given preference in recruitment to Category C and D in concerned Company subject to suitability and observance of laid down procedure of employment exchange.
6   Training to be arranged by the concerned Company for eligible persons to enable them to take up the job.

Environmental impact after mitigation measures

The environmental impact of the project after implementation of the mitigation measures is presented in Table 4.6. It may be observed that the project can be implemented without significant adverse impact. The impact score reduces to − 425 after mitigation compared to − 2900 without implementation of control measures.

Cost estimates for environmental protection measures

In keeping with the mitigation measures proposed, the major costs of capital expenditure are given hereunder. The format for presentation is in keeping with the guidelines of the Department of Environment, Forests and Wildlife, Government of India, for Coal Projects. Even if certain costs are not incurred, all items have been presented so as to give an idea of items to be considered.

Cost of rehabilitation

Identify the following:

1   total number of families to be rehabilitated
2   number of jobs to be given to land oustees
3   additional likely demand for jobs

Capital estimation
● Compensation of land to be acquired for rehabilitation at 0.02 ha per family and Rs. 0.5 lakhs/ha for total number of families in 1 above
● Cost of development of land plots at Rs. 6000 per plot for total number of families in 1 above
● Shifting charges at Rs 2000 per family
● Compensation in lieu of earnings at Rs. 500 per month per person for 20 years (240 months) as alternative to persons in 3 above
● Establishment of schools/hospitals/roads/well etc. in case village is rehabilitated.
  Sub-total (provision made in absence of detailed
  enumeration)   Rs. 50.00 lakhs

Cost of compensatory afforestation

Identify the following:

● Total forest land diverted	283 ha
● Forest cover (density)	0.3
● Number of existing trees removed	Under enumeration
● Cost of tree	Rs. 50–4500
● Cost of afforestation charged by State Forest Department in Bihar	Rs. 6200/ha

Capital estimation
● Cost of revenue land for compensatory afforestation at Rs. 0.5 lakhs/ha for 283 ha	Rs. 141.50 lakhs
● Cost of existing trees	Under estimation
● Cost of afforestation at Rs. 6200/ha for 283 ha	Rs. 17.55 lakhs
Sub-total	Rs. 159.05 lakhs + cost of trees

Capital cost for restoration

● HEMM for reclamation	Rs 93.96 lakhs
● Biological reclamation of dumps of area 227.5 ha at Rs. 28985/ha	Rs. 65.94 lakhs
● Housing for reclamation personnel	Rs. 7.70 lakhs
● Cost of testing/laboratory equipment	Rs. 15.00 lakhs
Sub-total	Rs. 182.60 lakhs

Capital cost for anti-pollution measures in mine and industrial area

● Water sprinkler	Rs. 0.50 lakhs
● Separate water tank for dust suppression on haul road	Rs. 1.20 lakhs
● Environmental control measures in CHP (dust extraction/suppression)	Rs. 15.00 lakhs
● Effluent treatment plant in workshop	Rs. 4.30 lakhs
● Surface water storage, settling tank and garland canal diversion of drains if any in this item)	Rs. 12.92 lakhs
● Arboriculture on roads and industrial area of 76 ha at Rs. 28985/ha	Rs. 22.03 lakhs
● Cost of environmental monitoring	Rs. 2.00 lakhs
● Housing for pollution control personnel	Rs. 6.60
Sub-total	Rs. 64.55 lakhs

Environmental   control   meaasures   in   township

- Sewerage   Rs. 7.80 lakhs
- Water treatment plant and distribution
  system   Rs. 10.72 lakhs
- Storm water drainage   Rs. 3.50 lakhs
- Horticulture on about 3 ha + tree guards etc.   Rs. 2.00 lakhs
- Other development measures in township
  which improve cleanliness and aesthetics   Rs. 5.00 lakhs
  Sub-total   Rs. 29.02 lakhs

Compensation for land

Compensation of acquired tenancy land of about
12 ha at Rs 0.5 lakhs/ha   Rs. 6.00 lakhs
Sub-total   Rs. 6.00 lakhs

Cost of environmental protection measures

The capital costs of individual items have been detailed in the earlier sections. The total capital cost based on a cost index of 341 in May 1987 (reference 100 in October 1976) is Rs. 491.22 lakhs.

The cost of the existing trees has not been included in this as it is under evaluation by the State Forest Department. This cost is estimated as losses of timber, fuelwood, minor forest produce including loss of man hours of people deriving livelihood by harvesting this produce, animal husbandry productivity, fodder and cycle, wildlife habitat, microclimate (upsetting ecological balance). As a rule of thumb the environmental value of one hectare of fully stocked forest (density 1.0) is taken as Rs. 126.74 lakhs to accrue over a period of 50 years. The value reduces with density. The compensatory afforestation and land reclamation measures are expected to recoup this loss.

The total capital investment for the project including environment protection is estimated to be Rs. 4828.83 lakhs. It should be noted that of the 10 per cent of total cost for environment protection measures, only 5 per cent of the total cost is the incremental cost as provision for HEMM, water supply, sewerage, housing etc. has already been considered in the project cost.

5

Strategy for a sustainable programme of thermal power generation
Rajendra Kumar and A. K. Singh

Ancient wisdom of India regarded that life (flora and fauna) in the biosphere was sustained by five elements of nature: air, water, fire (energy), earth (lithosphere) and 'akash' (solar system). The ecosystem inherited by mankind in the early 19th century reflected the state of equilibrium established after a millennium of evolutionary development of flora and fauna in a manner that had made not only their continued co-existence mutually complementary but had simultaneously ensured that their, including mankind's continued survival, depended essentially upon renewable organic resources; depletion of the life-sustaining vital resources was fully compensated by their regeneration through the continued, uninterrupted occurrence of the so-called water, carbon and nitrogen cycles. While fauna inhaled oxygen from atmosphere to combust the carbohydrates slowly in their bodies to meet the physiological requirements of energy and exhaled carbon dioxide, the flora assimilated the very carbon dioxide through photosynthetic reactions occurring in their chlorophyll material and released oxygen back into the atmosphere. As a result the atmosphere contained nearly 79 per cent nitrogen and 21 per cent oxygen (by volume) with only about 3.50 p.p.m. of carbon dioxide, besides acting as the carrier of water vapour.

Energy requirements of the world until about the 18th century were almost entirely met through renewable forest and agricultural resources. Nature had until then reigned supreme; it had its own ways to check undue pressures of population growth through famine and epidemics of now preventable diseases. In other words, science and technology had then not begun to interfere with nature in any serious manner, mankind had not yet learnt to draw upon the inherited resources of fossil fuel and of mineral resources.

The advent of sciences and their popularization in the early 19th century has been universally heralded as a great leap forward in the direction of unravelling the secrets of nature and for using them to free mankind from superstition and to improve the quality of life. Interference with nature gave rise to unprecedented growth in population which simultaneously put undue pressures on both renewable and non-renewable resources.

The concurrent growth of industralization through exploitation of stored resources of energy and of minerals helped to sustain a sudden expansion of population through generation of new employment.

Industrialization introduced new concepts of trade to sustain the new techno-economic system, concepts of gross national production, per capita income and of per capita consumption of industrial products such as iron, steel, cement, copper, aluminium, sugar, energy etc. Industrial countries joined in a mad race to excel one another in terms of these new concepts. As a result 'economic activity has multiplied to create a $13 trillion world economy (in 1985–86) and this could grow five or ten-fold in the coming half century. Industrial production has grown more than fifty-fold over the past century, four-fifths of this growth since 1950. Such figures reflect and presage profound impacts upon the biosphere, as the world invests in houses, transport, farms and industries. Much of the economic growth pulls raw material from forests, soils, seas and waterways' (World Commission on Environment and Development, 1987).

Successes and failure of technology

Science and technology have thus ushered in a new era of economic satisfaction and there are many physically visible signs of their impact on society; among them are the following:

- falling infant mortality, increasing human life expectancy, better medical amenities;
- increasing amount of literacy, spread of education among females and elimination of drudgery of physical labour;
- increasing food production and enhanced quality of life;
- faster communication systems etc.

Against the background of successes, the list of failures can be as alarming and serious as the impact of 200 years of industralization (and economic growth) on environment which today, threatens the very existence of the ecosystems which nature took millions of years to establish. 'Each year 6 million hectares of productive dry land turns into worthless deserts ... more than 11 million hectares of forests are destroyed freely and would equal an area about the size of India in just three decades ... in Europe acid precipitation kills forests and lakes ... and it may have acidified vast tracts of soil beyond reasonable hope of repair' (World Commission on Environment and Development, 1987).

The World Commission on Environment and Development (1987) has poignantly drawn attention to the seriousness of the situation by stating that in its existence of 900 days between October 1984 and April 1987 the world faced the following crises:

1 The drought-triggered, environment-development crisis in Africa peaked, putting 35 million people at risk, killing perhaps a million.
2 A leak from a pesticides factory in Bhopal, India killed more than 2000 people and blinded and injured over 20 000 more.

3   Liquid gas tanks exploded in Mexico city, killing 1000 and leaving thousands more homeless.
4   The Chernobyl nuclear reactor explosion sent nuclear fallout across Europe, increasing the risk of future human cancers.
5   Agricultural chemicals, solvents and mercury flowed into the Rhine River during a warehouse fire in Switzerland, killing millions of fish and threatening drinking water in Germany and the Netherlands.
6   An estimated 60 million people died of diarrhoeal diseases related to unsafe drinking water and malnutrition; most of the victims were children.

It is now being increasingly realized that environmental issues cannot be separated from those of economic growth through industrial development because widespread industrialization in its wake may subject the ecology to great stress through degradation of soil, water regimes, forests and atmosphere. Despite rapid strides in science and technology 'during the 1970s, twice as many people suffered each year from "natural" disasters as during the 1960s. The disasters most directly associated with environment/development mismanagement – droughts and floods – affected the most people and increased most sharply in terms of numbers affected. Some 18.5 million people were affected by drought annually in the 1960s, 24.4 million in the 1970s. There were 5.2 million flood victims yearly in the 1960s, 15.4 million in the 1970s. Number of victims of cyclones and earthquakes also shot up as growing numbers of poor people built unsafe houses on dangerous ground' (World Commission on Environment and Development, 1987).

While industrialization has the potential to usher in an era of prosperity and is regarded as a messiah to solve the problem of providing the basic needs of mankind – food, shelter and gainful employment, it creates new problems, which if they remain unmanaged or not corrected in time could destroy the world.

Importance of thermal energy in development

The twin discoveries that fire can be created and confined within space and that thermal energy can be transformed into electrical energy truly triggered off the industrial development of human society to an extent that energy has become as vital a component of human survival as are water, clean air and food. Today, energy is required in the form of both heat and electricity and is used for both domestic (cooking, lighting and temperature control of residential premises) and industrial applications in the manufacturing and transport industries. There is no wonder that the per capita consumption of energy is at once indicative of the state of economic development of any country. There could be an 80–100-fold difference between its per capita consumptions in the economically weak and developing countries and the technologically advanced countries of Europe, North America. Soviet Union and Japan. The economic disparity between the two groups of countries can be appreciated when it is realized that only a quarter of the world population residing in the industrial countries consume nearly three-quarters of the world's primary energy. Since development plans for economic growth of many Third World countries tend to follow that of the industrial countries, their energy production and consumption through the use of primary fuels is bound to increase.

It will thus be seen that the energy requirements of modern man have far exceeded that which could be replenished through the capture of solar radiation by trees and plants. The shortfall is predominantly met through the combustion of fossil fuel which is an exhaustible gift of nature.

Wood as a vanishing resource

It has been estimated that 70 per cent of people in the developing countries meet their elementary requirements of thermal energy through the combustion of wood; the per capita per annum consumption varies between 350–2900 kg of dry wood. Its ever increasing demand has led to rapid deforestation; some of the contributing factors for which are:

1 Wood being collected faster than it grows.
2 Rapid growth of profitable agriculture with consequent deforestation through encroachment of forest land.
3 Urbanization putting pressures on wood based building materials.
4 Inability of the other commercial fuels such as kerosene LPG, gas and electricity to penetrate villages, either due to economic weakness of the rural people or on account of lack of development of effective transportation systems.

The non-availability of firewood or other fuels at reasonable prices has forced the rural Indian masses to use cow dung, crop stems, roots and husks, dry and fallen leaves etc. for their hearths. While the burning of some of them may be innocuous, that of others such as cow dung and roots of leguminous plants could deprive the soil of much needed nutrients, the fact that this does not happen on a large scale in India is more due to the traditional wisdom of the Indian farmer than to anything else. Extensive deforestation has led to the following:

● soil erosion,
● general environmental degradation,
● change in climate, and
● progressive desertification.

Indian forest cover has drastically shrunk – more so perhaps in the post-independence era and estimates of the forest cap vary between 8–11 per cent of the geographical area. The National Remote Science Agency data shows that during the period 1972–75 to 1980–82, 1.3 million hectares of forest cover was permanently destroyed (The Hindustan Times, 1988).

India's annual requirement of wood is of 150 million tonnes of which nearly 80 per cent is used as firewood. Against this, the quantity of wood that can be obtained on a renewable basis is a mere third of anticipated consumption. The shortfall of 100 million tonnes a year makes a mockery of governmental directives to conserve forest wealth particularly when much of the officially inspired afforestation of trees is of the commercial variety not excluding eucalyptus and teak. Commercial forestry is rarely effective in providing fuelwood to rural areas as they help only to meet the commercial, urban and industrial needs. Apprehensions have also begun to be expressed that plantation of the same variety of trees over vast tracts of land could in the long run reduce the fertility of the soil. Natural forests are usually a conglomerate of trees of different varieties.

The most important task facing the enlightened intelligentsia of the country is to provide a plan for expeditious action that is capable of satisfying the basic human need of energy for the hearths of their surging population. In this task easy and large availability of thermal/electrical energy plays a pivotal role as energy provides the motive power for rapid industrialization as well as for the development of agricultural and agri-based industries.

The primordial and traditional sources of energy in many developing countries are mostly renewable and are derived from human and animal muscle power, wind and sun. However, energy requirements of an industrialized society are mostly met through the use of non-renewable natural gas, oil and coal besides nuclear energy, the renewable and non-polluting hydropower also makes a substantial contribution to the energy scenario.

The national development plans have accorded highest priority for increasing the availability of electrical energy by adopting a three-faceted approach of achieving the targets of power generation mostly through thermal and hydroelectric generation and marginally through nuclear energy. If the submergence of land/forest areas is ignored, hydroelectric generation is renewable, does not pollute the environment and should be less costly than power from other sources despite the longer gestation period required for the construction of dams and associated systems. The establishment of thermal power stations has received priority in India on account of large resources of coal/lignite being available in different parts of the country and the fact that its gestation period is considerably less. Welcome in itself as the establishment of large thermal power stations was, it appears in retrospect that both the experts and the political leaders were, in the first place concerned with making electrical energy available for the commencement of industrial development processes; perhaps there was then no time to pause and reflect that unabashed industrial growth, on the pattern of Europe and United States could bring new problems which, if untackled, could lead to disastrous consequences. Was this indifference because environmental consciousness had not then grown?

Pollution and generation of energy from coal

The conversion of stored thermal energy of coal into thermal/electrical energy occurs through the simultaneous occurrence of three independent processes:

1   combustion of pulverized coal in the furnace of a boiler with the help of oxygen drawn from atmospheric air;
2   conversion of demineralized water circulating through thousands of water and steam tubes which are heated by the heat energy released by the combustion of coal and
3   conversion of the heat energy of superheated steam into mechanical energy inside the steam turbine in a manner that helps to drive the generator producing electricity.

On average, the production of 1 kWh of electrical energy requires about 0.70–0.72 kg of Indian coal containing 30–35 per cent ash. Thus for every 100 kWh of electrical energy, the requirements are:

coal   72 kg (besides furnace oil)
oxygen   130 kg
(if the combustible matter in coal consisted entirely of carbon)
which produces:

carbon dixoide	180 kg
hot nitrogen with some NO_x	520 kg
ash	24 kg
sulphur dioxide (0.5% S in coal)	0.7 kg

Since 20 per cent excess air is ordinarily used in the boiler, the exhaust gases will additionally contain 104 kg nitrogen and about 26 kg oxygen. On the basis of the above, figures for annual per capita consumption of coal and consequent generation of waste products at different levels of energy consumption are computed in Table 5.1.

Disposal of products of combustion

Nearly 20 per cent of ash is collected in hoppers placed below the furnace in the form of clinker containing variable amounts of unburnt carbon in the range of 6–12 per cent. The rest of the ash, now called fly ash, is carried with flue gases, into the electrostatic precipitators which are provided to arrest its discharge into the atmosphere through the chimney which may be about 100–150 m. The efficiency of dust collection in the electrostatic

Table 5.1   *Consumption of coal and production of waste products*

Energy consumption in kW year/year	Coal (kg)	CO_2	Nitrogen (kg)	SO_2	Ash (kg)
$0.1^* \equiv 876\,kWh$	630	1575	4550	6	210
$0.2^* \equiv 1752\,kWh$	1260	3150	9100	12	420
$0.5 \equiv 4380kWh$	3150	7875	22 750	31	1050
$1.0^{**} \equiv 8760kWh$	6300	15 750	45 500	62	2100
$2.0^{***} \equiv 17520kWh$	12 600	31 500	91 000	124	4200

*Total of developing countries; **of Europe and ***USA

precipitators is seldom 100%; when operating at their best, the efficiency may be about 98–99 per cent. The chimneys thus eject large quantities of particulate matter of great fineness along with gases at 150–200°C.

The quantity of coal used for thermal power generation is continually rising; nearly 60 million tonnes in 1984–85, producing more than 20 million tonnes of ash rising to 100 million tonnes of coal in 1986-87 corresponding to about 35 million tonnes of ash. According to the projections of the Advisory Board on Energy, energy requirements in the year 2004-5 will be nearly four times more than for 1984–85, when the inevitable generation of fly ash would be approaching a hundred million tonnes annually in view of ever increasing quantities of ash in coal.

Environmental consequences of thermal generation

DISCHARGE OF CARBON DIOXIDE

The advent of industrialization in the early nineteenth century and its growth by leaps and bounds thereafter, has today threatened the continuation of the life-sustaining, otherwise fragile, carbon dioxide–oxygen cyclic conversion cycle. This is because carbon dioxide is incessantly being belched out into the atmosphere in high concentrations by the chimneys of thermal power stations and of other industries which are dependent for their energy or process requirements on the combustion of fossil fuel besides that from the exhausts of large numbers of automobiles etc. When compounded with the decreased amount of vegetative cover and with industrial consumption of oxygen in steel making etc., the consequences could easily assume serious proportions. The cumulative effect of the two mutually unrelated human activities has been to increase the concentration of carbon dioxide in atmospheric air to 340 p.p.m. in 1980; mathematical modelling suggests that if the pace of industrial development and degeneration of the ecology continues as at present, the concentration could rise to as much as 560 p.p.m. in the early 21st century.

Accumulation of increasingly greater amounts of carbon dioxide in the atmosphere strengthens the 'greenhouse effect' of trapping solar radiation near earth's surface. A consequence of this would be general global warming; modelling studies and experiments suggest that surface temperatures could increase by 1.5–4.5°C for an effective doubling of the concentration of carbon dioxide; the warming being more pronounced at higher latitudes than at the equator. Another consequence of this could be melting of polar ice caps and consequent increase in sea level by 25–140 cm large enough to inundate low lying coastal areas and river deltas. This in turn, could also drastically upset agricultural production through increased salinity of soil. Today, global climatic change is a serious probability.

For a country like India, which depends upon seasonal winds for its annual, life-sustaining rainfall, the consequences of selective global warming could be even more disastrous because both the intensity and direction of the monsoon winds which are created by the difference between the equatorial and polar temperatures could be affected. Changes in ecology may have already affected the Indian scenario as suggested by the occurrence of continuing droughts in the western parts of the country and the prevalence of higher temperatures during summer months. There is no way to say whether or not this has already occurred except to compare the recent meteorological data with the past but then irrevocable ecological damage would have already occurred.

DISCHARGE OF NO_x

Discharge of highly toxic oxides of nitrogen (NO_x) and of sulphur into the atmosphere is also a serious matter as it may lead to acidification of the environment. It has been estimated that parts of the Europe and North America are receiving from the atmosphere more than 1 gm of sulphur per m² of ground area every year in the form of acid rain. Acidification of soil has also been reported from some of the developing countries as well. Spread of industrial pollution and acid rain do not respect national boundries for it is known that industrial atmosphere polluting discharges from central European sources have caused precipitation of acid rain in the Arctic zone Scandinavian countries. The consequence of acid rain on forests, farms and soils could be disastrous because it encourages erosion of soil and consequencial siltation of lakes and dams, reduces the water-holding capacity of soils and thus contributes to flash floods. Acid rain leaches out nutrients from leaves and soils and provides mobility to ions of aluminium and heavy metals with a result that they are taken up by the trees whose growth is then stunted. The only redeeming feature however is that technology is today available to arrest and neutralize the discharges of acidic nature in the atmosphere. However the technology to reduce the amount of the discharges of carbon dioxide is non-existent.

Though, Indian coals contain lower amounts of sulphur in comparison with those of the United States or Europe, discharges of sulphur dioxide into the atmosphere could yet bring about serious ecological changes in the Himalayan sub-terrain regions through precipitation of acid rain causing destruction of forests and consequential increase in erosion.

Need for new strategy

New strategies are therefore needed to control the amount of carbon dioxide in the atmosphere by reinvigorating the natural carbon dioxide oxygen cycle and by taking effective steps to arrest the discharge of acidic gases into the atmosphere through the installation of appropriate scrubbers.

This is the time to develop a global agenda for sustainable development because the hitherto uncontrolled withdrawal of natural resources and their consumption through industrial processing are rapidly degrading the environment towards a limit from where its reinvigoration may become impossible. While industrialization provides a proven means for rapidly bringing about economic redemption of large masses of people, uncontrolled industrialization must not be allowed to occur because science and technology have not reached a high enough level of maturity to protect and enhance the natural heritage. While exploitation of natural resources for human welfare is essential, the exploitation itself should be inspired by a policy of resource management for there exists a very close nexus between environmental degradation, poverty and resource mismanagement. Thus, 'unfortunately in the majority of developing countries, especially the least developed, the shortage of energy goes hand in hand with food shortages' (UNIDO, 1983). An alarmist view of the scenario emerging through unregulated, non-sustainable industrialization should not be dismissed as scientific fantasy but propagated with magnanimity for the purpose of driving home the point that the world stands on the brink of ecological disaster if urgent steps are not taken at this stage to reverse the already inflicted damage. National economy should be inter-woven with national ecology and the two together with industrialization.

Environmental illiteracy – a threat to human survival

Are we aware of the consequences of unmitigated discharges of carbon dioxide, oxides of sulphur, complex oxides of nitrogen and fine particulate matter besides, hot nitrogen in tonnage quantities from a single point source of a chimney of a modern thermal power station or of the accumulation of mountains of fly ashes – materials of low enough bulk density to make dust airborne at only a slight whizz of air and capable of remaining airborne over long distances with and without the formation of aerosols with the condensation of moisture on the surface of discharged particulate matter. The concentration of particulate matter in the vicinity of thermal power stations may be anything up to 500 $\mu g/m^3$ depending upon the efficiency of installed dust arresting systems and the particles remain floating in the atmosphere for durations which depend upon a number of factors, such as, the size and morphology of the particles, their bulk density and formation or otherwise of aerosols; their settlement also depends upon the local wind conditions, temperature distributions and thermally induced inversions of atmospheric air. The situation may become all the more devastating to human health when the airborne remnants of shattered cenospheric particles are inhaled because the particles are now most prone to get anchored within the soft tissues of human lungs and thereby create long-lasting pulmonary distresses. Fly ash particulate matter may also contain other toxic metals such as mercury, chromium, selenium and iron. Some of the fly ashes are known to be radio-active as well.

Dispersion of pollutants

Since thermal power generation is a necessary imperative for develop-ment, the atmospheric pollutants discharged, in its wake, into the environment from the stacks of power stations must either be neutralized or dispersed expeditiously so that concentration of harmful constituents in the immediate vicinity is sufficiently diluted with air and is less than the permissible limits and that the pollutants are not carried far away to bring about, imperceptibly but positively, environmental degradation in the long run. The use of tall stacks, with/without gas scrubbers, has until recently been considered as a viable engineering solution. While all the flue gases contain carbon dioxide, the situation becomes much more aggravated if the waste gases contain toxic substances such as SO_2, SO_3 CO, NO_x, hydrocarbons etc., besides fly ash. These substances are harmful for vegetation, animals and people even in low concentrations above the specified limits. Ordinarily gaseous pollutants from thermal power stations are discharged into the atmosphere through tall stacks. The fact of their being at high temperatures (120–130°C) powerfully accen-tuates their upward thrust into the atmosphere on being discharged from the stack.

Since the atmosphere is practically in continuous motion, it is now generally recognized that dispersal of the pollutants discharged from a single point source, for example, a stack, occurs into the atmospheric space under the influence of two components of atmospheric motion: (1) the mean wind field which transports the pollutants from one point to another and (2) the turbulent motions, including eddy currents, which disperse the pollutants about some central position. Atmosphere turbulence produces pulsation velocities in all the three directions which ensure mixing of flue gases with atmospheric air through widening of the plume as it is carried away in the direction of the wind.

Since the ground surface/atmosphere interface offers friction and as air, in common with other fluids possesses viscosity, both the direction and

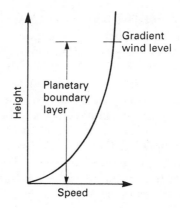

Figure 5.1   *Wind speed change with height above the ground*

speed of wind changes with height above ground level. Though the precise manner in which surface wind velocity could be used to compute the wind speed at stack height through quantifiable mathematical relationship is not known, power law types of relationships are described in many text books (Calvert and England, 1984). The change in wind speed with height is schematically shown in Figure 5.1.

The dispersal of pollutants is affected by motions that occur in the atmosphere near the ground and are influenced by the friction of the ground surface and surface heating and cooling.

The atmosphere above the ground surface can be divided into three zones:

1   surface boundary layer which extends up to 50–150 m where wind motion is affected by surface roughness and vertical temperature gradients;
2   transition layer in space above 100 m up to a height of 500–1000 m or more where wind motion is affected by surface friction, density or temperature gradient and earth's rotation;
3   free atmosphere where wind motions are unaffected by ground friction or by surface heating and cooling.

The three zones are schematically shown in Figure 5.2. The surface boundary and the transition layers together are called the 'planetary boundary layer'. Most of the motions and turbulence occur in the planetary boundary layer but once the pollutants reach the free atmosphere, they are rapidly carried away to far off places. The entry of pollutants into the free atmosphere is a common occurrence and is confirmed by scientific monitoring experiments for the transport of pollutants discharged in the atmosphere in Central United States or in Central Europe to places in Canada and beyond and to Scandinavian countries of the Arctic zone respectively. Some of the planetary boundary layer can be upset by the occurrence of intense convective activities associated with thunderstorms and cyclonic movements of air. When cold air is advected over a warm surface, such as may occur on a very warm spring day with strong sunshine the convective currents from the earth's surface may extend to a height of as much as 3000 metres and above.

Tall stacks do not provide the answer/solution to problems of environmental pollution; they merely shift the site of effective precipitation of pollution in the form of either the settling down of fine particulate matter or of gaseous pollutants in the form of acid rain. Environmental monitoring in the vicinity of tall stacks is, therefore, likely to generate misleading data and would not provide any indication with regard to the damage that may be caused at long distances away from the source. If pollution is considered as a 'global' problem on the concept of 'one world', tall stacks are not the answer. This awareness has given rise to the concept that the height of the stack should be determined by 'good engineering practice'. The term 'good engineering practice' is defined in the *Handbook of Air Pollution Technology* to mean the height necessary to ensure that emissions from the stack do not result in excessive concentrations of any air pollutants in the immediate vicinity of the source as a result of atmospheric downwash which may be created by the source itself, or as a result of nearby structures or terrain features. The height allowed by this new definition shall not exceed two and a half times the height of the source unless the owner affirmatively demonstrates that a greater height is necessary to prevent excessive pollutants 'downwash'.

Mathematical models

Turbulent pulsations and eddy currents in surface boundary and transition layers encourage tendencies for particulate and gaseous pollutants to disperse in the atmosphere. Ideally, the gaseous constituents should also have a tendency to diffuse in a molecular state, but as yet the problem has

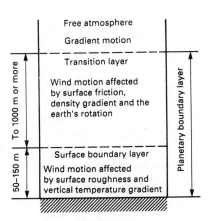

Figure 5.2   *Regions of atmospheric motions above the ground surface*

defied rigorous mathematical development. Most of the mathematical models for the dispersal of pollutants from a single point discharging source are inspired by models of diffusion in solid state which owe themselves to classical models of heat conduction. They form the basis of the 'gradient transport' approach models to predict the concentration profile of pollutants away from the source after their discharge into the atmosphere. In accordance with the gradient transport theory (K-theory) the rate of change of any quantity, q in a one dimensional system is related to the rate of change of the gradient

$$\frac{dz}{dt}\bar{q}=\frac{k\partial^2}{\partial x^2}q$$

where k is the eddy diffusivity coefficient (Calvert and England, 1984).

In three dimensional form the equation is:

$$\frac{d\bar{q}}{dt}=\frac{\partial}{\partial x}\left(k_x\frac{\partial\bar{q}}{dx}\right)+\frac{\partial}{\partial y}\left(k_y\frac{\partial\bar{q}}{\partial y}\right)+\frac{\partial}{\partial z}\left(\frac{k_z\partial\bar{q}}{\partial z}\right)$$

This equation implies that dispersal of pollutants from a concentrated single point source occurs in three dimensional space where the diffusivity coefficients in the three directions are independent and mutually unrelated.

A number of solutions to these differential equations have been proposed by a number of workers.

One important limitation of the K-theory is that it assumes that diffusivity is constant; in as far as the boundary planetary layer is concerned this assumption is not correct because of the existence of large variations in the vertical temperature gradients due to different surface heating conditions and the wind being simultaneously subjected to shearing forces. Atmospheric turbulence in the three directions is introduced by both the surface roughness and convection; mechanically induced eddies are much weaker than the thermally induced eddy currents.

In view of the inherent difficulties of measuring three dimensional dispersion coefficients models for mathematical representation for the dispersion of gaseous and particulate matter in atmosphere based on statistical (Gaussian) distribution in space began to gain favour, the space being fully defined with the help of a three dimensional coordinate system where x direction is the direction of plume travel in the direction of mean wind motion, y axis is in the horizontal plane perpendicular to the x axis and the z axis extends vertically. This is schematically shown in Figure 5.3. The lateral dispersion coefficient (σ_y) represents the horizontal spread of the plume in the direction of plume travel; the vertical dispersion coefficient (σ_z) represents its spread in the vertical direction.

The *Handbook of Air Pollution Technology* provides the following fundamental dispersion equation by the Gaussian theory:

$$C(x,y,z,H)=\frac{Q}{2\pi\sigma_y\cdot\sigma_z\cdot u}\exp\left[-\frac{1}{2}\left(\frac{y}{\sigma_y}\right)^2\right]\left\{\exp\left[-\frac{1}{2}\left(\frac{z-H}{\sigma_z}\right)^2\right]\right.$$
$$\left.+\exp\left[-\frac{1}{2}\left(\frac{z-H}{\sigma_z}\right)^2\right]\right\}$$

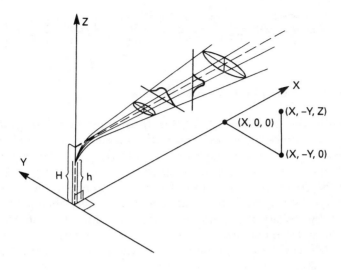

Figure 5.3 *Coordinate system showing Gaussian distributions in the horizontal and vertical*

where C, the concentration at any coordinate position (x, y, z) given, an emission Q, at an effective height (H), is represented by the Gaussian distribution. H is the plume centreline for an elevated source which is the sum of the physical stack height and the plume rise. The following assumptions are made:

1 The plume spread has a Gaussian distribution in both the horizontal and vertical planes with standard deviations of plume concentration distribution in the horizontal and vertical of σ_y and σ_z respectively.
2 The mean wind speed affecting the plume is u.
3 The uniform emission rate of pollutants is Q.
4 Total reflection of the plume takes place at the earth's surface, that is, there is no deposition or reaction at the surface which is why there is a double exponential in the z and H terms.
5 The normal units utilized in the Gaussian model are concentration in grams per cubic metre, with Q the emission rate in grams per second, u in metres per second; σ_y, σ_z and H, and all coordinates are in metres.

The basic assumptions of this model are that the turbulence is everywhere the same; σ_y and σ_z are functions of distance from the source; the wind speed is constant throughout the layer where the plume is being transported; and the wind direction remains constant during travel' (Calvert and Englund, 1984).

There are many equations which may be used in special circumstances that are much simpler than the full equation. When concentrations are calculated only at ground level and perfect reflection is assumed, the following equation may be used:

$$C(x, y, o, H) = \frac{Q}{\pi \sigma_y \cdot \sigma_z \cdot u} \exp\left[-\frac{1}{2}\left(\frac{y}{\sigma_y}\right)^2\right] \exp\left[-\frac{1}{2}\left(\frac{H}{\sigma_z}\right)^2\right]$$

ESTIMATION OF COEFFICIENTS FOR DISPERSION

In terms of the Gaussian distribution theory, dispersion of pollutants is favoured by atmospheric turbulence; the magnitude of turbulence however varies a great deal during the course of a day and every day along the year. A knowledge of distribution coefficients is necessary to be able to predict the concentration profile of the dispersion of pollutants into the atmosphere. Widely used dispersion coefficients were obtained by Pasquill in 1959 by collating experimental data of dispersion in the United Kingdom and United States with theoretical models with the help of computers. His values are graphically shown in Figures 5.4 and 5.5. Each of the six collating lines in the figures represents a different level of atmospheric stability; line A is for high turbulence as with light winds on a sunny afternoon and line F for relatively little turbulence.

Pasquill used the letters (A–F) arbitrarily to define different levels of stability of atmosphere according to incoming solar radiation; the categories are listed in Table 5.2 in accordance with surface wind speeds. 'During the daytime when incoming solar radiation is strong and the wind speed is light, the stability category is A. With strong incoming solar radiation and wind speeds greater than 6 m/s, the stability category is C, the assumption being that the strong winds would not permit thermal convection to develop to the degree that it does with light winds' (Calvert and Englund, 1984).

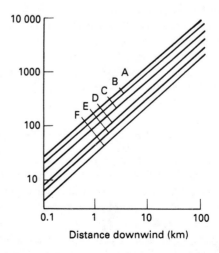

Distance downwind (km)

Figure 5.4   *Horizontal dispersion coefficient as a function of downwind distance from the source*

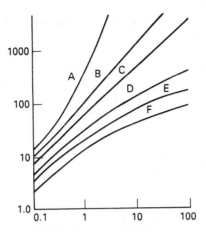

Figure 5.5   *Vertical dispersion coefficient as a function of downwind distance from the source*

Table 5.3 lists the stability classifications as a function of vertical fluctuations if a vane is available from which the standard deviation of the vertical wind direction may be calculated (Calvert and Englund, 1984).

Plume rise above stack exit

The gaseous effluent plume also contains particulate matter on discharge in to the atmosphere from the stack up to a certain height which depends upon two factors: (1) the hydrodynamic rise on account of the kinetic

Table 5.2   *Key to stability categories*

	Day*			Night*	
Surface wind speed (at 10 m) (m/s)	Incoming solar radiation			Thinly overcast or $\geqslant \frac{4}{8}$ Low cloud	$\leqslant \frac{3}{8}$ Cloud
	Strong	Moderate	Slight		
<2	A	A–B	B		
2–3	A–B	B	C	E	E
3–5	B	B–C	C	D	E
5–6	C	C–D	D	D	D
>6	C	D	D	D	D

*The neutral class, D, should be assumed for overcast conditions during day or night

Table 5.3   *Pasquill–Gifford stability category versus vertical wind direction fluctuation**

P–G stability category	Standard deviation of vertical wind direction σ_ϕ† (degrees)
A	> 12–12
B	10–12
C	7.8–10
D	5–7.8
E	2.4–5
F	< 2.4

*(From appendix C in *Guideline on Air Quality Models*: Environment protection agency USA. OAQPS guideline series, Triangle Park 1980)
†These values Should be adjusted for surface roughness by multiplying σ_ϕ by $(z_0/15 \text{ cm})^{0.2}$, where z_0 is the average surface roughness length within a 1 to 3 km radius of the source.

energy of the upward travelling flue gases in the stack, and (2) the thermal rise due to the difference in the densities of the plume and surrounding air. The extent of the plume rise depends, in a complex manner, on a number of factors, including the meteorological conditions.

Hydro-dynamic rise has been considered proportional to the square roots of the gas volume being discharged per second, and of the gas velocity at the exit, (hence on the stack diameter) and inversely proportional to the wind velocity at the level of the stack. On the other hand, the thermal rise component is neither influenced by the stack exit diameter nor the exit speed of gases; it depends upon three factors: (1) the quantity of heat contained in the effluent gases relative to the surrounding medium; (2) wind velocity; and (3) extent of atmospheric turbulence, particularly in the horizontal direction (y). For the same wind velocity and turbulence, the thermal rise depends only on the magnitude of heat ejection; it does not distinguish the quantum of heat supplied by a relatively small volume of gases with a high temperature difference between flue gas and air or due to greater volume of gases at a lower temperature difference.

A number of different approaches have been developed to compare the plume rise but those adopted by the Environment Protection Agency of USA are derived from Brigg's equations which are based on the theory of the entrainment of air into a jet or buoyant plume with coefficients determined empirically from a wide variety of sources. Accordingly:

$$\Delta h = 1.6 F^{1/3} U^{-1} \rho^{2/3} \qquad \text{for } \rho \leqslant 3.5 X^*$$

and

$$\Delta h = 1.6 F^{1/3} U^{-1} (3.5 X^*)^{2/3} \text{ for } \rho > 3.5 X^*$$
$$X^* = 14 F^{5/8} \quad \text{if } F \leqslant 55$$
$$X^* = 34 F^{2/5} \quad \text{if } F > 55$$

where

Δh = plume rise, m

F = $g\ V_s R_s [(T_s - T_a)/T_s]$. It is the vertical flux of the buoyant plume.

g = acceleration due to gravity.

V_s = average exit gas velocity of gases of plume m/s.

R_s = inner radius of the stack, m.

T_s = average temperature of gases in plume °K.

T_a = ambient temperature, °K.

U = wind speed at stack height, m/s.

ρ = distance from source to receptor.

The distance to the point downward of the stack where the plume is no longer rising is given as 3.5 X∗ and is incorporated in the plume rise equation.

Knowledge of rise of plume above the stack exit can now be used to determine the concentration of pollutants at any place due to the dispersion of pollutants according to the Gaussian model.

Macroscopic morphology of plume

There are five principal shapes of plume and are shown schematically in Figure 5.6.

LOOPING PLUME

The plume spreads in wavy manner with a large angle of widening and high degree of turbulence i.e. it is observed under conditions of unstable atmosphere. The plume reaches earth's surface rather quickly after discharge and being not far away from the stack, the concentration of toxic gases may not have been diluted to safe levels. The situation is essentially due to thermal stratification in the atmosphere resulting in daytime on clear days when earth's surface is intensely heated up by solar radiation i.e. under conditions of super adiabatic vertical lapse rate (temperature gradient).

CONING PLUME

The plume reaches earth at a somewhat greater distance than does the looping plume. It is formed under conditions of stable atmosphere with nearly isotropic turbulence in the horizontal and vertical direction, as could occur with overcast sky and windy weather during either day or night. The vertical lapse rate is somewhere between dry adiabatic and isothermal ($dT/dz = 0$).

FANNING PLUME

This type of dispersion is observed at inversion or at slightly isothermal

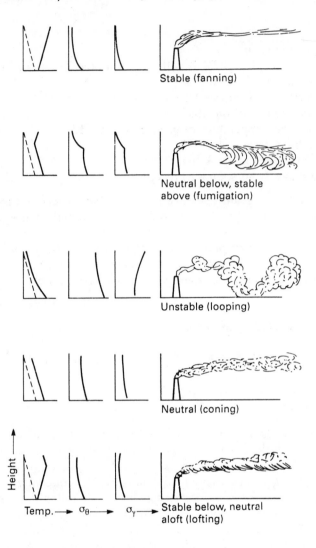

Figure 5.6   *Shapes of smoke plume*

lapse rates. This kind of atmospheric structure typically occurs at night times when the ground temperature is lower than that of the air and is favoured by light winds and clear sky (and snow cover). The plume, spreading mainly in the horizontal direction, (and only slightly vertically) becomes 'fan-like'; the plume does not touch earth at all, if it does, it does so at great distances away from the stack. This kind of plume disperses the pollutants widely and extensively.

LOFTING PLUME

This kind of plume forms when an inverted thermal structure exists in the lower portions of the atmosphere in the zone of the stack height and a normal one with negative lapse rate above it. The zone of the highest concentrations is at the upper boundary of the inverted layer. A lofting plume when formed from high stacks, throws the pollutants into the high atmospheric layers; the pollutants are thus dispersed globally, though not seemingly affecting local scenario.

FUMIGATION PLUME

This kind of plume forms when an atmospheric layer with a normal negative lapse rate extends from the surface to beyond the stack height and plume rise, and is followed by an inversion layer above. Such a stratification of the atmosphere may occur early in the morning when the night inversion is being dispersed under the action of solar radiation. Under such conditions dispersion of the pollutants occurs near the earth's surface and is most undesirable.

Energy afforestation

However impressive the gains of technological monoculture involving exploitation of minerals and ever increasing generation of electrical power through combustion of fossil fuel may be, it has, nevertheless lead mankind to a cul-de-sac of widespread environmental pollution, acidification and ecological degradation. The threat to global ecology from increased concentration of carbon dioxide in the atmosphere through the greenhouse effect alone is chilling (its concentration in pre-industrial times was 280 p.p.m., rose to about 340 p.p.m. in 1980 and unless reversed, is poised to become 560 p.p.m. towards the middle of the next century). Except its biological reconversion into oxygen and plant organic materials through photosynthesis, there is no known technology which can achieve the laudable objective of reducing the atmospheric carbon dioxide once again into oxygen and organic compounds of carbon.

Unlike industrial processes, the dynamics of biological conversion of carbon dioxide and moisture into the plant system defined by leaves, stalk and roots, cannot yet be described in truly mathematical terms. It is however known that photosynthetic activity is influenced by a number of factors such as the photosynthetic active radiation (PAR), concentration of carbon dioxide, ambient temperatures, water supply and atmospheric humidity, concentration of mineral elements (nitrogen, phosphorus and calcium) and other nutrients in the soil etc.

Green plants can use only light of wavelength 400–700 nm which in tropical countries constitutes about 0.43 of total solar radiation. The efficiency of conversion of PAR into biomass (carbohydrate, starch and cellulose considered as a network of glucose sub-units) works out to only

0.0984 of the total i.e. less than 1 per cent for most forest trees. Higher efficiencies of conversion are however found in some plants; the highest at 3.3 per cent is found with sugarcane (a so-called C-4 plant) because of the added metabolic pathway of four carbon acids. The other C-4 type plants (sorghum and maize) have evolved in semi-arid tropical and sub-tropical areas. Generally, C-4 plants are more efficient at (1) high light intensities as they avoid the wasteful process of photorespiration which occurs in other plants, (2) at higher tropical temperatures and (3) low partial pressures of carbon dioxide such as in air (0.03 per cent).

Photosynthesis in some plants occurs through a three-chain carbon skeleton (rice, wheat, barley, alfalfa, cotton, soyabean, peanut, sugar beet). At the natural level of carbon dioxide in the atmosphere, corn and sugarcane grow faster than the non C-4 plants but when the level of carbon dioxide in a greenhouse is raised by a factor of three or so, rice and other temperate zone plants grow faster as shown in Table 5.4.

Since food crops can never be used for the generation of electrical energy, there is a great challenge for genetic engineering to evolve new species of trees with greater biomass potential. A major task today is to expand and deepen basic research and to make its findings work in practical fields.

Short rotation forestry

Despite its having low efficiency of conversion, there is at present no alternative to photosynthetic conversion of solar energy into fuel. The use of biomass for decentralized power generation is advocated because it also holds the seeds of stopping any further increase in the concentration of carbon dioxide in atmosphere. Since seeding and crowning on maturity of trees is not an annual affair, the present is the time for initiating world-

Table 5.4   *Rate of photosynthesis at air levels and elevated levels of carbon dioxide*

Plant	Air	$mg\ CO_2/dm^2$ per hour Elevated CO_2
Corn, grain sorghum		
Sugarcane	60–75	100
Rice	40–75	135
Sunflower	50–65	130
Soyabean, sunflower	30–40	56
Cotton	40–50	100

Data from Bassham, J.A. (1977) *Biological Solar Energy Conversion.* (Eds. Mitsui, Miyachi, Pietro and Tamura), Academic Press

wide action for energy afforestation on wastelands, so that there is no further encroachment on natural forests for meeting the fuel/energy needs.

Selection of tree species for energy plantation depends on several factors. There can be no one solution for all the developing countries as competing uses of high economic value of wood for fibres, chipboards etc. may also have to be considered along with (1) the mean annual increment (MAI) in the quantity of wood mass in energy forests; (2) the total leaf area in the canopy of the tree should be large enough so that the energy tree plantation is able to recycle fully the carbon dioxide released into the atmosphere; and (3) its amenability to adjust to local soil and climatic conditions. The world average MAI for natural forests is about 2 t/ha per year but through well managed forestry can be substantially raised.

Trees suitable for energy forestation can be selected after taking into account the pattern of rainfall distribution and soil conditions. The eucalyptus is however considered by some as a good choice as it grows rapidly on all types of soils and in climates with annual rainfalls as high as 300 cm to arid regions with less than 30 cm rainfall. It is said to have inherent eco-adjusting qualities and has been successfully grown on degraded sites, disturbed overburdens of working mines, deep ravines, hard lateritic or loose sandy soils. Whereas high yields of 25 t/ha per year are common, values up to 156 t/ha per year have also been reported from Brazil through biotechnological development of forests involving tissue culture, supply of micronutrients etc. There is also a very vocal, anti-eucalyptus lobby on the grounds of its putting heavy demands on ground water and soil nutrients.

Since photosynthesis of carbon dioxide occurs at measurable rates, it is theoretically possible to calculate the total leaf area required to fully neutralize the quantity of carbon dioxide emitted into the atmosphere by the combustion process. Precise data in terms of the rate as influenced by the tree species or the leaf area and its variation with the age of the plant/tree is not known. The data presented in Table 5.5 may be taken as an attempt to develop a model for the calculations. The table lists the assumptions and calculates the forest area required per one MW generating unit.

Conclusion

Carbon dioxide coming out of a low height stack diffuses to the ground at a short distance from the stack and in that area carbon dioxide level can go very high, which may affect the habitat of that area. If very tall stacks are used, the carbon dioxide may not diffuse back in the lower atmosphere but may enter in the upper atmosphere. High concentrations of carbon dioxide in the upper atmosphere will cause the greenhouse effect. Therefore, large stacks do not solve the pollution problem. Calculations regarding the spread of carbon dioxide coming out of a low height stack, have been

Table 5.5   *Forest area required for complete reconversion of carbon dioxide discharged from a 1 MW generating station*

Basis of Calculations:
Power plant capacity: 1MW
40% of carbon in wood (by weight)
Photosynthesis rate: 1g/m^2 per h (on yearly average basis)
Power value of wood: 1.5 kg of wood = 1 kWh
Tree plantation density: 1 tree/25 m^2

Calculations
Carbon dioxide produced: 2.2 t/h
Wood required to produce 1MW year electrical power: 13 000 t

Leaf area/trees (sq)	No. of trees	Area of plantation (Ha)
5	440 000	1100
8	274 800	687
10	220 000	550
15	146 400	366
50	44 000	110
100	22 000	55

done based on the Gaussian model of dispersion of gases in the atmosphere. It shows that a thermal power plant, consuming 100 t of coal per hour will raise the carbon dioxide level to more than 700 p.p.m. at ground level around a distance of 800 m from the stack.

Planting of the areas where carbon dioxide concentration rises very high, will assimilate the excess carbon dioxide and bring the carbon dioxide level to normal. Besides that biomass produced due to plantation will be utilized for producing power using a wood-fired thermal power plant.

In remote areas, where there is no production of electricity, electricity is supplied by very long power transmission lines which have a high transmission loss. In such areas small power plants will be more beneficial. Planting of areas near wood-fired thermal power plants, assimilates the excess carbon dioxide coming out of the stack, thus controlling pollution and producing biomass for energy generation.

References

Calvert, S. and Englund H. M. (eds) (1984) *Handbook of Air Pollution Technology* John Wiley & Sons, New York.

Editorial (1988) Deceptive forest data *The Hindustan Times*; New Delhi 1st April.

UNIDO (1983) *Implications of Biomass Energy Technology for Developing Countries*, UNIDO Document ID/WG 384/6 Rev.

World Commission on Environment and Development (1987) *Our Common Future*, Oxford University Press, Delhi.

6

Ambient air impact assessment of Feroze Gandhi Unchahar thermal power plant

A. K. Gupta, M. K. Ghosh, P. K. Singh and Ambrish Goel

With rapid industrialization, urbanization and agricultural development, electric power in India has increased tremendously. The demand always exceeds the generating capacity. This shortfall in demand is being met by the construction of new thermal power plants, in accordance with the Government of India's policy of emphasis on coal for power generation. These power plants are also a major source of atmospheric pollution. The total effect of pollution loading on the environment due to a thermal power plant is dependent on the location, size and pollution control technologies employed in the plant.

The present case study relates to the monitoring of ambient air quality in and around F. G. Unchahar Power Plant in Rae-Bareilly District of Uttar Pradesh, India. The objective of the ambient air quality observations was to determine the average background pollution level at the plant site. The plant has two 210 MW units under construction, which are expected to be fully operational by late 1988. The primary source of fuel is coal obtained from Jharia. Background pollution level was measured at the plant site during 1988 and at distance's up to 6 km from the power plant. The methods followed were as prescribed by IS:5182. The ambient air quality monitoring (background level) was measured with a view to establish baseline air quality for future use and to observe long-term trends. These are also helpful in investigating specific ambient air quality problems and to evaluate and formulate pollution control strategy.

This chapter also aims to predict the concentrations of pollutants when the two units are operational. To determine the concentration level with average background pollutant loading superimposed, due to the two units under construction the Gaussian diffusion model was developed based on single point source and due consideration was given to meteorological data. Based on the model pollutant level assessment at varying distance from the plant was done. The model was also used to predict additional loadings in case extension was undertaken at a later date. Lucas formula was used to estimate the plume rise and hence determine the effective stack height. The choice of differential co-efficients was based on Pasquill's stability criterion. The prediction was made to give a graphical representation of the concentrations in areas in downwind direction. The chapter also highlights that more effective dispersion of pollutant is possible with increase of stack height of thermal power plant.

An attempt is also made to suggest the appropriate environmental management plans that should be undertaken on a continuous basis.

Introduction

Thermal power plants contribute significantly towards economic growth as a result of electrical energy generated by them. Electricity is a clean form of energy at the point of consumption. Its uses range from the industrial sector to the agricultural sector. The availability of power has always been short of its demand. Thermal power plants are of course necessary for the economic development of the area but these also bring lots of environmental problems. Most of these relate to air and water pollution. The thermal power station (TPS) needs special efforts to reduce pollution level to within limits. Feroze Gandhi Thermal Power Station, Unchahar is under construction by U. P. Rajya Vidyut Utpadan Nigam Ltd and the two units of 210 MW each were expected to be in operation during 1988–89. It is proposed to extend this project to 3×210 MW units. The plant is located where there are no forests, sanctuaries or tourist attractions within 20 km. Ambient air impact assessment studies were carried out at this power plant so as to find the background level concentration of air pollutants in and around the plant site before the units became operational. These values are superimposed on expected emissions from 2×210 MW units to predict the ground level concentrations by using an air dispersion model. The ground level concentrations for the extension 3×210 MW units was also forecasted in the study after superimposing the above values of concentration of pollutants. A survey of plant site was carried out to identify land use, agriculture, human settlements, industrial activities etc.

Materials and methods

The ambient air samples were collected from in and around the thermal power station site up to a distance of 60 km, so as to find out the average concentration of pollutants in the ambient air. These measurement data are useful for investigating the specific problems of ambient air quality besides establishing baseline air quality for future use and to evaluate and formulate pollution control strategy.

The plant

U. P. Rajya Vidyut Utpadan Nigam has a thermal power unit under erection at Unchahar, district of Rae-Bareilley. It has two units of 210 MW each and three units of 210 MW each are proposed. The technical data for the units is as follows:

	2 × 210 MW	3 × 210 MW
Number and type of stacks	Single stack	Multiflue single stack
Height of each stack	160 m	220 m
Diameter of each stack	14–15 m	14–15 m
Exit gas velocity	25 m/s	25 m/s
Flue gas temperature	140°C	140°C
Flue gas density	0–8 kg/m³	0–8 kg/m³
Inter-stack distance	187.5 m	—
Flue gas volume	448 m³/s for ultimate capacity of 1050 MW.	

The units also have an electrostatic precipitator with the following technical data:

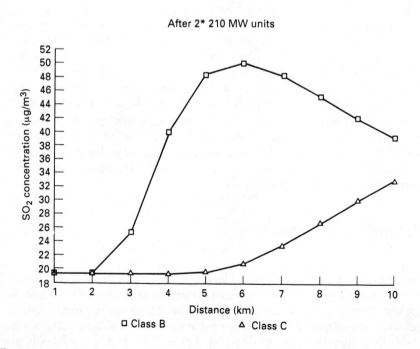

Figure 6.1 *Distant vs. SPM concentration*

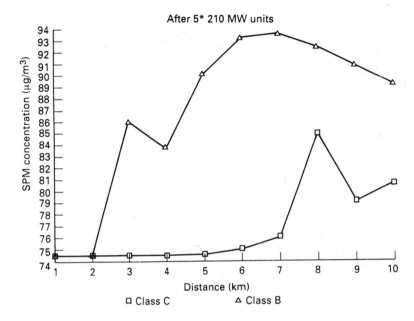

Figure 6.2 *Distant vs. SPM concentration*

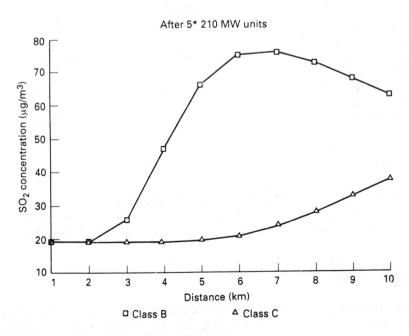

Figure 6.3 *Distant vs. SO₂ concentration*

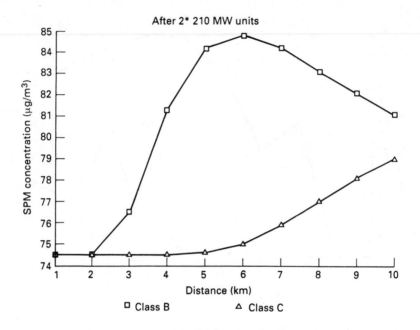

Figure 6.4   *Distant vs. SO$_2$ concentration*

	Normal conditions	Worst coal firing
Collection efficiency	99.46%	99.57%
Flue gas flow	355.5 m³/s	355.9 m³/s
Temperature of flue gas at inlet of Esp	145°C	139°C
Dust concentration of flue gas at inlet of Esp	55.2 gm/nm³	68.9 gm/nm³
Dust concentration of flue gas at outlet of Esp	300 mg/nm³	300 mg/nm³

Location and layout

Unchahar is situated 135 km from Lucknow, the capital of Uttar Pradesh, on the Lucknow — Allahabad road. The nearest railway station is Unchahar. Unchahar is at 81° 19'E longitude and 25° 55'N latitude.

Weather conditions

Wide fluctuations in temperature are reported. The observed maximum and minimum temperatures are 42.1°C and 1.1°C. The relative humidity varies from 15 to 100 per cent. Monsoon starts in July.

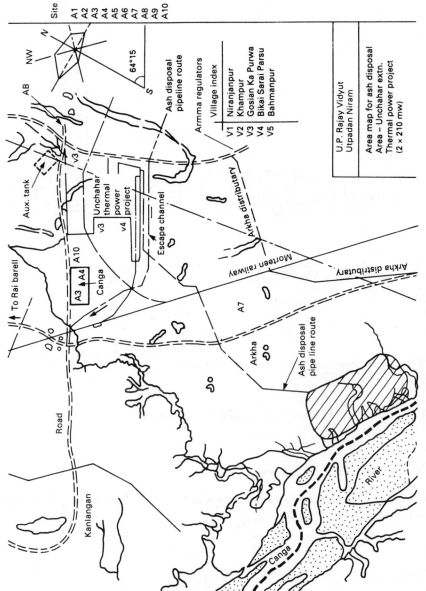

Figure 6.5 *Map of area round Unchahar Thermal Power Project*

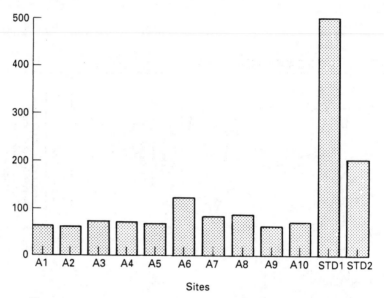

Sites
A1 – Coal handling
A2 – Administrative building
A3 – Field hostel
A4 – D.A.V. public school
A5 – Unchahar Hospital
A6 – Unchahar city 33kv
       (sub-station)

A7 – Cold storage
A8 – Vill. paterwa
A9 – Water intake to C.W
       pump house
A10 – Bank of Baroda

Graph from showing average values and
permissible limits

Figure 6.6   *Background level of SPM at Unchahar*

Human population

The total human population within a radius of 10 km of the plant site is between 8000 and 10 000.

Topography and physiography

Unchahar is almost flat, partly agricultural and partly ushar.

Water sources

Water sources used for TPS are Sarda Sahyak Canal and Pawa Canal.

Crops and vegetation

Wheat, rice, grain, pea, pulses etc. are the main crops grown in the area. Shrubs are mainly babul.

Surroundings

There are no forests, sanctuaries, cultural, historic or tourist attractions within 20 km of the plant.

Residential and commercial locations

The plant is situated at a distance of about 35 km from the populated residential areas of Rae-Bareilly city. The residential colony of the thermal power plant is situated near the plant. The residential area of Unchahar town is at around 4 km from the plant.

Fuel

The fuel used is pulverized coal. The sulphur content in the coal is in the range of 0.5–0.77 per cent and an ash content of 35 per cent. The source of supply is from middlings of Jharra coal fields for 2 × 210 MW units. Some 90 t/day of furnace oil is also required for the TPS.

Ambient air quality for background level at Unchahar

The following parameters were monitored for background ambient air monitoring at Unchahar TPS:

1   suspended particulate matter,
2   sulphur dioxide,
3   nitrogen oxides.

The results of the ambient monitoring are summarized in Table 6.1.

Mathematical modelling

Large power stations may affect the environment in more ways than one by contaminating the human habitat, flora and fauna if proper control measures are not taken. In order to forecast the extent of air pollution due to F. G. Thermal Power Station due to 2×210 MW units and the extension, computer modelling for the forecasting of ground level concentrations of airborne pollutants (suspended particulate matter and sulphur dioxide) was undertaken. The computer model is based on IS:8829–1978.

Methodology

Although owing to the complexity of the problem it is highly improbable that one single, unifying model can take into account all combinations of meteorological, topographical and source parameters, the most widely used dispersion model to compute pollutant concentration profiles is the Gaussian model. The model is based as recommended in IS:8829–1978. This model which is a steady state form of deterministic model is capable of computing pollutant concentrations in the ambient air using solutions to various equations representing the relevant physical processes. Independent meteorological variables are comprehensively used in the model which are important for dispersion of pollutants in air. Concentration of pollutants in air released from the stack (emission sources) is calculated using Gaussian diffusion:

$$X(0, 0, 0) = \frac{Q_v}{\pi, \sigma y \sigma z u} \exp\ 0.5(he/\sigma z)^2$$

where:
X is the GLC concentration
Q_v is the source strength in g/s
y and z are dispersion coefficients in metres.
u is the horizontal wind speed m/s.

Table 6.1   *Background levels of pollutants*

Site	Site name	Distance in km	Concentration in $\mu g/m^3$		
			SPM	SO_2	NO_x
A1	Coal handling	1.0	62	60	21
A2	Irrigation canal	6.5	61	5	2
A3	Field hostel	3.0	121	31	N.D.
A4	DAV school	4.0	82	10	3
A5	Unchahar hospital	5.0	65	21	1
A6	33 KV sub-station	4.0	70	20	2
A7	Cold storage	6.0	72	N.D.	11
A8	Village Paterwa	4.0	67	13	N.D.
A9	Pump house	1.5	60	14	N.D.
A10	Bank of Baroda	1.0	67	13	N.D.

N.D. Not detected

The coordinate system is such that the origin (0, 0, 0) at the source X is in the mean downwind direction. Effective stack height he is dependent on plume site h. For hot effluent with heat release of the order of $.10E\ 06$ Cal/s or more, IS:8829 prescribes the modified Lucas formula for plume rise calculations.

$$he = \frac{0.84\ (12.4 + 0.09\ hp)}{u}\ Q_h$$

Where:
hp = physical stack height
Δh = plume rise
u = mean wind speed at the stack top in m/s
Q_h = head release rate in Cal/sec. Heat release rate Q_h is calculated from the mass flow rate and exit temperature of stack. IS:8829–1978 prescribes the Sutton's empirical law to extrapolate wind speed from one level to another. This is given in the equation:

$$u = u,\ (z/zh)^{(n/Q - n)}$$

Where:
  u and u are wind speed at heights z and z, respectively.
  The effective stack height from ground is given by the equation:

$$he = hp + \Delta H$$

Emission factors are calculated from the data available in the form of quantities and composition of the stack exhaust. These are used to calculate source strength Q_v (g/s) of pollutants from each stack. The vertical dispersion coefficient z (M) and horizontal dispersion coefficient y (M) are found based on Pasquill's stability criteria and they can be expressed in the following form:

$$y(x) = (ay)(X)^b y$$
$$Z(x) = (az)(X)^b z$$

Where X is the downwind distance.

Pollution concentrations measured decrease as the sampling time decreases. A correction factor is applied to the resultant concentrations for longer sampling times, and may be obtained from

$$X_s = X_{10} X\ (10/ts)^{0.17}$$

Where:
X_s = the desired concentration at the relevant interval.
X_{10} = calculated concentration based on 10 min interval
ts = desired time interval in minutes

By putting the appropriate values for ts, the concentration can be obtained for 8 h sampling time.

Pasquill stability criteria

Atmospheric stability is an important factor in governing the extent of pollutant dispersion. Atmospheric stability has been divided into six classes from Class F. Class A describes the most unstable condition with strong daytime insolation (solar radiation) and a wind speed lower than 2.5 m/s. Class B describes unstable atmospheric conditions with moderate daytime insolation and a wind speed 3–5 m/s. Class C describes mildly unstable conditions with strong daytime insolation and a wind speed of 2–5 m/s. Class D is a neutral condition with moderate solar conditions and a wind speed greater than 5 m/s or slight daytime insolation and a wind speed greater than 5 m/s or night with less cloud and wind speed greater than 5 m/s or night with less and more cloudiness and wind speed 3–5 m/s and 2–3 m/s respectively. The overall result is that the greater the instability in atmosphere, the better the transport and diffusion of pollutants.

The stability Classes B and C were found to be relevant for maximum duration based on the meteorological data provided for F. G. Thermal Power Station. The results for forecasting includes concentrations based on both stability classes B and C.

Conclusion

The air pollution dispersion model has been computerized for single point source for existing units and multipoint sources, with proposed extension. The data used in the modelling are the design values of units under installation as well as the proposed units. The average background levels which are actually measured are superimposed on the modelling results to get the total ground level concentration of SPM and SO_2 around Unchahar TPS.

From the results it is observed that the expected ground level concentration after the installation of 2×210 MW units are well within the limits, both in the case of sulphur dioxide and suspended particulate matter. The permissible ambient SO_2 limit for industrial areas is 120 mg/m³ and for SPM it is 500 μg/m³ whereas the permissible limits of SO_2 and dust for residential and rural areas are 80 μg/m³ and 200 μg/m³ respectively. After the installation of two units the maximum SO_2 concentration is estimated to be 75 μg/m³ and that of dust 93.1 μg/m³ for 8 h sampling time at a distance of 2 km and wind speed of 20 km/h for stability class B, which are well within permissible limits.

Additional 3×210 MW units when commissioned are expected to contribute slightly to the pollution level in the atmosphere. The maximum SPM concentration in ambient air after the proposed expansion is expected to be 108 $\mu g/m^3$ for 8 h sampling time at a distance of 3 km and windspeed of 14 km/h for class B.

Although this value slightly exceeds the permissible limit prescribed by the Central Board for the Prevention and Control of Water Pollution for residential and rural areas, it may be noted that the modelling is done only for the downwind direction and then levels are only possible if the wind speed and wind direction is constant throughout the day. Thus the modelling is done for the extreme conditions and the results are usually biased upward. Since only few values are exceeding the permissible limit, it can be expected that the ground level concentration of SO_2 may remain almost within the limits in the normal conditions.

It is essential that actual emissions levels from 2×210 MW are measured and the ground level concentration at different distances are measured after these units are in operation. These values could be superimposed on the design values of proposed extension.

In the case build up of the green belt around thermal power plant, ESPs should be maintained properly.

References

Central Board for the Prevention of Water Pollution (1984) *Emissions Regulations*, July New Delhi.

Cheremisnoff, P. N. and Young, R. A. (1977) *Air Pollution Control and Design Handbook*. Part 1 & 2, Marcel Dekker Inc., New York.

Environmental Impact Statement of F. G. Unchahar Thermal Power Project, December 1984.

IS:8829 (1978), *Guidelines for Micrometeorological Techniques in Air Pollution Studies.*

Parker, A. (1979) *Industrial Air Pollution Handbook* McGraw Hill Book Company Ltd., London

Stern A. C. (1978) *Air Quality Management*, Vol V, Academic Press, London.

7

Evaluation of environmental impact of a new aluminium factory
Mario Polelli

Description of the area

The evaluation study of environmental impact proposed here constitutes the methodological basis in the case of the installation of an aluminium factory in an area which is underdeveloped in terms of commerce and service industries and where there is a level of agriculture of relatively modest productivity compared with large-scale cultivations, vineyards and herds.

Fishing allows the local families to add to their income. The predominant activity is agriculture which is conditioned by the climate, with very limited rainfall in the spring and summer months and the unavailability of water in the irrigation canals because the rainfall in the winter is also not high.

As a result, the cultivated land has been transformed into pastureland which produces very limited yields.

The prevailing soil conditions are clayey soil in the north-east and mainly sandy in the other areas.

An area of approximately 3,000 ha was considered in this evaluation, mostly situated to the south-west of the factory in the direction of the north-west wind which is the prevailing wind in this area Figure 7.1.

Description of the characteristics of the factory

The factory to be installed has a production capacity of 125 000 tonnes per year and will employ 1200 people. The production process starts with bauxite which is processed into aluminium and primary aluminium.

This processing is carried out in electrolytic chambers containing 348 cells. Cryolite and fluorite are used as fluxes. Fluorine and hydrofluoric acid are emitted into the atmosphere, the latter being particularly damaging to plant life. Fluorine pollution was identified up to 10 km away from the source. The distribution and extent will be described in detail later in this document. The amount of this pollution was extremely high and varied as

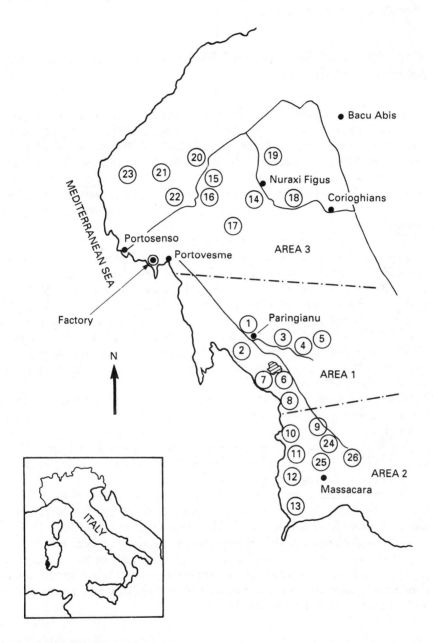

Figure 7.1 *Evaluation area*

a function of the production cycle, amounts varying between 100 p.p.m. and 800 p.p.m. in the various zones.

The effects of fluorine and hydrofluoric acid on the soil, plants, animals and man

Fluorides act on plants gradually producing a build-up which produces acute and chronic damage to plant life (Polelli, 1977). Acute damage is caused by high concentrations of pollutants in the atmosphere which become highly acid because of the presence of compounds which tend to condense as hydrofluoric acid.

The resulting damage is particularly obvious on the leaves, which change colour, and in the drying up of various organs of the plant (Zimmermann, 1958).

Chronic damage is caused by constant pollution at lower levels of concentration. During the first stage damage is comparatively modest and is shown by poor growth of the plant and premature shedding of the leaves. It is interesting that the action of these gases becomes evident only when they have penetrated the leaf structure through the stomata and this explains why the damage is much less at night and when the vegetation is dormant. Effects on plant life are measured against a scale of plant sensitivity to pollutants and in some cases plants are known as 'spy plants' because of their ability to react to fluorine compounds even at very low concentrations (Bossavy, 1968).

Numerous studies have demonstrated that the more sensitive plants show negative symptoms at levels of 20 p.p.m. upwards and the more resistant ones at 500 p.p.m.

The damage threshold is considered to be around 100 p.p.m. This damage is manifested by a reduction in the production of leaves and a shortening of the vegetative life cycle.

Normally humans and animals ingest small quantities of fluorides in their diets without suffering any ill effects; however, the situation is different when food and animal fodder contain large quantities.

In the higher animals, the fluorides affect the skeleton because they are highly reactive with calcium, in fact the F ion replaces the hydrophilic groups and causes fluoride hepatitis producing such typical symptoms as dental decay, damage to the bones, difficulty in walking and a reduction in weight and productivity (Enne, 1984).

Methodological approach for the evaluation of the environmental impact

The methodology indicated in Figure 7.2 was adopted for this study.

The research was divided into two correlated sections, qualitative and

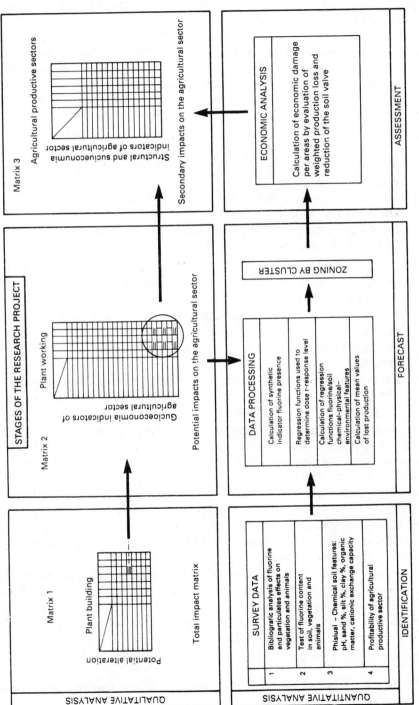

Figure 7.2

quantitative, and was carried out in three stages: identification — forecasts — evaluation (Polelli, 1988a).

The adoption of this method permitted the formulation and identification of the general matrices of the impact and thus the identification of the sectors which are specifically or potentially involved and, subsequently, the quantification of the impact itself (Clark, 1980).

The indications contained in Moore's methodology were used for the construction of the matrix of inter-relationship (Moore, 1973).

1   Identification of the activities and operations connected with the phases of construction and operation of the plant.
2   Identification of all the possible sources of impact during the operating phase.
3   Identification of possible systems which can be applied to minimize the effects of the impact.
4   Identification of potential alterations to the environment on the basis of reports from experts.

This first qualitative matrix relates the activities involved in the implementation of the plant to the potential alterations and provides the following indications (Matrix 1):

1   The possible duration of the alteration as a function of the action produced, in other words classification as long or short term;
2   the possibility of introducing measures to mitigate or correct these effects;
3   the possible partial dimension of the effects i.e. will the impact produce changes only in the areas around the plant or will much larger geographical areas be involved.

The second matrix is a weighted representation of the impact with the plant in operation, when the environmental and socio-urbanistic effects are greater (Lee and Wood, 1980). At this stage a relative weighting is attributed to the effect on the environment by means of a judgment based on a hierarchy of values using the criteria suggested by the Delphi method. Once the objectives of acceptability of the single effects which must be considered as standards has been established, the degree of compliance of the proposed plant is identified on the basis of a series of global evaluations (Matrix 2).

Finally, a matrix which correlates the possible alterations in the agricultural and socio-economic sectors is created. Compared with the first, this matrix represents an enlargement of the sections which identify a long-term irreversible effect in the agricultural sector caused by the operation of the plant (Matrix 3).

Criteria adopted for the definition of homogeneous areas

There are some exceedingly interesting models for the study of pollution (Weber, 1982). The basic data utilized by us in the preliminary stage of the

Matrix 1	Felling plants	Soil levelling	Accesses and roads to yard	Industry building	New workers houses building	Port widening and arrangement for docking ships
Landscape alteration	ilz	ilz	ilz	ilz	ilz	ilz
Loss of outspace light	ilz	ilz	ilz	ilz	ilz	ilz
Changes in soil stability	ilz	ilz	—	—	—	—
Changes in general characteristics of soil	ilz	ilz	ilz	ilz	—	ilz
Growth of air pollution	—	—	ilz	ibz	—	—
Growth of water pollution	—	—	ilz	ilz	—	ilz
Changes in town and country payout	—	—	ilz	ilz	ilz	ilz
Loss of visibility	—	—	—	ilz	—	—
Growth of population in nearby villages	—	—	—	ilr	ilz	ilr
Changes in agricultural sector	ilz	—	ilz	—	ilz	ilz
Changes in labour market	—	—	ibz	ilz	ilz	ilz
Changes in income distribution	—	—	—	—	—	—
Alteration of economic activities using local resources	ilz	—	ibz	ilr	—	ilr
Alteration of population health and hygienical conditions	—	—	—	ilr	ilz	—

EFFECTS

r = reversible; b = short-term; z = local level; i = irreversible; l = long-term;
r = regional level

Matrix 2

	Bantite transportation	Bantite loading and unloading	Bantite stocking	Emission of particulates	Gas emmission	Acid rain	Heavy metal	Material transportation to dump	Accesses to factory	Stocking finisher products	Water pollution	Noise
Socio-economic indicators of agricultural sector												
A1 Structural indicators												
Total land area									−liz	−liz		
Arable land area									−liz	−liz		
Total number of farms												
Total number of livestock farms												
Average land per farm												
<5 ha												
5–20 ha												
20–50 ha												
>50 ha												
Average arable land per farm												
Title deed: owner												
tenant farming												
System of farming:												
owner occupation												
with workers												
Farm machinery												
Irrigation												
Real estate market				−Rlz	−Rlz	−Rlz	−Rlz					−liz
Family capital flow:												
self-financing												
agricultural credit												
ordinary credit												
housing				−liz								−liz
improvement of farm structure				−liz	−liz	−liz	−liz					
improvement of farm machinery and equipment												
working capital												
B1 Socio-economic indicators												
Agricultural sector's workers	−lir	−lir	−lir									
Manufacturing sector's workers	−lir	−lir	−lir							+liz		
Services sector's workers	+lir	+lir	+lir						+liz	+liz		
Owner occupated												
Simple workers												
Feminilization												
Senilization												
Farm job done by:												
family members												
full-time workers			−liz	−liz								
temporary workers												
Owner working: only in the farm												
in other farms												
in other sectors												
Arable land												
maize unit production/ha				−liz	−Rlz	−Rlz	−liz				−liz	
wheat unit production/ha				−liz	−Rlz	−Rlz	−liz				−liz	
barley unit production/ha				−liz	−Rlz	−Rlz	−liz				−liz	
Permanent meadow area												
unit production/ha				−liz	−Rlz	−Rlz	−liz				−liz	
Wool				−liz	−Rlz	−Rlz	−liz				−liz	
Livestock – Cattle: number												
unit production								−liz				
Pigs: number												
unit production									−liz			

Matrix 3	Secondary actions — Production loss caused by primary actions							
	Pasture	Arable land	Permanent meadow	Market garden	Vineyard	Eucalypti	Cattle	Sheep
Socio-economic indicators of agricultural sector								
A) Structural indicators								
Total land area	−	−	−	−	−	−		
Arable land area	−	−	−	−	−	−		
Total number of farms	−	−	−	−	−	−	−	−
Total number of livestock farms	−		−	−	−	−	−	−
Average land per farm								
<5 ha	−	−	−	−	−	−		
5–20 ha	−	−	−	−	−	−		
20–50 ha								
>50 ha								
Average arable land per farm	−	−	−	−	−	−		
Title deed: owner								
Tenant farming	−	−	−	−	−	−		
System of farming:								
owner occupation								
with workers	−	−	−	−	−	−		
Farm machinery	−	−	−	−	−	−		
Irrigation	−					−		
Real estate market	−	−	−	−	−	−		
Family capital flow:								
self-financing	−	−	−	−	−	−	−	−
agricultural credit	−	−	−	−	−	−	−	−
ordinary credit	−	−	−	−	−	−	−	−
housing	−	−	−	−	−	−	−	−
improvement of farm structure	−	−	−	−	−	−	−	−
improvement of farm machinery and equipment	−	−	−	−	−	−	−	−
working capital	−	−	−	−	−	−	−	−
B) Socio-economic indicators								
Agricultural sector's workers	−	−	−	−	−	−	−	−
Manufacturing sector's workers	+	+	+	+	+	+	+	+
Services sector's workers	+	+	+	+	+	+	+	+
Simple workers	−	−	−	−	−	−	−	−
Utility machinery company	+	+	+	+	+	+	+	+
Feminilization	+	+	+	+	+	+	+	+
Senilization	+	+	+	+	+	+	+	+
Farm job done by:								
family members	+	+	+	+	+	+	+	+
Temporary workers	−	−	−	−	−	−	−	−
full-time workers	−	−	−	−	−	−	−	−
Owner working: only in the farm	−	−	−	−	−	−	−	−
in other farms								
in other sectors	+	+	+	+	+	+	+	+

impact on the environment were those obtained from a survey of the area, including 26 samples. The objective was to construct an index in order to quantify the presence of fluorine on the basis of the results of the analyses carried out on the samples.

Samples of vegetables and grape juice taken at many of the survey points were analysed in order to identify the amounts of fluorine they contained. Thus we obtained the amounts of fluorine contained in the soil, leaves, must and pasture land at the 26 sampling points (Tables 7.1 and 7.2).

A statistical analysis of these data was then performed in order to define a single index of the presence of fluorine for each point (Polelli, 1987).

This index was linked to the characteristics which also have an undoubted influence on the presence of metals in the soil and plant life in a given place.

Authoritative sources indicate that the soil characteristics which determine the presence and mobility of metals are the texture, the pH, the quantity of organic sand and the level of cation exchange. Therefore, these values were monitored in correspondence to the clayey sand.

Another parameter which is extremely important for the explanation of the presence of metals in the soil was also included—the distance of the survey point from the source of pollution (Table 7.4).

The following formula was used to standardize the variables:

$$Z_i = \frac{X_i - U}{Q_x} \tag{1}$$

in other words, each element X_i of the variable X is transformed by subtracting the mean value of the variable X and dividing the result by the standard deviation of the variable itself. Thus all the variables considered have a mean value equal to zero and a standard deviation equal to one.

This eliminates all the differences caused by different units of measurement of the variables. For each dependent variable Y, a linear function was obtained by a multiple regression of the independent variable X.

$$\begin{aligned} Y_1 &= f(X_1, X_2, \ldots, X_n) \\ Y_g &= g(X_1, X_2, \ldots, X_n) \\ &\ldots\ldots\ldots\ldots\ldots\ldots \\ Y_p &= h(X_1, X_2, \ldots, X_n) \end{aligned} \tag{2}$$

The regression functions of the fluorine contents to the environmental variables are shown in Table 7.3.

Each value estimated according to the regression functions was compared with the effective value obtained from the analysis of the samples (Table 7.4). The percentage difference between these two values was used as a coefficient of inverse proportionality for the definition of the weighted average of these indices. Thus a 'Presence Index' (I_p) was identified using the following formula:

Table 7.1   *Survey sites features and fluorine amount: vineyard*

Site	Distance X_1	pH X_2	Sand X_3	Silt clay X_4	Index leaves X_5	Total Y_1	Soil NaCl Y_2	Canes Y_3	Leaves Y_4	Must Y_5
1	3·6	6·1	77·30	23·20	5	862	14·22	0·51	810	8·31
2	4·1	6·5	86·50	15·10	5	465	10·12	0·27	924	6·96
3	4·1	6·7	91·60	11·30	5	510	10·26	0·30	665	5·92
4	5·6	6·4	61·20	37·10	5	675	9·66	0·27	560	5·31
5	6·2	6·3	88·20	18·20	4	445	8·54	0·15	492	5·10
6	6·2	6·5	89·20	14·40	5	442	9·16	0·37	488	4·71
7	5·6	6·7	66·20	33·10	5	384	7·16	0·61	495	4·51
8	6·1	7·0	65·10	38·20	4	310	7·15	0·57	510	5·10
9	8·2	6·5	88·15	15·40	4	285	6·42	0·27	385	2·31
10	7·6	6·3	93·20	11·10	3	296	6·28	0·26	365	1·97
11	3·1	6·4	94·20	12·20	3	301	5·48	0·47	384	2·27
12	8·4	6·5	64·30	36·10	3	206	4·08	0·36	371	2·96
13	9·4	6·6	93·20	20·10	3	281	4·88	0·35	365	2·31
14	3·6	6·5	81·30	23·20	2	164	3·28	0·46	261	2·36
15	3·0	6·8	94·20	15·10	2	155	4·08	0·28	172	3·71
16	2·5	6·5	80·30	24·10	2	160	3·08	0·38	145	1·42
17	2·1	6·5	82·10	23·20	2	191	4·28	0·45	132	1·10
18	4·4	6·1	83·20	18·10	2	171	4·88	0·29	170	2·05
19	5·1	6·3	89·10	12·20	3	157	3·88	0·89	165	1·97
20	3·4	6·6	78·30	20·10	2	147	4·28	0·51	147	1·89
21	3·1	6·2	97·40	8·50	2	153	3·88	0·36	129	1·05
22	2·1	6·5	99·20	9·20	2	156	3·70	0·34	134	1·47
23	3·4	6·8	95·10	7·40	2	164	2·08	0·46	139	1·43
24	8·4	6·4	93·10	10·20	3	273	6·48	0·28	277	1·51
25	9·1	6·3	88·50	11·10	3	276	6·48	0·38	263	1·61
26	9·4	6·7	65·30	35·10	3	286	5·48	0·46	272	2·86

$$Ip_i = \frac{\sum\limits_{j=1}^{p} \dfrac{Y_{ij}}{D_{ij}}}{\sum\limits_{j=1}^{p} \dfrac{1}{D_{ij}}} \tag{3}$$

when:

Y_{ij} = the estimated value for the ith point by means of the jth regression function.

D_{ij} = the percentage difference between the observed value of the ith point and the value estimated by meansof the jth function.

All the values Ip_i ($i = 1, 2, ..., 36$) were finally varied between 0 and 1 in order to complete the index found, both conceptually and operatively (Table 7.5).

By means of aggregation into homogeneous areas, three zones with the following indices were identified:

Zone	Synthesized indices
A	0.757
B	0.498
C	0.261

Table 7.2   *Survey sites features and fluorine amount: pasture*

Site	Distance X_1	pH X_2	Sand X_3	Silt clay X_4	Soil tot. Y_6	NaCl Y_7
1	3.6	6.1	77.30	23.20	321.00	13.12
4	5.6	6.4	61.20	37.10	300.00	15.23
6	6.2	6.5	89.20	14.40	254.00	11.22
8	6.1	7.0	65.10	38.20	380.00	13.21
10	7.6	6.3	93.20	11.10	157.00	8.40
13	9.4	6.6	93.20	20.10	171.00	7.29
16	2.5	6.5	80.30	24.10	102.17	4.81
17	2.1	6.5	82.10	23.20	81.29	3.36
23	3.4	6.8	95.10	7.40	93.47	2.41
26	9.4	6.7	65.30	35.10	209.07	8.21

Table 7.3   *Regression functions*

Y1 = 1007.69 − 11.966 ÷ X_1	− 235.720 ÷ X_2	3.879 ÷ X_3	6.886
Y2 = 17.449 − 0.128 ÷ X_1	− 3.187 ÷ X_2	0.027 ÷ X_3	0.031
Y3 = 1.252 − 0.011 ÷ X_1	0.118 ÷ X_2	− 0.015 ÷ X_3	− 0.013
Y4 = − 391.350 − 10.207 ÷ X_1	− 69.179 ÷ X_2	6.372 ÷ X_3	7.699
Y5 = − 4.762 − 0.245 ÷ X_1	− 0.287 ÷ X_2	0.053 ÷ X_3	0.092
Y6 = 1062.02 11.156 ÷ X_1	− 39.590 ÷ X_2	− 7.364 ÷ X_3	− 2.905
Y7 = 74.379 0.605 ÷ X_1	− 6.070 ÷ X_2	− 0.326 ÷ X_3	− 0.136

Economic evaluation

The indices defined in this way were used to establish the loss of productivity and the devaluation of the soil in each zone (Polelli, 1988b).

To identify these values, the dose/response regression lines and the fluorine/physical–chemical environmental characteristics regression lines were calculated.

The evaluations were divided into two parts:

- evaluation of the areas planted with vines;
- evaluation of the arable land and pastures.

For the vineyards, the differential value $V_0 - V_{01}$, was defined:

where:
V_0 = the value of the vineyard in normal conditions
V_{01} = the value of the vineyard when polluted with fluorine.

$$V_0 = \frac{\sum_0^n Bf}{q^n - 1}$$

Bf equals the sum of the income during the economic cycle of plants. The value $V - V_1$ was applied in the case of arable land and pastureland

where:

$V = \dfrac{Bf}{r}$ the income deriving from transformation without pollution.

$V_1 = \dfrac{Bf_1}{r}$ the income as above when polluted with fluorine.

The correlations for zones B and C were established on the basis of these values for zone A. These values were high in zone A with a 65 per cent devaluation of the soil for the vineyards and 53 per cent for the arable land/pastures. The figures for zone B were respectively 43 per cent and 38 per cent and for zone C 17 per cent and 15 per cent.

This economic evaluation constituted an integration of the qualitative analyses carried out and a useful component in the evaluation of the global impact.

Table 7.4 Regression function values and per cent spread

Site	Y_1		Y_2		Y_3		Y_4		Y_5		Y_6		Y_7	
	Estimated value	Spread %	Estimated value	Spread %	Estimated value	Spread %	Estimated value	Spread %	Estimated value	Spread %	Estimated value	Spread %	Estimated value	Spread %
1	652.304	−32.1	11.435	−24.3	0.382	−33.6	694.519	−16.6	6.359	−30.7	224.027	−43.3	11.164	−17.5
2	531.948	12.6	10.094	−0.3	0.396	31.9	658.007	−40.4	5.859	−18.8				
3	478.423	−6.6	9.477	−8.3	0.396	24.2	647.414	−2.7	5.720	−3.5				
4	590.913	−14.2	10.219	5.5	0.447	39.6	657.773	14.9	6.217	14.6	312.649	4.0	13.915	−9.4
5	448.714	0.8	8.391	−1.8	0.303	50.5	510.423	3.6	4.269	−19.5				
6	512.473	13.8	9.877	7.3	0.343	−7.7	648.388	24.7	5.423	12.6	175.126	−45.0	7.624	−47.2
7	512.051	25.0	9.275	22.8	0.462	−32.0	638.085	22.4	6.025	25.1				
8	333.015	6.9	6.169	−15.9	0.460	−24.0	469.798	−8.6	4.719	−8.1	262.557	−44.7	9.154	−44.3
9	358.164	20.4	7.410	13.4	0.344	21.5	454.297	15.3	3.461	33.3				
10	269.279	−9.9	5.913	−6.2	0.329	21.1	298.647	−22.2	2.026	2.8	178.792	12.2	8.829	4.9
11	311.010	3.2	6.231	12.0	0.360	−30.6	352.503	−8.9	3.253	30.2				
12	272.598	24.4	5.167	21.0	0.436	17.4	284.961	−30.2	2.555	−15.9				
13	238.997	−17.6	5.007	2.5	0.225	−55.7	328.810	−11.0	2.328	0.8	160.852	−6.3	6.874	−6.0
14	173.968	5.7	3.626	9.5	0.429	−7.2	168.283	−55.1	1.927	−22.5				
15	104.700	−48.0	2.844	−43.4	0.389	28.0	173.494	0.9	1.920	−93.2				
16	189.449	15.5	3.768	18.3	0.443	14.3	180.068	19.5	2.227	36.2	171.211	40.3	6.970	31.0
17	195.021	2.1	3.840	−11.5	0.433	−3.9	188.692	30.0	2.337	52.9	156.107	47.9	6.263	46.4
18	230.934	26.0	4.692	−4.0	0.414	29.9	160.632	−5.8	1.476	−38.9				
19	290.865	46.0	6.156	37.0	0.402	−121.4	306.508	46.2	2.523	21.9				
20	119.806	−22.7	3.155	−35.6	0.529	3.6	120.424	−22.1	1.504	−25.7				
21	211.901	27.8	4.626	16.1	0.358	−0.4	183.559	29.7	1.629	35.5				
22	164.955	5.4	3.868	4.3	0.369	7.8	189.872	29.4	1.947	24.5				
23	50.384	−225.5	2.578	19.3	0.475	3.1	115.865	−20.0	1.160	−23.3	108.897	14.2	3.136	23.2
24	229.549	−18.9	5.461	−18.7	0.346	19.1	275.997	−0.4	1.713	11.8				
25	233.097	−18.4	5.594	−15.8	0.383	0.7	253.387	−3.8	1.411	−14.1				
26	210.481	−35.9	4.398	−24.6	0.447	−2.8	259.592	−4.8	2.213	−29.2	318.782	34.4	13.328	38.4

Table 7.5 *Fluorine presence index*

Site	Area 1	Area 2	Area 3
1	0.72500		
2	0.77312		
3	0.75453		
4	0.76238		
5	0.63743		
6	1.00000		
7	0.75817		
8	0.64381		
9		0.51109	
10		0.59571	
11		0.49847	
12		0.58471	
13		0.44419	
14			0.00000
15			0.30051
16			0.39194
17			0.07765
18			0.30449
19			0.39832
20			0.11615
21			0.35684
22			0.32297
23			0.33711
24		0.40090	
25		0.46308	
26		0.48493	
Average index	0.75700	0.49800	0.26100

References

Bossavy, J. (1968) Air pollution. In *Proceedings of the 1° Eur. Congr. on the Influence of Air Pollution on Plants and Animals*, Wageningen, pp. 111–136.

Clark, B. D. (1980) A manual for the assessment of major development proposal, Scottish Development, *Department of the Environment and the Welsh Office, Research Report* No. 13.

Enne, G. (1983) Valuation criteria of fluorine in scheeps. V *Conference on animal Production*, Tokyo, 14–19 August.

Lee, N. and Wood C. (1980) *Methods of Environmental Impact Assessment for use in Project Appraisal and Physical Planning.* University of Manchester Department of Town and Country Planning.

Moore, S. L. (1973) A methodology for evaluation manufacturing environmental impact assessment for Delaware coastal zone, *Study Report D. Battelle Columbus Laboratories.*

Polelli, M. (1977) Criteri per la stima dei danni alle piante da emanazione gassose. *Genio Rurale 12.*

Polelli, M. (1987) *Valutazione di Impatto Ambientale,* Reda, Roma.

Polelli M. (1988a) The environmental impact assessment of the electric power plants. International meeting, Capri.

Polelli, M. (1988b) La valutazione di impatto ambientale caso di inquinamento da metalli pesanti in un'area rura *Convegno Italo-Sovietico 'Ecologia 88',* Donetsk, Ukraine. USSR.

Weber, E. (1982) *Air Pollution Assessment Methodology and Modelling,* Plenum Press, New York.

Zimmermann, P. W. (1958) Hirchoch. *Contribution from the Boyce Thompson Institute,* **18**, 263, 279.

8

Environmental impact assessment of Jubail Industrial City, 1978–1988

Patrick L. O'Brien, David E. Jones, and Saleh A. Abotteen

Jubail Industrial City is located on the southern coast of the Arabian Gulf, in the kingdom of Saudi Arabia (see Figure 8.1). The Industrial City has only been in existence as such since 1978. Studies of marine and terrestrial ecosystems in the region were undertaken as the major industrial facilities planned for the area were developed. Data is available at present, to show most of the effects of the development of Jubail Industrial City on the regional air and water quality. Surveys of local terrestrial and marine flora for comparison with the base line studies are to be made in the near future.

The original environment

The proposed site for Jubail Industrial City, including both industrial and community developments, covered an area of about 170 km². The main geographic feature of the area was the 'sabkha' — a flat, highly saline, sandy-clay substrate, lying just above the normal high tide level. The sabkha was bordered on the west by aeolean sand dunes (up to 15 m in height), and on the east and south by low sand dunes, oolithic limestone terraces, and marine deposits. The sabkhas are wet and waterlogged during the winter months, and covered by a hard, dry crust for most of the remainder of the year, and consequently have no vegetative cover. There is little local relief, although elevations of up to 33 m exist some 20–30 km to the south-west.

The geology of the Jubail area is one of sedimentary formations, overlain by quaternary deposits. The hydrology is characterized by mostly saline aquifers that are close to the surface, and display regional hydraulic gradients to the north and east.

Plant communities recorded in baseline ecological studies were of the species shown in Tables 8.1 and 8.2. The local vegetation reflected the topography and climate of the area, with different plant communities established for the stable sand dunes, deep salt sand areas, shallow salt sand areas, and sub-tidal exposed flatlands. The dominant plant was

Panicum turgitum – a forage grass for camels, and an influential factor in sand dune stabilization.

The Arabian Gulf is sometimes referred to as a marginal sea. It is located between north latitudes 24° and 30°. The general circulatory pattern of the gulf waters is a counterclockwise gyre. Dense water leaves the gulf through the straits of Hormuz, beneath less dense, incoming water from the Gulf of Oman. The arid climate and latitudinal position of the Arabian Gulf contribute to the high salinities and temperatures of the gulf waters, which result in a relative paucity of marine biota.

The climate in Jubail is similar to the larger-scale, regional climate, and is

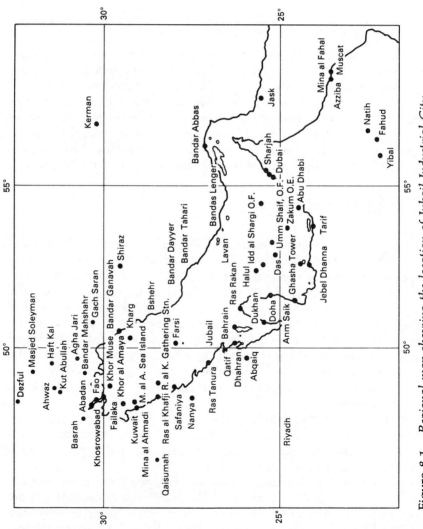

Figure 8.1   *Regional map showing the location of Jubail Industrial City*

Table 8.1   *Dominant species of plants*
in the Jubail area

Plant species	Dominance (%)
Poaceae	20
Chenopodiaceae	18
Cyperaceae	10
Leguminosae	8
Zygophyllacaea*	8
Palmae	8

9 plant families constitute the remaining 28% of plant cover in the study area
* Dominant family in the deep and shallow salt sand communities

referred to as a 'hot, desert' climate. Rainfall is low (< 100 mm per year), summer temperatures are high (> 45°C), and there is little cloud cover for most of the year. Synoptic winds are influenced by the regional air flows of the Arabian Gulf. Local marine/land/air interactions also affect coastal temperatures and humidities, and cause mesoscale air mass circulations Predominant winds are north-northeasterly to northwesterly, but nocturnal surface-based air temperature inversions and associated low-level air flows are common, and variable sea and land breezes are often produced by the local sea/land/air interactions. A typical set of wind roses for Jubail is shown in Figure 8.2.

Industrial and community development

Construction of Jubail Industrial City began in 1977. Sand dunes and substrate from sourrounding areas were removed for use as landfill in the

Table 8.2   *Extent of plant communities in the Jubail area*

Terrain	Area covered (km²)	Percentage of total area
Stable dunes	476	37.5
Unstable dunes	354	28.0
Sabkha	256	20.2
Deep salt sands	134	10.6
Shallow salt sands	42	3.3
Sub-tidal flats	5	0.4
Total	1267	100.0

Plant species from the families Poaceae, Chenopodiaceae, Cyperaceae, and Palmae are found in the stable/unstable dunes and in the deep and shallow salt sands. These three plant families comprise 50% of the dominant plant cover in the area.

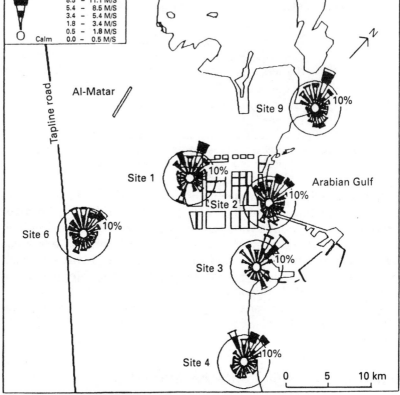

Madinat Al-Jubail Al-Sinaiyah wind roses
Jan 87 to Dec 87. Hours of day – 1 to 24

Figure 8.2   *Typical wind rose set for Jubail Industrial City*

primary industrial area (40 km²). Material that was dredged from the sea bed during the construction of the industrial harbour and waterways was also added to the land-fill. The land-filling was done in order to:

1   ensure that the developed area was above the tidal flood plain;
2   provide an adequate gradient for rainfall drainage;
3   provide a firm substrate for building foundations;
4   increase the depth of the ground water below the substrate, to protect plants, and to minimize the corrosive effects of the saline ground water on underground utilities and building foundations.

A large, three-channel, concrete-lined, high-capacity, sea water canal was constructed. The canal extends from the coast line to about 7 km inland, and supplies non-contact cooling water to the major works located in the primary industrial area.

Large-scale dredging of the sea bed was carried out, to create the Jubail industrial harbour and shipping channels. Causeways, piers, breakwaters, and other shipping facilities were constructed.

After the site preparation was completed, construction of the industries began in 1980, along with the construction of major highways and the development of infrastructure facilities – power and sea water desalination plants, telecommunications network, airport, community facilities, etc.

Considerable gardening/landscaping work was done after the completion of the primary industry and community areas. Most of the plant species used were introduced to the Jubail area for the first time. The introduced species came primarily from the USA, Mexico, Australia, Sri Lanka, Indonesia, Spain, and other parts of Saudi Arabia. The plants were irrigated with fresh water, by a network of PVC water pipes.

The first industrial works commissioning in Jubail Industrial City began in 1980.

Table 8.3 lists the major primary industries in Jubail Industrial City in chronological order, as they started to come on-line. The nature of the products and processes associated with these industries is also briefly described in Table 8.3. The first official start-ups were in 1983, with other industries commencing operation between 1983 and 1987. Development of both primary and secondary industries in Jubail Industrial City is continuing. Several major industrial works started operations in 1987.

The Jubail environmental monitoring programme

From the outset, the Royal Commission for Jubail and Yanbu – a Saudi Government body – undertook to ensure that the development of Jubail Industrial City would be done in accordance with 'sound environmental practice'. The complete transformation of a large, relatively untouched coastal stretch into an industrial city and harbour required the implementation of a comprehensive environmental study and monitoring plan. Particular attention was paid to specific environmental contamination by operational discharges of industrial and municipal pollutants to the air, water, and land. The effects of the construction activities themselves on the local terrestrial and marine flora and fauna are currently being reviewed, and appropriate studies are planned for the near future.

The environmental guidelines and standards that were established are based on:

1   the Royal Commission's own findings on the pollutants most likely to have an impact on the Jubail environment;
2   international environmental standards and criteria; and
3   environmental criteria applicable to, and acceptable to industries.

The environmental monitoring plan for Jubail Industrial City has been

Table 8.3   *Summary of the major primary industries operating in Jubail Industrial City*

Start date	Company	Major products	Processes
1983	Saudi Iron and Steel (HADEED)	Direct reduced iron. Steel billets. Reinforcing bars. Wire rods.	Direct reduction (Midrex), electric arc furnace, rolling mill.
1983	Saudi Methanol Company (AR-RAZI)	Methanol	Steam reforming, compression, catalytic reaction, separation.
1983	Al Jubail Fertilizer Company (SAMAD)	Ammonia (intermediate). Urea.	Catalytic reforming, compression, catalytic reaction, liquefaction, distillation, evaporation, prilling.
1984	Sulphur Prilling (ARAMCO)	Prilled sulphur	Prilling tower.
1984/85	National Industrial Gases Company (GAS)	Gaseous and cryogenic nitrogen and oxygen.	Air separation.
1984	National Methanol Company (IBN SINA)	Methanol (future vinyl acetate, acetic acid, ethylene glycol).	Steam reforming, compression, catalytic reaction.
1985	Petromin Shell Refinery Company	Fuel oil, naptha, kerosene, diesel oil, LPG, benzene, sulphur.	Atmospheric and vacuum distillation, desulphurization, hydrocracking, visbreaking, hydrodealkylation, platforming.
1984/85	Saudi Petrochemical Company (SADAF)	Caustic soda, crude ethanol, styrene, ethylene, ethylene dichloride.	Cracking furnace, compression, de-ethanizer, demethanizer, catalytic reaction, distillation, brine purification, electrolysis, separation.
1984	Al Jubail Petrochemical Company (KEMYA)	Linear low-density polyethylene (LLDPE)	(UCC) polymerization through fluidized bed with catalyst.
1985	Arabian Petrochemical Company (PETROKEMYA)	Ethylene (future polystyrene)	Cracking furnace, compression, drying, de-ethanizer, demethanizer.

Table 8.3—*continued*

Start date	Company	Major products	Processes
1985	Eastern Petrochemical Company (SHARQ)	Mono-, Di-, and Tri-ethylene glycols, Linear low-density polyethylene (LLDPE) (future ethylene)	Glycols-catalytic direct oxidation of ethylene, polyethylene-(UCC) catalytic polymerization of ethylene.
1986	National Plastics Company (IBN HAYYAN)	Vinyl chloride monomer (VCM), polyvinyl chloride (PVC)	Oxidation, pyrolysis, caustic wash, separation polymerization, compression, centrifuging.
1986	Petromin Lubricant Blending and Grease Manufacturing Plant	Turbine oil, motor oil, diesel oil, gas oil, multi-purpose greases.	Proportioning and blending units, heat reactor, filtration, milling and drying.
1987	Bulk Oil Terminals (PETMARK)	Sales of bunker fuel, diesels, gasoline, jet fuel.	Bulk storage tanks and facilities.
1987	National Chemical Fertiliser Company (IBN AL BAYTAR)	Anhydrous ammonia.	Catalytic reforming, compression, synthesis, liquefaction.
1987	Saudi European Petrochemical Company (IBN ZAHAR)	Methyl tertiary butyl ether (MTBE), butadiene, butene-1.	Information not available.

implemented by a number of contractors and sub-contractors since 1978, under the supervision of Royal Commission contract specialists.

The Jubail Air Monitoring Network

Installation of a network of automatic air monitoring stations to monitor the air quality in and around Jubail Industrial City was begun in 1978.

The Jubail location is particularly hard on environmental monitoring and computer equipment, because of the climate (heat and humidity ranges encountered), the levels of airborne dust, and the need for portable diesel generators for electric power – in 1978, no mains electric power was available at all and, at present, mains electric power is still not available at two sites in the network. Substantial modifications were needed in order to obtain satisfactory performance from the equipment. As a result of the need for such development work, data recorded before 1980 are rather sporadic and of dubious validity. Only data recorded from 1980 onwards are considered here. The data used here as a baseline reference were recorded after the start of construction of Jubail Industrial City, but before the start of industrial operations.

Figure 8.3 shows the Jubail Air Monitoring network. Some changes have been made to the network over the years. The present site locations are shown in Figure 8.3.

The pollutants measured are: oxides of nitrogen (NO, NO_2, NO_x), sulphur dioxide (SO_2), hydrogen sulphide (H_2S), ozone (O_3), carbon monoxide (CO), non-methane hydrocarbons (NMHC), and inhalable suspended particulate matter (ISP). In addition, several meteorological parameters are also measured. These are: wind speed and direction, variability of wind direction, air temperature and dew point, total solar radiation, soil temperature, rainfall, evaporation rate, and atmospheric pressure.

The stations have real-time data logging and reporting systems, and operate continuously. A data set that includes data from 1978 to the present is available on magnetic tape. Data from the network are used for the assessment of the current air quality in the Jubail region, the management of industrial incidents or accidents that may have an effect on the Jubail environment (real-time data), and as input to pollutant dispersion models, that are used as tools for planning for the future development of Jubail.

The Jubail Receiving Water Quality Network

Gulf waters are sampled monthly to monitor their physical, chemical, and biological integrity. The sampling is done at a network of 10 sampling stations that are located in inshore and offshore waters adjacent to Jubail Industrial City. The number and disposition of the samplers has been changed over the years. The present disposition of the marine samplers is shown in Figure 8.4. *In situ* measured parameters are: temperature, pH, dissolved oxygen concentration, electrical conductivity, oxidation/ reduction potential, salinity, and water depth. Samples are also returned to an analytical laboratory for heavy metal content analysis.

Data from the Jubail Receiving Water Quality Network are entered into a computer data set, and used in a similar manner to the Jubail Air Monitoring Network data.

Land surveys

Routine inspections of the Jubail Industrial City area, the municipal sanitary landfill, and the surrounding terrain and beaches are made on a semi-regular basis, to monitor waste dumping, accidental spills of liquid or solid industrial waste, deposition of marine oil spills on beaches, etc. Noise levels in the industrial and residential areas are also monitored.

The terrestrial and marine flora in the Jubail area were surveyed and assessed before construction work started. Further surveys are planned for the near future, to assess the extent to which they have recovered from the upheavals of the Jubail Industrial City and harbour construction work.

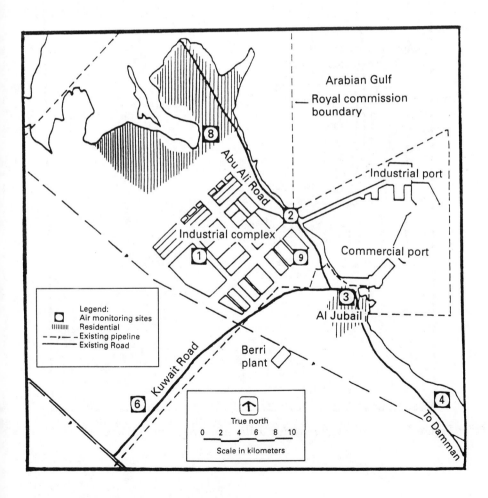

Figure 8.3   *The Jubail air monitoring network*

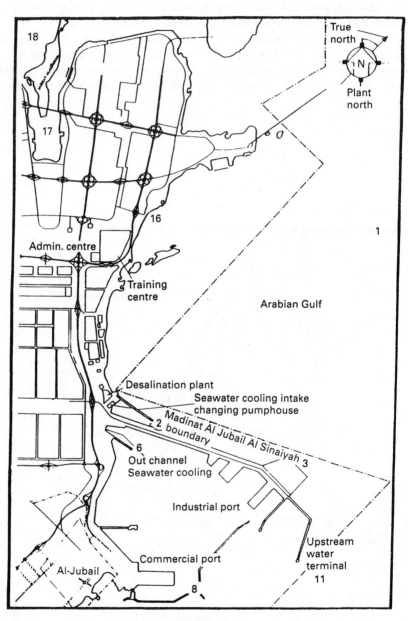

Figure 8.4   *The Jubail receiving water quality monitoring network*

Survey results

Air quality

There are a number of dominant pollutant sources both within and outside the immediate area of Jubail Industrial City. The apparent wind directions associated with these sources vary, depending on the pollutant under consideration. For example, a typical set of air pollution roses for SO_2 in Jubail Industrial City is shown in Figure 8.5. The works areas in the Industrial City are obviously major sources of SO_2. However, there are other contributing sources – there is a gas/oil separating plant located 5–10 km to the south, and there are a number of oil drilling platforms in the Berri oil fields, offshore to the north of Jubail. H_2S is another source-specific pollutant that is readily traced to major industrial developments both within and outside the Jubail area.

While CO, NO_x, and NMOC are released in substantial quantities in

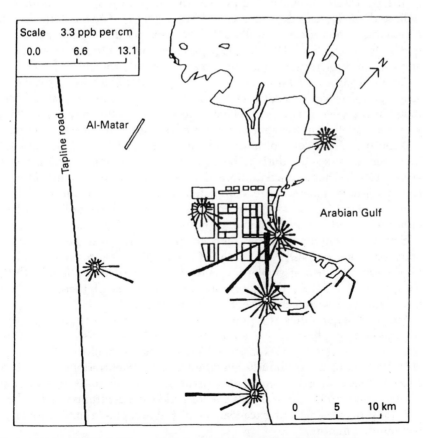

Figure 8.5   *Typical SO_2 pollution roses for Jubail Industrial City*

the Industrial City and port area, there are also major sources associated with the urban areas, the old city of Jubail and the major highways that pass through the region – indicating that motor vehicle traffic and domestic urban activities are also major souces of these pollutants.

Tropospheric ozone is difficult to reconcile with any particular source because it is a secondary pollutant, formed over a period of time, from the reaction of oxides of nitrogen with atmospheric oxygen, in the presence of sunlight and reaction catalysts (mostly NMHC). In a stagnant air mass, a general photochemical O_3 precursor source reconciliation is possible. However, where air masses are mobile, and especially where complex, multi-layered ar flows can occur, obvious sources of photochemical O_3 precursors become masked, and ozone pollution roses simply echo the climatic wind roses. This has been found to be the case for Jubail.

The variation over time of the air quality in Jubail Industrial City is shown in Figures 8.6a–8.6n. These figures show the month by month hourly-maximum and monthly-mean concentrations of the main pollutants as measured at sites 1, 2, 3, 4, and 6, between the years 1980 and 1988. These sites have been chosen because they were in continuous operation, at the positions shown in Figure 8.3, for the entire study period. Also indicated on Figures 8.6a–6n, where applicable, are the criteria for the acceptable levels for each pollutant. The units used are parts per billion (p.p.b.) for NO_x, SO_2, H_2S, and O_3, parts per million (p.p.m.) for NMHC and CO, and micrograms per cubic metre ($\mu g/m^3$) for ISP.

Concentrations of NO_x, SO_2, H_2S, O_3, and ISP show a substantial seasonal influence, reflecting changes in climatic conditions at different times of the year. Larger variability in source strengths may mask similar seasonal variation in the concentrations of the other monitored pollutants.

Monthly mean concentrations of NO_x, SO_2, H_2S, NMHC, and CO increased significantly during the early industrial commissioning phases (1981–1983). These concentrations decreased by large amounts after the commissioning phases were completed, and on-line operations began. From 1983 to the present, the concentrations of these pollutants have either remained relatively stable, or have been gradually decreasing.

Similar variations can be seen in the hourly-averaged maximum concentrations of NO_x, SO_2, NMHC, and CO. The concentrations of NO_x have remained at similar levels to those recorded in 1980. With the exception of NMHC, the hourly-averaged maxima of these pollutants have remained within the acceptable limit criteria.

Substantial quantities of H_2S were emitted by the industries during their commissioning phases between 1980 and 1983, and also during 1987, when several industries experienced operational difficulties. The acceptable limit criteria for hourly-averaged H_2S concentrations have been exceeded on a substantial number of occasions, and by quite large amounts during 1980–1983. Since 1983, the recorded concentrations have been generally decreasing, but exceedances of the acceptable limit criteria are still quite common.

Although not considered as a harmful primary pollutant in itself,

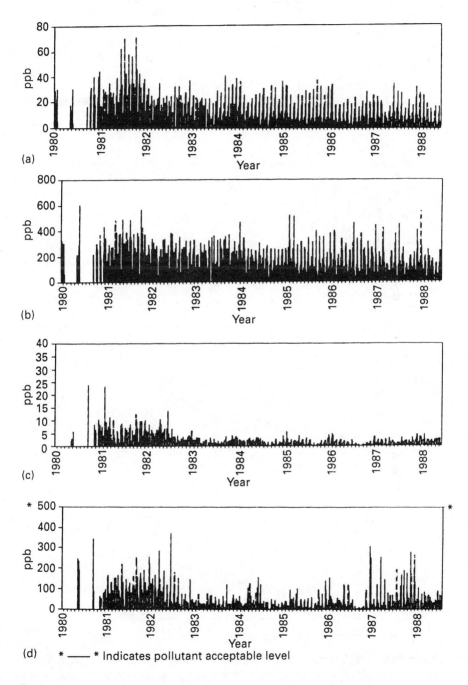

Figure 8.6a
Figure 8.6b   *NO_x variation: 1980–1988 (hourly maxima, Sites 1, 2, 3, 4, & 6)*
Figure 8.6c   *SO_2 variation: 1980–1988 (monthly means, Sites 1, 2, 3, 4, & 6)*
Figure 8.6d   *SO_2 variation: 1980–1988 (hourly maxima, Sites 1, 2, 3, 4, & 6)*

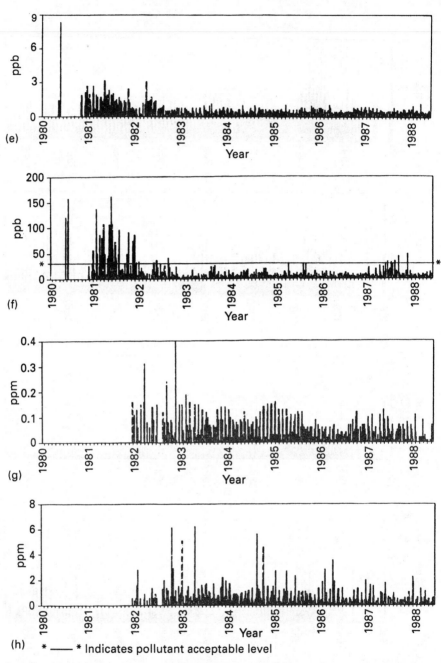

(e)

(f)

(g)

(h)   * ——— * Indicates pollutant acceptable level

Figure 8.6e   *H_2S variation: 1980–1988 (monthly means, sites 1, 2, 3, 4 & 6)*
Figure 8.6f   *H_2S variation: 1980–1988 (hourly maxima, sites 1, 2, 3, 4 & 6)*
Figure 8.6g   *NMHC variation: 1980–1988 (monthly means, sites 1, 2, 3, 4 & 6)*
Figure 8.6h   *NMHC variation: 1980–1988 (hourly maxima, sites 1, 2, 3, 4 & 6)*

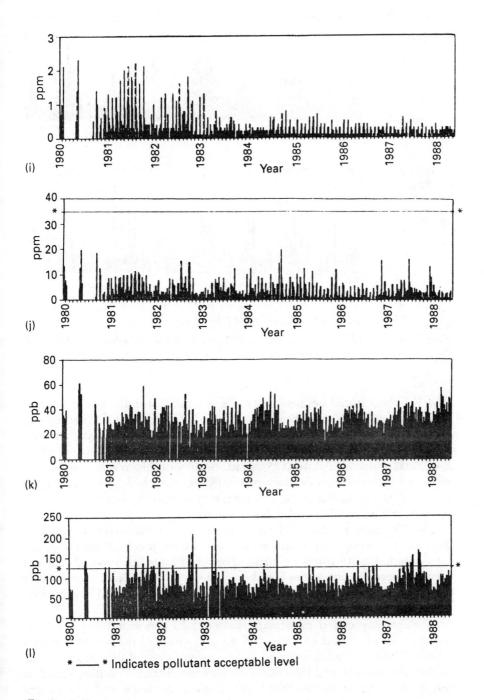

Figure 8.6i

Figure 8.6j   *CO variation: 1980–1988 (hourly maxima, sites 1, 2, 3, 4 & 6)*

Figure 8.6k   *Ozone variation: 1980–1988 (monthly means, sites 1, 2, 3, 4 & 6)*

Figure 8.6l   *Ozone variation: 1980–1988 (hourly maxima, sites 1, 2, 3, 4 & 6)*

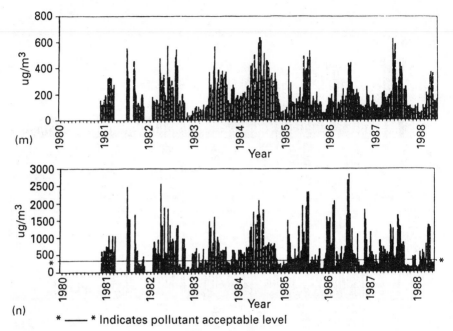

Figure 8.6m   *ISP variation: 1980–1988 (monthly means, sites 1, 2, 3, 4 & 6)*
Figure 8.6n   *ISP variation: 1980–1988 (hourly maxima, sites 1, 2, 3, 4 & 6)*

NMHC is monitored because of its role as a catalyst in the photochemical production of O_3. Significant concentrations of NMHC, particularly during the summer months, are undesirable. the acceptable limit criterion for NMHC is that the concentration averaged between the hours of 06.00 and 09.00 must be below 0.25 p.p.m. Both monthly mean and hourly-averaged maximum concentrations of NMHC have been decreasing since 1983, but the recorded levels still remain unacceptably high, and exceedances of the acceptable limit criteria are quite common.

The O_3 concentrations show a distinct seasonal cycle, peaking in summer, and troughing in winter. The acceptable level criteria for ozone are exceeded quite often in Jubail. The variation with time of ambient ozone concentrations in the Jubail area shows no significant trend at this time. This suggests that the industrial developments in Jubail have had no significant effect on the local ambient O_3 concentrations.

Inhalable suspended particulate matter (SIP) concentrations have frequently exceeded, and continue to frequently exceed the acceptable limit criteria. These exceedances may be the consequences of the natural effects of the local climate and the nature of the topsoil (sand), or they could be due to the effects of the Jubail site preparation work and consequent defoliation and soil/sand destabilization in the area. The absence of pre-site preparation data makes this a difficult question to resolve. Daily and monthly mean ISP concentrations are shown in Figures 8.6m and 8.6n. The figures show no significant trends between 1980 and the present –

indicating either no significant recovery of soil/sand stabilizing vegetation, or no significant effect of the construction work.

Gulf receiving water quality

Some of the works in the primary industrial area discharge waste water
into the sea water cooling canal. Guidelines for acceptable levels of
pollutants in this wastewater are set out, but these guidelines are not
always complied with. There is, as a result of this, the possibility that
discharges from the cooling water canal could adversely affect adjacent
gulf waters. Particular attention is paid to monitoring the sea water
cooling canal outfall.

The variation in time of the parameters measured by three sampling
stations from the Jubail Receiving Water Quality Monitoring Network is
shown in Figures 8.7a to 8.7g). The selected stations sample at the sea
water cooling canal intake (station 2), outfall (station 6), and in the open
gulf waters near the Berri oilfields (station 1).

Seasonal temperature variations for gulf waters adjacent to Jubail are
shown in Figure 8.7a. During the summer, surface water temperatures of
up to 32°C in offshore waters, and up to 36°C in inshore waters have been
recorded. Surface water temperatures may fall below 18°C in winter. There
are no obvious effects of the Jubail Industrial City development on local
sea surface water temperatures.

For gulf waters, surface water salinity increases from about 36.6 parts
per thousand (p.p.t.) in the Hormuz region, to about 40.6 p.p.t. in the
northwestern gulf region. The high salinity of gulf waters is attributed to
the high rate of loss of water through evaporation, which is not made up
by precipitation and river inflow. Figure 8.7b shows the variation in
salinity of the waters adjacent to Jubail, from 1982 to the present. Seasonal
variability in salinity is apparent, with higher salinities being recorded
during the warmer months. From Figure 8.7b, it would appear that salinity
values for the gulf waters adjacent to Jubail have decreased, possibly due
to a significant fresh water input from extensive irrigation practices in the
Jubail area.

Dissolved oxygen (Figure 8.7c) displays a seasonal variation, with
higher values being observed during the cooler months. Variation in
dissolved oxygen content is influenced by temperature and salinity
factors. There is a slight upward trend in dissolved oxygen content of the
gulf waters adjacent to Jubail.

The pH range for Jubail gulf waters is maintained between 7.3 and 8.5
(Figure 8.7d). This suggests that any influences of Jubail developments on
the pH of the Jubail gulf waters are within the buffering capacity of the sea
water. Seasonal variations in pH may be correlated with phytoplankton
development.

In general, the organic carbon content of the gulf is low due to a

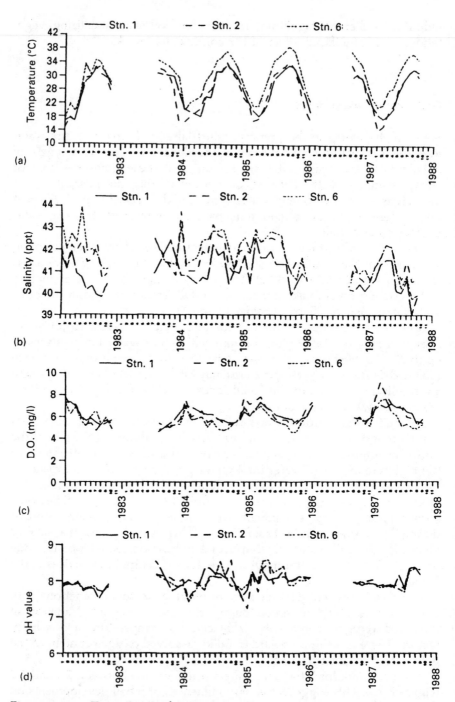

Figure 8.7a   *Temperature plot (1983–1988)*
Figure 8.7b   *Salinity plot (1983–1988)*
Figure 8.7c   *Dissolved oxygen plot (1983–1988)*
Figure 8.7d   *pH plot (1983–1988)*

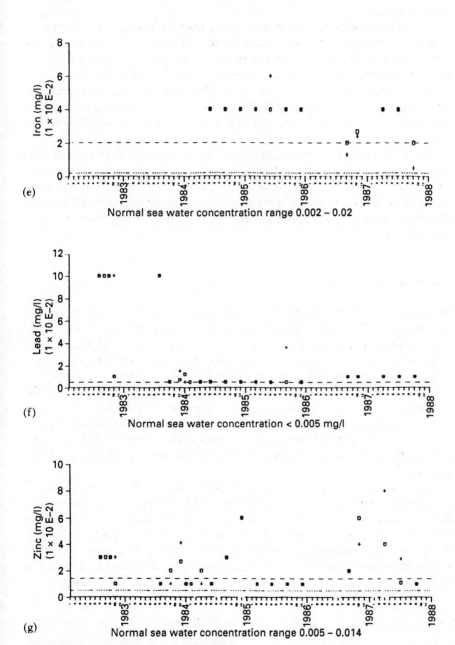

Figure 8.7e   *Iron plot (1983–1988)*
Figure 8.7f   *Lead plot (1983–1988)*
Figure 8.7g   *Zinc plots (1983–1988)*

nutrient deficiency in the western basin. The data showed a significant upward trend.

Suspended solids have decreased somewhat, following the cessation of dredging activities in the near shore Jubail gulf waters in 1983/84. Inshore waters tend to be higher in phosphorus content than offshore waters, a factor related to the general circulatory pattern of the gulf.

Figures 8.7h to 8.7j show the concentrations of iron, lead, and zinc measured at sampling stations 2 and 6 (the sea water cooling canal intake and outfall). The concentrations of iron and lead have remained within the normal background range.

Zinc is of particular concern as it is used in corrosion-retarding sacrificial anodes in the sea water cooling canal. As Figure 8.7j shows, zinc concentrations above the normal background range have been measured on at least three occasions. However, these concentrations were lower than the maximum acceptable concentrations cited in the Jubail environmental criteria.

Marine and terrestrial

Deep water dredging during the construction of the Jubail industrial port destroyed shellfish beds, and increased the concentrations of suspended solids in offshore waters. The extent to which the sea bed and marine biota may have recovered since the dredging operations is not yet known. Follow-up studies in this area are planned for the near future.

The removal of large quantities of sand from surrounding areas, for land-filling operations, destroyed the indigenous vegetation growing in those areas, possibly destabilizing the remaining sand, which could worsen local sand and dust storms and encourage the development of large, migratory sand dunes. Studies to assess the extent of regrowth are planned for the near future.

The local elevation of the groundwater surface has been increased significantly by the Jubail Industrial City development. Before the development, the groundwater recharge was by rainfall only, and was balanced by discharge and evaporation through the sabkhas. Ground-filling has eliminated large areas of the sabkhas. Recharge has been substantially increased by excess irrigation of plants in the Jubail area. The groundwater levels are being monitored for further developments.

Conclusions

The impact of the industrial developments in Jubail on the local air quality has been significant and, on occasion, unacceptable. However, since 1983, recorded concentrations of most airborne gaseous pollutants have decreased and remained below the acceptable limit criteria.

Air quality in the Jubail Industrial City area has been relatively stable – in some instances gradually improving – even though considerable industrial development has taken place during the last 10 years. Recorded levels of hydrogen sulphide (H_2S) and inhalable suspended particulate matter (ISP) remain a cause for concern.

There is reason to believe that the acceptable level criteria currently used in Jubail for ozone (O_3) and inhalable suspended particulate matter (ISP) may not be realistic, considering the local climate and conditions. The acceptable levels for all pollutants in Jubail are based on the criteria used by the United States Environment Protection Authority (USEPA). These criteria are generally applicable to all man-made, primary pollutants (NO_x, SO_2, H_2S, NMHC, CO), but O_3 and ISP have a very strong dependence on local climate and conditions. The USEPA criteria were established for the temperate climate of North America, and may be unrealistically low for the hot, desert climate of Saudi Arabia. Further studies should be made to resolve this matter.

In general, the water quality parameters monitored in the Arabian Gulf adjacent to Jubail show no major variation over the study period.

Observed reductions in salinity level are possibly attributable to irrigation practices in the industrial and residential areas of Jubail.

Total organic carbon levels appear to have increased. The observed increases in total organic carbon may have derived from anthropogenic sources.

The deep water dredging for the construction of the Jubail industrial port had a considerable effect on the concentrations of total suspended solids in the Arabian Gulf waters adjacent to Jubail. The time required for the suspended solids to settle back to normal levels appears to have been about 3–4 years.

Existing data on heavy metals in Arabian Gulf waters adjacent to Jubail indicate no significant upward trend above background levels. However, concentrations of zinc that were above the normal background levels have been observed on occasions. Studies on the possible impact of zinc on marine biota (for example *Meretrix meretrix*) are being undertaken. The general agreement among marine chemists is that metal determinations made over the past decade are not accurate due to problems associated with salt matrix interference in sea water samples. Baseline monitoring for heavy metals in gulf waters is currently being done using methodology to eliminate such interference factors.

9

Environmental aspects of hazardous wastes disposal in India

N. C. Trehan

With increasing economic activities and technological developments, production of hazardous wastes in India, as well as many other developing countries, has increased in recent years. Current trends indicate that the production of hazardous wastes in India is likely to increase at a much faster rate during the present decade than during the previous decade. While no one will argue with the observation that to the end of the present century and beyond in India and other developing countries in a similar stage of economic development, the production of hazardous wastes will continue to increase in the foreseeable future, not much is known about the characteristics of the hazardous wastes produced at present, total quantities produced or the existing disposal practices.

With increasing environmental awareness, the problem of disposal of hazardous wastes in an environmentally-sound fashion is also receiving a higher level of attention from the media, appropriate central and provincial regulatory agencies and also the general population. This heightening of interest has gradually contributed to the tightening of disposal regulation. While such developments are unquestionably a step in the right direction, it is clear that an accelerated programme is essential for efficient hazardous wastes disposal in India and other developing countries. Equally, a programme by itself will not be enough. It must be so designed that it will not only have full public support but also can be implemented properly.

Hazardous wastes

There is no one definition of hazardous wastes. While the definition could vary from one country to another, and also between different international organizations, there is clearly considerable commonality among such definitions. Only two definitions of hazardous wastes have been given below as an indication of this commonality.

United States: 'one that may cause or significantly contribute to serious illness or death or that poses a substantial threat to human health or the environment when improperly managed.'

UNEP: 'wastes other than radioactive wastes which, by reason of their chemical reactivity or toxic, explosive, corrosive or other characteristics causing danger or likely to cause danger to health or the environment, whether alone or coming into contact with other wastes, are legally defined hazardous in the State in which they are generated or in which they are disposed of or through which they are transported.'

Using a definition that is considered to be appropriate in a specific country, it is possible to compile a list of hazardous wastes. Some countries, for example the United States or Canada, have compiled such lists, which are updated as and when necessary. The Environmental Protection Agency (EPA) of the United States defines any waste as hazardous if it meets with one of the following four criteria:

1   Ignitability: Wastes that pose a fire hazard during routine management. Fires not only present immediate dangers of heat and smoke but also can spread harmful particles over wide areas.
2   Corrosivity: Wastes requiring special containers or segregation from other wastes because of their ability to dissolve toxic contaminants.
3   Reactivity: Wastes that tend to react spontaneously, to react vigorously with air or water, to be unstable to shock or heat, to generate gases or to explode.
4   Toxicity: Wastes that, when improperly managed, may release toxicants in sufficient quantities to pose a substantial hazard to human health or the environment.

Although hazardous wastes are generated in many different segments of society, industry is by far the largest producer. While the amount may vary from country to country, generally the chemical and allied products industry account for nearly 50 to 70 per cent of all hazardous wastes produced. For the United States, current estimates indicate that some 60 per cent of all industrial hazardous wastes is generated by the chemical and allied products sector. It is likely that the situation is somewhat similar in India and other major developing countries.

Reliable estimates of hazardous wastes currently being generated are not available for most developing countries. However, in the absence of reliable estimates, it can be assumed that as a general rule of thumb some 10 to 15 per cent of wastes produced by industry are likely to be hazardous. On this basis, it is likely that the generation of hazardous wastes is increasing at the rate of 2 to 5 per cent per year.

Estimates of the quantities of hazardous wastes generated by industry indicate that the total production in the OECD countries was some 300 million tonnes annually in 1985, out of which the United States accounted for some 268 million tonnes, European OECD countries 24 million tonnes, and the balance of 8 million tonnes was contributed by the Pacific OECD countries. Very little information is available at present on the extent of hazardous wastes produced in most developing countries and their waste disposal and management practices. A UNEP-WHO *ad-hoc* Working Group of Experts on Environmentally-sound Management of Hazardous

Wastes concluded in 1984 that 'it is safe to say that virtually all developing countries have yet to develop a comprehensive hazardous waste management scheme, as compared to those already established in most industrialized countries'. Regrettably, some 7 years later, very little improvement can be noted in nearly all developing countries.

From an environmental and health viewpoint it is not only important to determine the source, extent and type of hazardous wastes being produced, but it is also essential to have similar information on the amount of such wastes generated in the past, how and where they were disposed, how they are being managed at present, and in case of improper disposals, what the existing and potential problems could be, and how they can be resolved.

It is not surprising that the bases for information in developing countries are so poor. Even for an advanced country like the United States, as late as mid-1979, its Council on Environmental Quality reported that 'existing estimates on the extent of the problem vary so widely they are only marginally helpful'. In addition, the number of existing disposal sites was 'one of the major unknowns'. The same year, USEPA estimated that only about 10 per cent of hazardous wastes were being disposed of in a manner that was likely to comply with the regulations the Agency was planning to adopt. Similarly, estimates of the cost of cleaning up abandoned hazardous waste dumps in the United States varied widely, ranging from a low of $28.4 billion to a high of $55 billion.

Hazardous wastes management

Sound management of hazardous wastes must consider more than only safe storage and disposal practices. It would require a holistic approach that will consider comprehensively all alternatives available to institute a cradle-to-grave management system. It should consider not only the characteristics, volume and location of the wastes, but also how and why wastes are being produced and what effective steps can be taken to reduce substantially the quantity of wastes eventually to be disposed of.

A systems approach to hazardous wastes management must include consideration of the following six steps:

1   Minimization of hazardous wastes generation: By modifying production processes, it may be possible to reduce the quantity of hazardous wastes finally generated. If the quantity of wastes generated is less, the quantity to be disposed of in an environmentally sound manner will also be less. For example, introduction of a new ferrosilicon furnace in Norway has contributed to higher yields, less raw materials and energy consumption and reduced waste generation. In Bulgaria, the introduction of low-waste technology has reduced the production of industrial wastes by about 5.5 million tonnes annually. Often a move to such low-waste technology is more economical than the processes

they replace. It makes good sense in terms of both good economic and environmental housekeeping. Introduction of such technology also enables industry to comply with environmental regulations more effectively.

2   Reprocessing and re-use of wastes: Many wastes may contain useful materials, which can be reclaimed and re-used. In many cases extraction of resources from concentrated wastes requires less energy and contributes to less air and water pollution and solid wastes generation than the mining and processing of virgin raw materials. Recovery of energy and raw materials from wastes has increased significantly in recent years. For example, in the German Democratic Republic, approximately 30 million tonnes of wastes have been recycled annually. In Hungary, of about 22.5 million tonnes of industrial wastes generated every year, some 6.5 million tonnes are recycled. The re-use of wastes from the chemical, pharmaceutical, food processing and mining industries in Bulgaria has increased significantly in recent years. The recycling of aluminium cans in the United States increased more than twenty-one-fold, from 24 000 tonnes to 510 000 tonnes, within a ten-year period from 1972 to 1982. However, since only a small fraction of wastes is economically suitable for recovery at present, new low-waste technologies need to be developed before recovery can become a more widely viable alternative for many different industrial processes.

3   Transfer of wastes to another industry: In certain cases, hazardous wastes from one industry can be transferred to another industry which can use them as raw materials. An information exchange can be set up to act as a clearing-house, which can assist in matching producers of wastes with potential purchasers and users. The first such information exchange was set up in the Netherlands in 1972. Similar information exchanges and materials exchanges now operate in Canada, United States and several other countries. It should, however, be noted that probably only a small fraction of hazardous wastes may be suitable for exchange.

4   Separation of hazardous and non-hazardous wastes: If hazardous and non-hazardous wastes can be separated at source, only a limited quantity of hazardous wastes need to be handled. This will naturally reduce the final handling, transportation, storage and disposal efforts and costs.

5   Transform hazardous wastes to non-hazardous: Hazardous wastes can be made non-hazardous by incineration and physical and biological processing. Some toxic organic wastes can be destroyed by incineration. If carried out properly, it will not contribute to environmental degradation. Incineration, however, is an energy-intensive and expensive process. Chemical and biological processes can be used to transform hazardous to less hazardous or non-hazardous wastes. Among the physical processes used are carbon or resin adsorption, distillation, centrifugation, flocculation, sedimentation, reverse osmosis

and ultrafiltration. Chemical processes include neutralization, oxidation, precipitation and material exchanges to remove heavy metals. Some of the biological processes that can be used are activated sludge treatment, trickling filter and controlled land application.

6   Disposal of wastes in a controlled landfill: After consideration of the above five options, whatever hazardous waste remains has to be disposed of in secure landfills. Siting, planning and operation of secure landfills must be properly carried out. Regular monitoring of disposal sites is essential, even after they are closed, to ensure potential health hazards and environmental contamination do not occur. Sound disposal of hazardous wastes is not cheap, but in the long run it will invariably turn out to be significantly less expensive than inadequate disposal. For example, the estimated cost of sound disposal at Love Canal would have been less than $2 million, but by May 1980, more than $36 million had been already spent for the clean-up and associated expenses. The final bill was much higher.

Rational management of hazardous wastes in India can only be possible when the following constraints can be successfully overcome:

1   Absence of reliable data on type, nature and sources of hazardous wastes from different types of industry – especially chemical industry, the quantities produced, present inventories, storage practices, and methods of and sites for disposal.
2   Lack of adequate resource available to the regulatory agencies which would allow them to develop and implement proper management policies and practices.
3   Lack of expertise avilable to regulatory agencies and various industries (this is especially important since numerous types of hazardous wastes are produced each year, and may require different expertise to plan, design and implement appropriate disposal practices).
4   Absence of a comprehensive set of legislations and regulations which could holistically control the present and foreseeable situations.
5   Absence of co-ordination between the various regulatory agencies.
6   Lack of incentives available to industry to reduce the total production of hazardous wastes.
7   General absence of political will to enforce the existing legislations on a priority basis.

Unless these constraints are overcome, management of hazardous wastes will continue to remain suboptimal in developing countries.

Incineration

There is no doubt that after the adoption of low-waste technologies, controlled incineration is probably the best solution for disposal of hazardous wastes in most serious cases. Some countries like Denmark and the Federal Republic of Germany had already reached this conclusion. For example, in Denmark, the main policy at present is central waste disposal services, with materials recovery and recycling and power generation, in properly sited industrial parks.

While incinerators have been used for disposal of municipal solid wastes for some considerable time, it should be noted that a hazardous wastes incinerator is very different from the former for the following four important reasons:

1   Hazardous wastes incinerators are generally specially designed to burn specific undesirable byproducts in contrast to the municipal types, which generally can accept a wide variety of municipal wastes.
2   The input feed is more homogeneous and less variable for hazardous wastes incinerators.
3   Most hazardous wastes incinerators are generally small-scale, ranging from burning a few to a few hundred tons of wastes per day.
4   Hazardous wastes incinerators require more stringent effluent monitoring processes because such wastes are more dangerous and complex when compared to municipal wastes.

Globally, there are at least 1,500 operating incinerators of municipal wastes, with an average waste-burning capacity of at least 220 tons per day. There are, of course, many more smaller units. The technology has now been clearly proven over many years of experiences in many different countries of the world. Monitoring the performances of the recently installed units indicates that the emissions of chlorinated hydrocarbons have been substantially reduced to very low, and thus acceptable, levels. However, emissions of heavy metals with fly ash and leaching from bottom ash could still contribute to environmental problems, but such problems now appear to be on the verge of solutions through techniques like bag-house clean-up.

Another type of incinerator worth mentioning is that designed specially for hospital and biomedical wastes. It is estimated that in the United States alone there are about 7,000 such units in hospitals. These units are small in character, burning between 1 to 25 tons of hospital wastes per day. The Pollution Control Research Institute is now experimenting with a small-scale incinerator to dispose primarily hospital wastes.

Conclusion

It is self-evident that as industrialization process progresses further in India, both quantities and types of solid wastes that will be generated will continue to increase in the foreseeable future. Accordingly, if full advantage is to be taken of the benefits of industrialization, wastes generated must be disposed of in an environmentally safe manner so that their adverse impacts on human and animal helath and biota can be reduced to acceptable levels. One of the major effective alternatives that is available at present for such disposal practices is incineration which, however, must be well planned and managed. Undoubtedly, incineration plants will play an increasingly significant role in solid wastes disposal in the future.

10
New monitor for process and accidental releases
Colin Doyle

This chapter is concerned with a new method for monitoring gaseous releases from industrial processes. But before getting down to the technical details of how this particular instrument functions, it will be useful first to look at the role of measurement instrumentation in general in the area of environmental pollution assessment.

The politics of environmental impact assessment has been well worked out, at least in Europe and the United States. Legislation now requires that quantitative assessments be made of the probable effect of any new industry on the surrounding population and ecosystem. As far as gaseous emissions are concerned this requires computer modelling of the transport of the process or fugitive emissions into the locality surrounding the plant. This, combined with the knowledge of the effects of the gas on man, and a benefit–risk analysis, leads to a decision on whether operation of the plant in the given area is acceptable or not. While much of the legislation and talk may be about the effects of process emissions, there is no doubt that what most people are afraid of is the possibility of accidental releases of large quantities of toxic gases to the environment with lethal consequences. In this respect too, computer modelling can be used at the planning stage to predict the worst case possible impact in the event of a massive release of toxic material. These computer dispersion models give valuable information on the optiumum siting of the plant, and on the precautions that need to be taken to protect the surrounding population in the event of an accident.

In this planning stage which has just been outlined, there may be little need for measurement instrumentation, as the environmental impact assessments can be modelled reliably by computer. In passing, it may however be pointed out that a gas measurement instrument can be very useful in determining the actual dispersion conditions at the plant site, by means of tracer gas measurement.

The role of gas monitors

Monitoring process emissions

When the plant is up and running what is the role of measurement instrumentation? As far as process gas emissions are concerned there is little doubt that in a well-run plant it is good practice to monitor the routine releases of these gases. Besides giving feedback to the plant manager on how well the plant is running, it also serves the purpose of providing documentation to the health and safety inspectors to verify that the authorized discharge limits are not exceeded. Such documentation would also prove useful to plant management many years into the future, as evidence in any litigation proceedings brought against them by people living near the plant who claim to have been damaged by the emissions.

Monitoring accidental releases

As regards accidental releases, rapid detection and subsequent monitoring of the releases in real-time would be of considerable benefit in deciding the optimum response activities to protect the surrounding population. Many chemical industries nowadays have computerized accident response systems. If a large accidental release occurs, the dispersion of the cloud can be modelled in real-time using a computer program developed for that site. The input data to this program must be as far as possible actual data collected on site. In modelling accidental releases, it is not good enough to make worse-case assumptions, except as a last resort, as this could precipitate unwarranted panic response, which may do more harm than good.

The correct estimation of the dispersion of the released gas is hampered by:

1   uncertainty in how much gas is being released (the source term);
2   uncertainty in the meteorological dispersion parameters around the plant, and the accuracy of the dispersional model itself.

I will address the question of the source term only. In the case of a breached storage tank for example, the size of the release can be estimated from the size of the hole and knowledge of the pressure and volatility of the substance in question, along with the energy available to drive the release. This approach is however subject to considerable practical difficulties and uncertainty. By actually measuring the concentration of the escaped gas at various points around the plant, using permanent monitors, it would be possible to quantify the source term more accurately. The information from the monitors placed around the plant can be fed back to the dispersion modelling computer, and the variables in the dispersion model can then be adjusted to get the best agreement with the actual measured concentrations. In addition, such a gas monitor or set of monitors if placed close to residential areas or staff quarters near the plant could be used to trigger a warning alarm.

Even without a sophisticated dispersion modelling system, an array of monitors placed around the plant can give accurate information on the location, concentration and direction of the cloud. This information can then be used in deciding whether evacuation is necessary.

The ideal monitor

Having discussed briefly the uses of a permanent gas monitor, the question may be asked what kind of monitor is best suited to this application. Some characteristics which would be desirable in such a monitor are as follows:

- It should be rugged and weatherproof for outdoor installation.
- It should be sufficiently sensitive and selective to the gas(es) of interest.
- It should be capable of meauring from the low p.p.m. or p.p.b. levels of process emissions, to several orders of magnitude higher to cover accidental emissions, with a linear response.
- It should yield absolute concentration measurement rather than simple yes/no indication.
- It should require minimal attention, and should have low enough drift so that frequent recalibration is not required.
- It should be possible to integrate the monitor into a computerized surveillance system.

A new type of gas monitor

The new type of gas monitor which is to be described has been designed with the foregoing desirable features in mind. The measurement method employed in this monitor will probably be novel to many, and I will therefore outline some of the background to the technique. The detection principle used in the monitor is based on the photoacoustic effect, which is described in detail in the standard reference literature. This is an effect whereby a gas in a sealed container emits an audible sound upon the absorption of modulated infra-red light.

Photoacoustic effect

The photoacoustic effect was discovered by Alexander Graham Bell during his investigation of acoustic transduction methods in the latter part of the last century. He discovered that a chopped light beam when shone on a sealed glass jar containing certain substances, evoked an audible sound. The strength of the sound signal depended on what substance was placed in the jar. We now know that this effect is due to rapid heating of the air in the jar following absorption of infra-red light by the substance in the jar. The rhythmic heating of the air in the closed container causes a corresponding rhythmic pressure fluctuation, which is perceived as sound. In principle then, any substance which absorbs in the infra-red region of the spectrum can be detected in this way by measuring the intensity of the sound produced.

The photoacoustic effect remained as a scientific curiosity for many years, but it was first put to practical use as a gas detector in the late 1930s, and ever since the technique has continued to be used, but mainly in specific research applications. It is therefore not as widely known as for example its companion technique, the well-known infra-red spectrometry, which is based on the measurement of the attenuation of an infra-red beam in the sample cell.

Design of the monitor

Due to the availability of accurate and stable measurement microphones, and digital electronics, it has been possible to develop a gas monitor suitable for outdoor use based on photoacoustic detection. As will be seen later there were good practical reasons for basing this monitor design on photoacoustic principles.

The monitor is shown schematically in Figure 10.1. A sample of air is pumped into the detection cell and the cell is sealed. The source of light is a tungsten lamp which gives an output spectrum approximating to that of a black body at about 700°C. This light is passed through an optical filter which transmits a certain pass-band of infra-red light into the cell. The pass-band of the filter is selected to correspond to a strong absorption band in the infra-red spectrum of the gas species which it is wished to detect. Therefore choice of an appropriate filter makes the monitor sensitive to a specific gas. The light is also chopped before it enters the cell, at a frequency of 20 Hz. This is required to produce a fluctuating stimulation of the cell, so that the resulting pressure fluctuation can be detected by a microphone. If there is any of the sought after gas present in the cell, it will absorb the infra-red radiation and result in heating in the cell with a corresponding pressure or sound signal which is detected by the microphone. The size of the signal from the microphone is proportional to the concentration of the gas in the cell. This signal is further processed in the electronics, converted to digital form and transmitted over the serial interface to a computer, where the result can be displayed on a screen.

The complete monitor is housed in a weatherproof box and can be mounted on a mast. It is powered by a 12 V DC supply, and connected to a computer over the serial interface, Figure 10.2. A typical monitoring system could consist of anything from a single monitor to tens of monitors

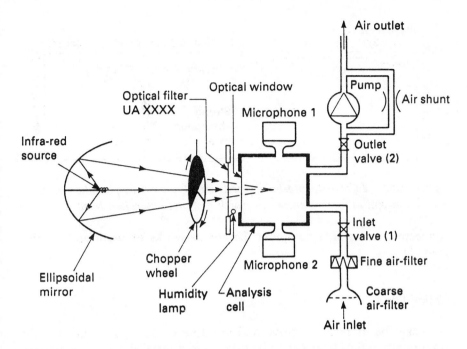

Figure 10.1   *Operation principles of the photoacoustic toxic gas monitor*

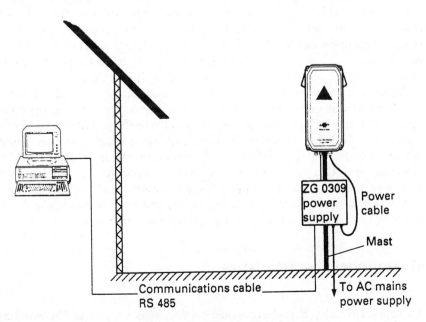

Figure 10.2   *Toxic gas monitor – mounting and connection*

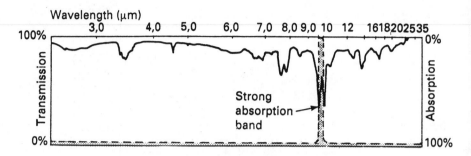

Figure 10.3   *Infra-red absorbtion spectrum of an organophosphorous compound. An optical filter is chosen to match a strong absorbtion band*

connected to a single computer. Larger networks of monitors are also possible.

Optical filters

To make the monitor sensitive and selective to the gas of interest, the appropriate optical filter has to be fitted before installation of the monitor on site. Choice of the correct filter requires knowledge of the infra-red absorption spectra of the gas of interest, which is easily obtained nowadays from the extensive literature on this subject. As an illustration of how a filter is chosen, suppose one wishes to tune the monitor to be specific for detection of a particular organophosphorous compound, which could conceivably be emitted from a pesticides plant. The infra-red spectrum of the substance is first examined, from which the regions of strong absorption can be identified. An optical filter is selected which has a pass-band matching a selected absorption band in the infra-red spectrum, thus making the monitor selective to this gas, Figure 10.3.

Before a monitoring system is installed consideration will also have to be given to the question of possible interferants, so that the optimum optical filter can be chosen to ensure selectivity to the gas of interest in the presence of the known interferants. One interferant which is almost always present is water vapour. Unfortunately water absorbs in all regions of the infra-red, and this must always be compensated for. In the monitor described there is a built-in facility for measurement of water concentration, based also on photoacoustic principles, and the interference from the water vapour is automatically compensated for within the monitor.

Operational characteristics

To appreciate why the photoacoustic effect was chosen as the working principle for the monitor, it will help to consider some of the characteristics of this monitor, which compare very favourably with other detection methods currently on the market.

Detection limits

The detection limits for a range of common industrial gases are shown in Table 1, from which it can be seen that the lower detection limits are typically in the low p.p.m. or p.p.b. range.

The upper limit of detection of a monitor based on the photoacoustic effect is four orders of magnitude greater than the lower limit of detection (10 000 times greater). The response is linear over this range.

Selectivity

For field measurements there is no point in having a very sensitive sensor unless it is selective with respect to the gas of interest. The good selectivity of the monitor described is based on the optical filter which is selected to best detect the gas of interest.

Table 10.1 *Detection limits achievable with the toxic gas monitor for a range of common industrial gases*

Gas	Detection limit (ppm)
Acrylonitrile	0.6
Ammonia	0.15
Benzene	0.8
Ethylene oxide	0.1
Freons	0.05
Hydrogen chloride	0.4
Hydrogen cyanide	0.3
Hydrogen sulphide	25
Methyl isocyanate	0.02
Methyl methacrylate	0.02
Methylenechloride	0.1
Phosgene	0.012
Styrene	0.2
Total hydrocarbons	0.02
Vinyl chloride monomer	0.15
Xylene	0.04

Response time

A complete measurement can be completed in one minute. A network of monitors can be measuring simultaneously so that in for example a monitoring system with ten sensors, the concentration at ten locations is obtained in one minute.

Recovery time

The monitor is completely purged after each measurement thus ensuring that residual traces of high concentration samples do not contaminate subsequent measurements. The monitor therefore responds accurately to a fluctuating gas concentration in the ambient air.

Drift

The high stability of the detecting microphone and of the electronic components ensures a sensitivity drift of less than 2.5 per cent/month, so recalibration is only required every few months. A very important point also is that the zero point of the monitor does not drift significantly, and this is a valuable protection against false alarms. This stable zero point is due to the fact that no photoacoustic signal can be produced unless there is a gas present in the cell which absorbs in the infra-red.

Accuracy

The photoacoustic monitor enables accurate results to be measured, with a repeatability of 1 percent. This accuracy means that reliable data is available for emission records and true estimation of danger in the case of accidental releases.

Conclusion

A new type of gas monitor has been developed suitable for permanent outdoor monitoring of gas concentrations around chemical industries. The monitor operates on the photoacoustic detection principle which results in an extremely stable, selective and compact unit. It is envisaged that this monitor will find application in the continuous surveillance of process emissions, as well as in real-time monitoring of accidental releases.

References

Pao, Yoh-Han (1977) *Optoacoustic Spectroscopy and Detection,* Academic Press, New York.

Rosencraig, A. (1980) *Photoacoustics and Photoacoustic Spectroscopy,* Wiley-Interscience, New York.

11

Stimulation modelling in environmental impact assessment
Kurt Fedra

Human activities, and in particular large scale industrial, energy, construction, or agricultural projects considerably affect the natural environment.
These impacts occur during the construction phase, the operational
lifetime of a project, and in many cases, such as with waste disposal sites,
may continue after closure of a plant or site. Consumption of natural
resources, including space, water, air, and biota, and the generation of
wastes including the dissipation of energy, usually lead to a degradation of
the natural environment.

Environmental considerations are increasingly becoming important
components of planning. Many countries, pioneered by the 1969 National
Environmental Policy Act (NEPA) of the United States, have introduced
appropriate legislation calling for the explicit consideration of environmental impacts in the planning and decision making process for large
projects. For an international comparison of EIA procedures and examples
from developing countries, see, e.g., Munn, 1979; Clark *et al.*, 1984.

Environmental Impact Assessment (EIA) approaches are often organized around checklists of data collection and analysis components (e.g.,
De Santo, 1978; Munn, 1979; Bisset, 1987; Biswas and Geping, 1987).

Basic components of the assessment are:

1   a description of the current environment, which usually includes such
    elements as rare or endangered species, special scenic or cultural
    components;
2   a description of the proposed project or activity, covering technologi-
    cal, socio-economic, and administrative and managerial aspects;
3   a description of expected impacts, with emphasis on irreversible
    change and the consideration of mitigation strategies and project
    alternatives, including the alternative to not undertake the project;
4   and, depending on the mandate given, a comparative evaluation of
    options.

Obviously, the prediction of future impacts is the most difficult part.
Approaches range from purely qualitative checklist-based matrix
approaches (Leopold *et al.*, 1971), expert panels and workshop techniques

(Holling, 1978), system diagrams and networks, to various computer-based modelling techniques (Patten, 1971; Kane *et al.*, 1973; Thompson, Vertinsky and Kane 1973; Walters, 1974; Gallopin, 1977; Bigelow *et al.*, 1977; Fedra, 1985b), and any combination of these approaches. However, most of the accepted and routinely used tools of EIA are not based on the use of computers, but on rather more-or-less formalized qualitative assessment procedures.

The use of computers as a major tool for EIA is, by far, not as common as it could or should be. Problems, in particular in developing countries, range from the availability of the necessary computer hardware to the expertise in developing, maintaining, and using more-or-less complex software systems (e.g., Ahmad and Sammy, 1985). Further, lack of quantitative data is often cited as a reason for not using computers and simulation models.

However, the availability of increasingly powerful and affordable computers grows rapidly (Fedra and Loucks, 1985; Loucks and Fedra, 1987), and so does computer literacy among technical professionals. Even very powerful super-micro computers have become somewhat more affordable, and technical workstations are approaching the price class of personal computers. And many of the reasons cited for not using computers in environmental assessment are in fact problems that the computer can help overcome.

Modelling in EIA

The two main problems, lack of expertise and lack of data, are good reasons to look into the use of computers, and in particular into new technologies such as expert systems, interactive modelling, and dynamic computer graphics. The basic idea of an expert system is to incorporate into a software system expertise, i.e., data, knowledge and heuristics, that are relevant to a given problem area. Application and problem-oriented rather than methodology-oriented systems are most often hybrid or embedded systems, where elements of AI technology are combined with more classical techniques of information processing and approaches of operations research and systems analysis. Here traditional numerical data processing is supplemented by symbolic elements, rules, and heuristics in the various forms of knowledge representation.

There are numerous applications where the addition of a quite small amount of 'knowledge' in the above sense, e.g., to an existing simulation model, may considerably extend its power and usefulness and at the same time make it much easier to use. Expert systems are not necessarily purely knowledge driven, relying on huge knowledge bases of thousands of rules. Applications containing only small knowledge bases, of at best a few dozen to a hundred rules, can dramatically extend the scope of standard computer applications in terms of application domains, as well as in terms of an enlarged non-technical user community.

Clearly, a model that 'knows' about the limits of its applicability, what kind of input data it needs, how to estimate its parameters from easily available information, how to format its inputs, how to run it, and how to interpret its output will require not only less computer expertise from its user, it will also make less demands on its domain expertise. Environmental impact assessment usally deals with rather complex problems that touch upon many disciplines, and rarely will an individual or a small group of individuals have all the necessary expertise at their disposal. The expert systems component of an EIA system can help to fill this gap and at the same time take over the role of a tutor. For recent surveys of the role and potential of expert systems technology in environmental planning and assessment, see Ortolano and Steineman, 1987; Beck, 1988; Gray and Stokoe, 1988.

The same line of argument holds for the missing data. A forecast of likely consequences and impacts has to be based on some kind of model. Whether that is a mental model, a set of 'rules of thumb' or heuristics an expert might use, or a formal mathematical model, the necessary information must be inserted in the (mental or mathematical) procedure somehow. If no specific data are available, one looks for similar problems for which information or experience exists and extrapolates and draws upon analogies. This role is usually filled by the expert's knowledge, or by handbooks and similar sources of information (Canter and Hill, 1979, Golden *et al.* 1979). Such information, however, can also be incorporated in a model or its interface, or be made available through dedicated databases connected to the models for the automatic downloading of parameters required. In a similar approach, basic parameters such as chemical properties relevant to environmental fate and transport calculations, for example, can be provided to the respective models through auxiliary models or estimation techniques (Lyman, Reehl and Rosenblatt 1982; Lyman, Potts and Magil, 1984).

An interactive approach

EIA is by definition a complex procedure that draws on numerous disciplines: the behaviour of highly interdependent, but usually ill-defined, systems needs to be understood and forecast. This interdisciplinary nature also calls for an array of related tools. At the same time, the subjective and discretionary human element must also be given due weight, in particular where aesthetic or cultural values are concerned that are difficult or impossible to express in monetary terms or measure reliably on any cardinal scale. This necessary subjective element calls for the direct and interactive involvement of users, allowing them to exert discretion and judgement wherever formal methods are insufficient.

Also, many information processing tasks such as recognition and comparison of complex patterns that depend on background information and an understanding of context, are often done more efficiently by man than by a machine. The direct integration of the user in turn requires a man–machine interface that is easy to use and error correcting, and thus minimizes problems of user error and user training.

The background information required for any comprehensive EIA is characterized by a broad range of disciplines and is subject to a variable degree of resolution and uncertainty. The assessment process therefore requires a strong element of human expertise and judgement in addition to the more formal, scientifically-based, analytical techniques based on technological, physiochemical, ecological, and economic principles. Computer-based methods of applied systems analysis, implemented using modern information processing technology, can now support such a comprehensive, interdisciplinary approach to environmental impact assessment. This approach can provide a powerful interactive tool for managers and planners, regulators and policy makers, because it makes access to a large number of relevant databases, problem simulation modules, and decision support tools easy and reliable.

At the core of this interactive approach, developed at the Advanced Computer Applications (ACA) group of the International Institute for Applied Systems Analysis, is an integrated set of modular software tools, building on existing models and computer-assisted procedures, that is intended for a broad class of users and should provide them with easy access to methods of analysis and information management which have previously been restricted to a small group of experts. To facilitate access to complex database systems and computer models by the non-expert user, it is necessary to build much of the accumulated knowledge of the subject areas into the user interface. The interface therefore incorporates elements of knowledge-based expert systems which assist the user to retrieve information or select, set up, run and interpret the specialized software relevant to his needs with a minimum of data preparation and manipulation effort.

By providing a coherent user interface, the interactions between different models, their databases and auxiliary software become more transparent to the user. Extensive use of symbolic representation with high-resolution colour graphics and menu-driven operations aids this transparency and makes the systems user friendly. Customizing the information and decision support systems for only a small set of specific applications, and then building the necessary background, context, and expertise into this special-purpose system, means trading off flexibility and generality for efficiency. However, as a consequence, a very efficient and largely error-free use of complex computer systems becomes possible even for users who have no expertise in the use of computers.

Application examples

The research and development carried out by IIASA's Advanced Computer Applications (ACA) project (Fedra, 1985a, 1986; Fedra and Otway, 1986; Fedra *et al.*, 1987a, b, c; Weigkricht and Winkelbauer, 1987) concentrates on integrated systems of software tools to make the scientific basis for planning and management directly available to planners, policy- and decision-makers.

Under contract to a number of international, governmental, and industrial clients, ACA is working on several projects that include or concentrate on environmental impacts of industrial activities and regional economic development. To support the complex tasks of comprehensive environmental assessment and management, the objective of these projects is to develop and implement an integrated set of software tools, building on existing models and computer-assisted procedures. Using concepts of artificial intelligence (AI) coupled with more traditional methods of applied systems analysis and operations research, these tools are designed to provide easy and direct access to scientific evidence, and allow the efficient use of formal methods of analysis and information management by non-technical users as well. The application examples from Europe, the United States, People's Republic of China (PRC) and India, discussed below, cover air, surface and groundwater modelling as well as risk analysis.

Air quality models

A number of atmospheric simulation models, including several Gaussian models for buoyant or heavy gases and dust, local Lagrangian and box models, and 2D finite-element models have been developed.

A long-range transport model based on a hybrid Lagrangian trajectory (Eliassen and Saltbones, 1982) and Gaussian model for large instantaneous sources describing e.g., major accidents, using a subset of the EMEP European synoptic wind field data, is implemented on a European scale with completely interactive problem definition, context driven auto-startup feature, and dynamic graphical display for the simulation (Figure 11.1).

The user can select the location for the accident by simply dragging a cross-hair cursor over the map of Europe. The magnitude of the emission, season, time of the day, and weather pattern can be selected by simply pointing at the appropriate description or icons symbolizing e.g., a repertoire of characteristic weather patterns. The appropriate input parameters are then automatically selected, scaled, or interpolated by the model system.

For the regional to local scale, and for continuous rather than accidental

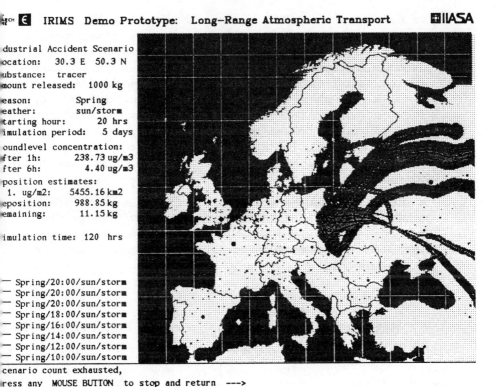

Figure 11.1   *Long-range atmospheric transport model*

emissions, the Industrial Source Complex model, a Gaussian air quality model for multiple point and area sources, was adapted. The implementation example described below was designed and implemented for industrial centres in the PRC (Figure 11.2). A simplified version, implemented on a personal computer (PC) with low-resolution colour graphics, was designed for the Pollution Control Research Institute (PCRI), Hardwar, India, and applied in a number of Indian examples.

The extensive use of coal, even of good quality, leads to considerable emissions of air pollutants such as SO_2 or dust, and, in consequence, may lead to high levels of local or regional air pollution, in and around industrial centres. Compounded by the widespread use of coal for cooking and heating, industrial centres such as Taiyuan City or Datong, situated in semi-enclosed, shallow valleys, can experience high levels of ambient pollutant concentration under adverse weather conditions.

To analyse the consequences of the current and increased use of coal under the various development scenaria as designed, e.g., with economic or technological models (Fedra *et al.*, 1987a), a Gaussian air pollution model for short-term concentration episodes, based on EPA's Industrial

Source Complex Model (ISC) has been implemented. The model is designed as a post-processor for production or energy scenaria based on coal, assessing environmental impacts at a given location (areas up to 50×50 km), characterized by a number of industrial point and area sources as well as domestic area sources. It translates emission characteristics for these sources into ambient SO_2 concentrations for a user-defined weather situation, e.g., a most likely or a worse-case assumption. The model provides information on the feasibility and desirability of a given development scenario in terms of selected environmental impacts.

The model input, defining a pollution scenario, comes from three distinct sources:

1 A site-specific data file, characterizing for one location (industrial installation or zone) the location (coordinates within a local grid) of the individual sources as well as the default values of emission characteristics. These include the yearly amount of coal burned for each source, stack height or height above ground for area sources, stack diameter,

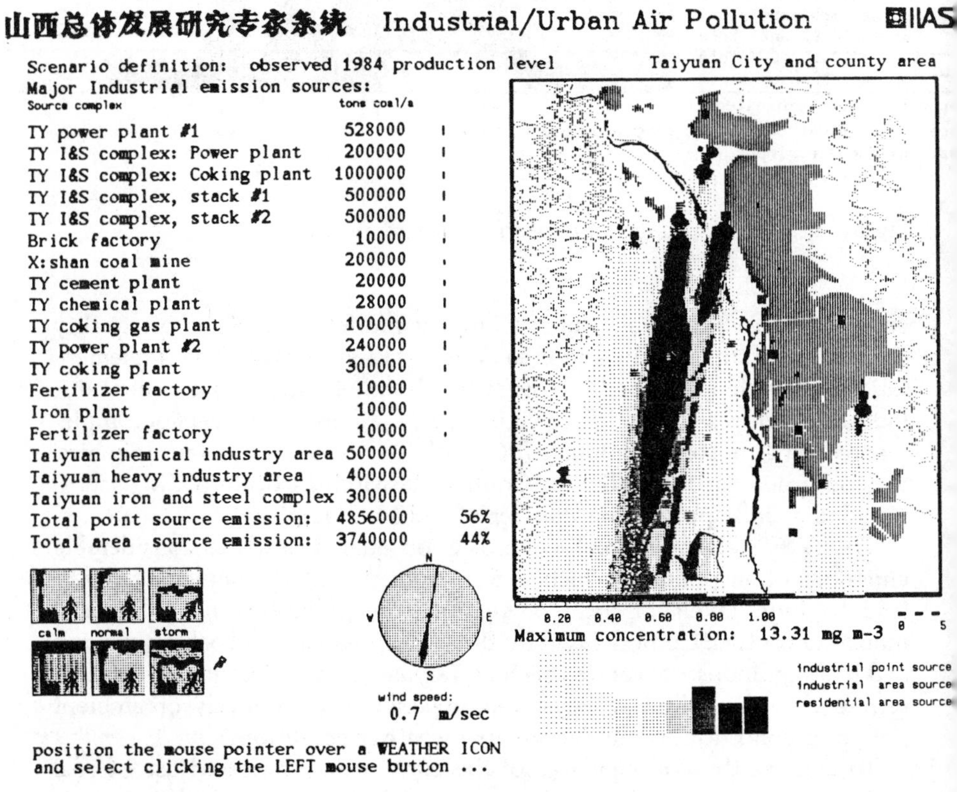

山西总体发展研究专家系统 Industrial/Urban Air Pollution ⊟IIAS

Figure 11.2 *Industrial Sources Complex model output for a heavy industry zone in Shanxi, PRC*

exit velocity, and exit temperature, and width of area sources. Where available, a background map from an appropriate Geographical Information System (GIS) is used.

2   Embedded in the code is the definition of a (generic) weather scenario (wind speed and direction, stability class, ambient air temperature, vertical mixing height, stability class).

3   The interactive user interface, allows modification of several of the above default or input values:
   ● the amount of coal burned for the first 18 sources,
   ● the season of the year (affecting domestic coal consumption as well as ambient air temperatures)
   ● wind speed and direction,
   ● weather characteristics by selecting one of six distinct weather patterns that translate into different stability classes used by the model.

The model interface lists up to 18 point and area sources (more can be used internally, but only the first 18 are listed and can be modified) and displays a background map of the area studied with the location of the sources indicated. Model results are shown as a colour-coded overlay on this map, a histogram (using the same colour code) of the frequency distribution of concentration values, and the maximum concentration value computed. The emissions from both point and area sources can be computed and the orography of the surrounding terrain can be taken into account in a simple manner.

Numerous program packages have been developed for this purpose, the so-called Gaussian dispersion model being the most commonly used basic model; this is probably the simplest kind of dispersion model, since it does not involve the solution of partial differential equations, but utilizes the fact that the concentration field resulting from a single point source can be reasonably described by a Gaussian or normal distribution (which is a solution to the diffusion equation). As a guideline for the implementation the user's guide for the Industrial Source Complex (ISC) model from the US Environmental Protection Agency (EPA, 1979) was used. A description of the meteorology and the physics of atmospheric dispersion can be found in standard textbooks (e.g., Seinfeld, 1975, or Pasquill and Smith, 1983; for the engineering aspects see e.g., Hanna, 1982).

Surface water quality models

There are several water quality models, ranging from EPA's SARAH (Ambrose and Vandergrift, 1986), a back calculating toxic waste reduction model or a simple dynamic river water quality model for toxic substances, extracted from the generic screening level USEPA model system TOXS-CREEN (Hetrick and McDowell-Boyer, 1984), to an integration of the chemical transport and fate model WASP and the fish gill uptake model

GETS (Ambrose, Hill and Mulkey, 1983; DiToro, Fitzpatrick and Thomann, 1983; Ambrose *et al.*, 1987).

The nearfield surface water model SARAH calculates the maximum allowable hazardous waste effluent concentrations based on predicted exposure to humans or aquatic life from contaminated surface water.

The surface water contamination pathways analysed in SARAH include:

● groundwater leachate from a land disposal facility.
● storm runoff from a land disposal facility.
● discharge through a waste treatment facility.

The human exposure pathways considered include:

● ingestion of treated drinking water,
● consumption of contaminated fish.

Acceptable leachate or industrial waste contaminant concentrations are computed by a back calculation procedure from chemical safety criteria in surface water, drinking water, or fish. The analytical solutions for contaminant behaviour in the catchment and stream near the facility allow rapid, multiple calculations required for good sensitivity and risk analysis.

GSARAH is an interactive, menu-driven implementation with a graphical user interface (Figure 11.3). The program initiates and guides the user dialog through prompt messages, and the user selects the desired option from a set of menus by means of a graphical input device (three-button mouse). Discrete choices such as selecting input data sets or contamination scenarios are accomplished by simply pointing at the desired option on the screen and pressing the left mouse button. Setting numbers to desired values is achieved by first identifying the respective number on the screen with the mouse, and then increasing or decreasing it by pressing the left or right mouse button, respectively.

At any stage, the model always offers a ready-to-run default that the user can run as a demonstration. The sequence of operations and problem definitions is therefore arbitrary. The user can go back and forth between scenario and data set selection, parameter editing, running the model, and performing sensitivity analysis in any desired sequence.

The user can select alternative data sets and scenarios from any of the data sets and scenario combinations offered by picking them with the mouse. While the number of contamination scenarios is currently fixed in the model structure, the data sets are defined external to the model. Whatever data sets are present in the data directory will be loaded and made available to the user.

The parameter values in the currently selected input data set can then be edited by the user to redefine the default data set (Figure 11.3). Any changes made will be only temporary, effective only during the current model run, and do not affect the original disk files. These can only be modified external to the program using any of the operating system's text editors.

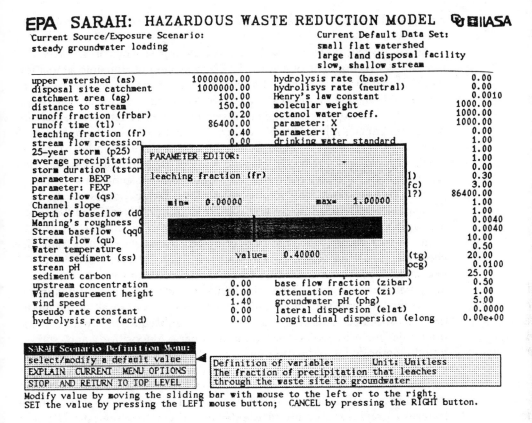

Figure 11.3   *Parameter editor for SARAH*

Running the current scenario will display a new page summarizing the results of a model run; maximum allowable leachate or raw waste concentration is displayed versus the respective target values for drinking water, concentration in fish biomass, and aquatic concentration.

Selecting a reference or target value by picking it with the mouse allows redefinition of the target value; this will then automatically rerun the model and recalculate the allowable concentrations. The lowest or constraining concentration of the three maximum allowable concentrations is highlighted by a box, indicating the most critical pathway or indicator in the current setup.

Selecting a target value for sensitivity analysis allows an upper and a lower bound to be set for the target. The bounds default to 50 per cent and 200 per cent of the current value, respectively. Within this range, the model will then be run a hundred times to calculate the allowable concentrations for the specified target range in 1 per cent increments. The resulting diagram plotting target versus maximum concentration is displayed.

Returning to the upper level allows either the current scenario parameters to be edited or another scenario and pathway combination to be selected.

As an alternative to the backward calculating scheme of SARAH, the river model component of TOXSCREEN, a system of dynamic simulation models, was adapted as part of an environmental risk assessment system (Fedra, 1985a). The model system TOXSCREEN, developed at Oak Ridge National Laboratory, is designed to assess the potential environmental fate of toxic chemicals released to air, water, or soil. It evaluates the potential of chemicals to accumulate in environmental media and is intended for use as a screening device. The model makes a number of simplifying assumptions and originally operates on a monthly time step. Assumptions include a generic (worst case) positioning of surface water bodies relative to atmospheric pollutant sources and contaminated land areas. The data used are typical of large geographic regions rather than of site-specific areas.

In TOXSCREEN, the physical/chemical processes which transport chemicals across air-water, air-soil, and soil-water interfaces are simulated explicitly. Deposition velocities, transfer rate coefficients, and mass loading parameters are used. Time-distributed pollutant concentrations in air, surface waters, and soil reflect both direct input to any or all of the media from a specified source or sources, and subsequent interaction via processes such as volatilization, atmospheric deposition, and surface runoff. Methods for estimating bioaccumulation in the food chain are also included.

The river model component of TOXSCREEN simulates pollutant dispersion in an arbitrary river segment. The model implementation features a graphical user interface, extensive interactive input modification based on predefined default values as well as animated graphical display of model results (Figure 11.4). The model is connected to the hazardous substances database, so that the parameters for specific substances can be loaded from this database after identifying a substance by one of the database access mechanisms.

To simulate dispersion in a river or part of a river, the river is divided into a number of geometrically equivalent reaches all of which have the same flow rate. An equation similar to the one used in EXAMS (Smith *et al.*, 1977; Burns, Cline and Lassiter, 1981) is used to estimate the pollutant mass in each timestep in each reach. Instantaneous mixing of pollutants upon entry into each reach is assumed; pollutant concentrations are computed for dissolved neutral, dissolved ionic, and adsorbed forms, according to chemical equilibria. Adsorption on sediment is also described. A number of first-order rate constants (e.g. biodegradation, hydrolysis, volatilization) are used to simulate decay phenomena. A more detailed description of the river model, the models it is based on, and various alternative models of higher resolution is given in Fedra (1985a).

In addition to the graphical display of dynamic model results, an important feature of the model is in its direct coupling to a database of hazardous substances, which also contains the rate coefficients required by the model for the simulation of a particular chemical. The user can either directly set these rate coefficients, or he can select a specific chemical from the database using several alternative styles of identifying a chemical. The corresponding parameters will then be automatically copied from the database into the river model.

EASE, a more complex assessment system, incorporates the WASP dynamic water quality model, coupled with the fish exposure and gill uptake model FGETS (Figure 11.5). The two models, dynamically linked, are connected to a set of databases and a simple GIS. The databases allow the user to select, by name or from the maps, a river and a certain reach within the river. The necessary hydrological and environmental parameters are then automatically loaded from an adaptation of the so-called Canonical Environments database, developed by the EPA. Two additional databases provide the necessary parameters for a toxic chemical and for a fish species. After selecting a loading scenario, representing either time variable area sources such as caused by agricultural runoff, or continuous loading from an industrial point source, a simulation run over 1 year traces the expected pollutant concentration in a multi-segment respresentation of the river and its sediments, as well as the bioaccumulation in the fish

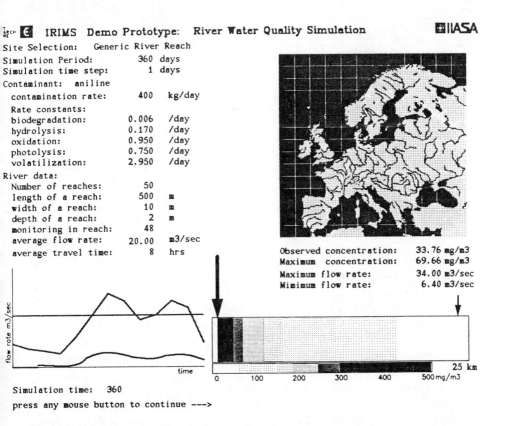

Figure 11.4   *River water quality simulation: TOXSCREEN*

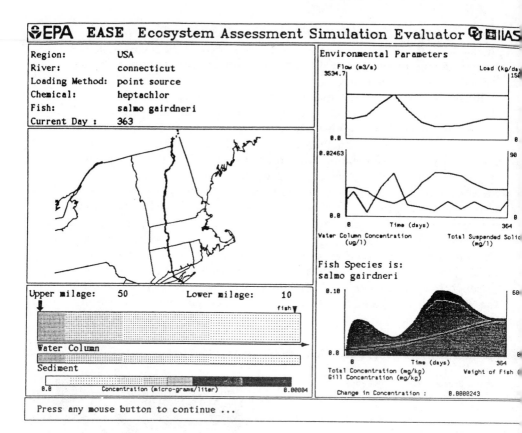

Figure 11.5   *Model output from a WASP/FGETS simulation run*

species selected. Again, dynamical graphical display of the simulation results and interactive problem definition are the main features of this system.

Groundwater quality modelling

FEFLOW, a 2D finite-element groundwater contamination model (Diersch, 1980), is being integrated in an interactive model support system. The software system supports problem selection from a library of site-specific and generic examples, as well as extensive problem editing features including a CAD system for mesh design and the definition of initial and boundary conditions. Problem representations as well as mesh design can use satellite maps such as LANDSAT or SPOT imagery or Digital Line Graph (DLG) vector maps as a background (Figure 11.6).

   Problem descriptions can be modified interactively, by setting pumping rates, activating or deactivating pumps or well galleries, specifying the concentration or mass flux of the pollutant source, and setting material parameters such as decay and adsorption rates. The model generates animated graphical output of flow fields and time-varying concentrations in the wells defined in a given problem, as well as a dynamic display of spatially distributed pollutant concentrations in horizontal or vertical projections, which again can be scaled or zoomed into under interactive control.

Risk analysis

An important part of environmental impact assessment is risk analysis. In a study for the Ministerie van Volkshuisvesting, Ruitmeljike Ordening en Milieubeheer (VROM), ACA has developed an interactive and graphics-oriented framework and post-processor for the risk assessment package SAFETI (Technica, 1984) to facilitate the quick generation, display, evaluation and comparison of policy alternatives and individual scenarios.

The SAFETI package is a computer-based system for risk analysis of process plants. The software package was developed under contract to VROM in association with the Dienst Centraal Milieubeheer Rijnmond, by Technica Inc., Consulting Scientists and Engineers, London.

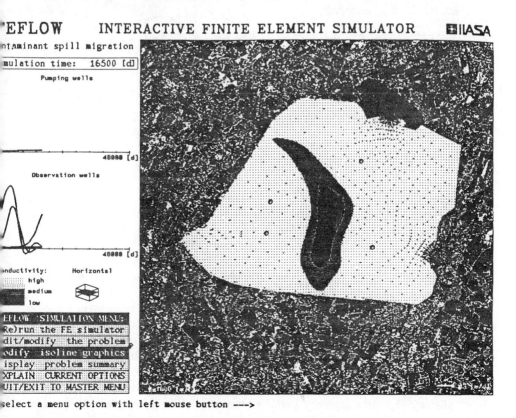

Figure 11.6 *FEFLOW, A 2D finite-element groundwater contamination model*

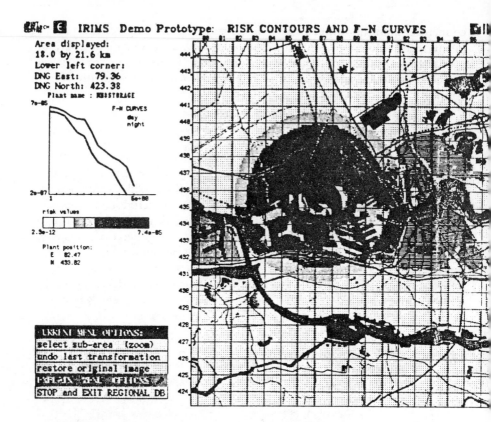

Figure 11.7   *Spatial display of risk contour from fault tree and consequence analysis*

SAFETI starts by generating a plant description; next, failure cases are generated and clustered; finally, the failure cases are processed by consequence analysis programs producing: radiation radii for early ignition of flammable gas; dense cloud dispersion profiles and associated flammable mass for late ignition; and toxic effect probabilities as 'appropriate' consequence parameters can be combined to produce risk contours and F–N curves. The SAFETI package itself is accessible from a master menu that also provides access to the graphical interfaces, and runs under its own interactive, line-oriented menu system.

The graphical interface to SAFETI's databases and consequence modelling results allows for the display of the raw data such as plant locations, weather data, or population distribution as thematic overlays on a map. Once risk analysis, using SAFETI's original interface, has been performed for a specific process plant, the results are available for graphical display and interpretation. In addition to the F–N curves, risk contours can be displayed as transparent overlays on a map of the Netherlands. This map allows arbitrary zooming to provide the appropriate level of detail and resolution for a given problem.

Discussion

Although they differ widely in their degree of sophistication, detail, and complexity, all of the above application examples have a common structure.

Built around one or more coupled simulation models, the systems feature:

1   An interactive, menu-driven user interface, that guides the user with prompt and explain messages through the application. No command language of special format of interaction is necessary, the computer assists the user in its proper use.
2   Dynamic colour graphics for the model output and a symbolic representation of major problem components, that allow for easy and immediate understanding of basic patterns and relationships. Rather than emphasizing the numerical results, symbolic representations and the visualization of complex patterns and time and space support an intuitive understanding of complex systems behaviour.
3   The coupling to one or several databases that provide necessary input information to the models. The user's choice or definition of a specific scenario can be expressed in an aggregated and symbolic, problem oriented manner without concern for the technical details of the computer implementation.
4   Embedded AI components such as specific knowledge bases allow user specifications in allowable ranges, to be checked and constrained and ensure the consistency of interactively defined scenaria.

In summary, the models are designed for easy and efficient use, even in data-poor situations, and do not require specific technical expertise from their user. The 'intelligent' interface and its pre- and post-processing functions free the user from the time consuming and error-prone tasks of data file preparation, the mechanics of model runs, and finally the interpretation and translation of numerical results into meaningful and problem-adequate terms. This not only allows the user to employ the models more freely in a more experimental and interesting way, it also allows the analyst to concentrate on the more important tasks he can do best, i.e., the recognition of emerging patterns, the comparative evaluation of complex alternatives, and the entire institutional aspects of any environmental impact assessment rather than its technicalities.

References

Ambrose, R. B., Hill, S. I. and Mulkey, L. A. (1983), *User's Manual for the Chemical Transport and Fate Model (TOXIWASP), Version 1 EPA/600/ 3–83/005*, Environmental Research Laboratory, Office of Research and Development, US Environmental Protection Agency, Athens, Georgia 30613, 178 pp.

Ambrose, R. B. and Vandergrift, S. B. (1986) *SARAH, A Surface Water Assessment Model for Back Calculating Reductions in Abiotic Hazardous Wastes*, EPA/600/3–86/058, Environmental Research Laboratory, Office of Research and Development, US Environmental Protection Agency, Athens, Georgia 30613, 95 pp.

Ambrose, R. B., Wool, T. A., Connolly, J. P. and Schanz, R. W. (1987) *WASP4, A Hydrodynamic and Water Quality Model – Model Theory, User's Manual, and Programmer's Guide*, Environmental Research Laboratory, US Environmental Protection Agency, Athens, Georgia 30613, 297 pp.

Ahmad, Y. J. and Sammy, G. K. (1985) *Guidelines to Environmental Impact Assessment in Developing Countries*, Hodder and Stoughton, London, 52 pp.

Beck, M. B. (1988) *Expert Systems in Environmental Systems Analysis and Control*, Dept,. of Civil Eng., Imperial College, London. Draft Expert Tutorial submitted to WHO.

Bigelow, J. H., De Haven, J. C., Dzitzer, C., *et al.* (1977) *Protecting an Estuary from Floods – A Policy Analysis of the Oosterschelde*, Vol. III, Assessment of Long-Run Ecological Balances, R-2121/4-NETH, Rand, Santa Monica, 215 pp.

Bisset, R. (1987) Methods for environmental impact assessment: a selective survey with case studies. In *Environmental Impact Assessment for Developing Countries* (eds A. K. Biswas and Q. Geping) Tycooly, London, pp. 3–64.

Biswas, A. K. and Geping, Q. (eds.) (1987) *Environmental Impact Assessment for Developing Countries*, Tycooly, London, 232 pp.

Burns, L. A., Cline, D. M. and Lassiter, R. R. (1981) *Exposure Analysis Modeling Systems (EXAMS): User Manual and Systems Documentation*, USEPA Environmental Research Laboratory, Athens, Georgia, 460 pp.

Canter, L. W. and Hill, L. G. (1979) *Handbook of Variables for Environmental Impact Assessment*, Ann Arbor Science, Ann Arbor, MI., 203 pp.

Clark, B. D., Gilad, A., Bisset, R. and Tomlinson, P. (1984) *Perspectives on Environmental Impact Assessment*, Reidel, Dordrecht, 520 pp.

De Santo, S. R. (1978) *Concepts of Applied Ecology*, Springer Heidelberg, 310 pp.

Diersch, H. J. (1980) *Finite-Element-Programmsystem FEFLOW. Program Description*, Institut für Mechanik der AdW DDR, Berlin (In German).

DiToro, D. M. Fitzpatrick, J. J. and Thomann, R. V. (1983) *Documentation for Water Quality Analysis Simulation Program (WASP) and Model*

Verification Program (MVP), EPA-600/3-81-044. Prepared for Environmental Protection Agency, Minnesota.

Eliassen, A. and Saltbones, J. (1982) *Modeling of Long-range Transport of Sulphur over Europe. A Two-year Model Run and Some Model Experiments*, EMEP/MSC-W. Report 1/82. Nor. Met. Inst., Oslo.

EPA (1979) *Industrial Source Complex (ISC) Model User's Guide*, Vol. I & II. EPA Report No. EPA-450/4-79-030/31, US Environmental Protection Agency, Research Triangle Park, North Carolina.

Fedra, K. (1985a) *Advanced Decision-oriented Software for the Management of Hazardous Substances. Part I: Structure and Design* (Final Report to Euratom CEC/JRC, Ispra, Italy). CP-85-18. International Institute for Applied Systems Analysis, A-2361 Laxenburg, Austria, 61 p.

Fedra, K. (1985b) A Modular Interactive Simulation System for Eutrophication and Regional Development *Water Resources Research*, **21** (2), 143–152.

Fedra, K. (1986a) *Advanced Decision-oriented Software for the Management of Hazardous Substances. Part II: A Prototype Demonstration System*, CP-86-10, International Institute for Applied Systems Analysis, A-2361 Laxenburg, Austria, 98 p.

Fedra, K. (1986b) *Decision Making in Water Resources Planning: Models and Computer Graphics*, Paper presented at the UNESCO/IHP-III Symposium on Decision Making in Water Resources Planning, Oslo, Norway, 5–7 May.

Fedra, K. and Loucks, D. P. (1985) Interactive Computer Technology for Planning and Policy Modeling. *Water Resources Research*, **21** (2), 114–122.

Fedra, K. and Otway, H. (1986) *Advanced Decision-oriented Software for the Management of Hazardous Substances. Part III: Decision Support and Expert Systems: Uses and Users*, CP-86-14, International Institute for Applied Systems Analysis, A-2361 Laxenburg, Austria, 44 pp.

Fedra, K., Li, Z., Wang, Z. and Zhao, C. (1987a) *Expert Systems for Integrated Development: A Case Study of Shanxi Province, The People's Republic of China*, SR-87-001. International Institute for Applied Systems Analysis, A-2361 Laxenburg, Austria.

Fedra, K., Karhu, M., Rys, T., *et al.*, (1987b) *Model-based Decision Support for Industry-Environment Interactions. A Pesticide Industry Example*, WP-87-97. International Institute for Applied Systems Analysis, A-2361 Laxenburg, Austria.

Fedra, K., Weigkricht, E. and Winkelbauer, L. (1987c) *A Hybrid Approach to Information and Decision Support Systems: Hazardous Substances and Industrial Risk Management*, RR-87-12, International Institute for Applied Systems Analysis, A-2361 Laxenburg, Austria. Reprinted from *Economics and Artificial Intelligence*, Pergamon Books, Ltd.

Gallopin, G. C., (1977) Modelling incompletely specified complex systems. *Third International Symposium on Trends in Mathematical Modelling*, S. C. Bariloche, December 1976, UNESCO-Fundacion Bariloche.

Golden, J., Ouellette, R. P., Saari, S., and Cheremisinoff, P. N. (1979)

Environmental Impact Data Book, Ann Arbor Science, Ann Arbor, MI, 864 pp.

Gray, A., and Stokoe, P. (1988) *Knowledge-based or Expert Systems and Decision Support Tools for Environmental Assessment and Management. Their Potential and Limitations*, School for Resource and Environmental Studies, Dalhousie University, Nova Scotia.

Hanna, S. R. (1982) Turbulent diffusion: chimneys and cooling towers, In *Engineering Meteorology* (ed. E. J. Plate) Elsevier, Amsterdam.

Hetrick, D. M., and McDowell-Boyer, L. M. (1984) *User's Manual for TOXSCREEN: A Multi-media Screening-level Program for Assessing the Potential Fate of Chemicals Released to the Environment*, ORNL-6041, Oak Ridge National Laboratory and EPA-560/5-83-024, USEPA, Washington, DC.

Holling, C. S. (ed.) (1978) *Adaptive Environmental Assessment and Management*, Wiley, Chichester, 377 pp.

Kane, J., *et al.* (1973) KSIM: a methodology for interactive resource simulation. *Water Resources Research* **9**, 65–80.

Leopold, L. B., *et al.* (1971) *A Procedure for Evaluating Environmental Impact*, US Geological Survey Circular 645. Washington DC: Highway Research Board.

Loucks, D. P. and Fedra, K. (1987) Impact of changing computer technology on hydrologic and water resource modeling. *Review of Geophysics*, **25**, 2.

Lyman, W. J., Reehl, W. F. and Rosenblatt, D. H. (1982) *Handbook of Chemical Property Estimation Methods. Environmental Behavior of Organic Compounds*, McGraw Hill, New York.

Lyman, W. J., Potts, R. G. and Magil, G. C. (1984) *User's Guide CHEMEST. A Program for Chemical Property Estimation*, Arthur D. Little Inc., Cambridge, MA.

Munn, R. E. (ed.) (1979) *Environmental Impact Assessment*, SCOPE5. 2nd edn, Wiley, Chichester, 190 pp.

Ortolano, L., and Steineman, A. C. (1987) New Expert Systems in Environmental Engineering, Proceedings of the American Society of Civil Engineers. *Journal of Computing in Civil Engineering*, **1** (4), 298–302.

Pasquill, F., and Smith, F. B. (1983) *Atmospheric Diffusion: Study of the Dispersion of Wind-borne Material from Industrial and Other Sources*, Ellis Horwood, Chichester, 480 pp.

Patten, B. C. (ed.) (1971) *Systems Analysis and Simulation in Ecology*, Vol I, Academic Press, NY, 607 pp.

Seinfeld, J. H. (1975) *Air Pollution. Physical and Chemical Fundamentals*, McGraw Hill, New York. Air Quality, AMS, Boston, Mass.

Smith, J. H., Mabey, W. R., Bohonos, N., *et al.* (1977) *Environmental Pathways of Selected Chemicals in Freshwater Systems*, EPA 600/7-77-113, US Environmental Protection Agency.

Technica (1984) *The SAFETI Package. Computer-Based System for Risk Analysis of Process Plants*, Vol. I–IV and Appendices. Tavistock Sq., London.

Thompson, W., Vertinsky, I. and Kane, J. (1973) Canadian industrial policy — simulation and analysis, *Long Range Planning* **6**, 66–73.

Walters, C. J. (1974) An interdisciplinary approach to watershed simulation models, *Technological Forecasting and Social Change*, **6**, 299–323.

Weigkricht, E. and Winkelbauer, L. (1987) *Knowledge-based Systems: Overview and Selected Examples*, WP-87-101. International Institute for Applied Systems Analysis, A-2361 Laxenburg, Austria, 102 pp.

Part III

National Experiences

12
Contribution of environmental impact assessment to decision-making: experiences from the Netherlands
Jules J. Scholten

The main objective for the execution of environmental impact assessment (EIA) is to offer the environment – next to other public interests – a full-fledged position in decision-making processes.

The subject of the conference was: EIA for developing countries. One of the conference objectives is 'to sensitize policy-makers and planners on the importance of EIA in developing countries'. This chapter attempts to highlight some of the factors that facilitate and inhibit the value of EIA as a tool in decision-making processes in the Netherlands. As such, this analysis may be of value to the development of EIA in developing countries. The Netherlands however, is a highly industrialized country with a well-developed infrastructure. It has an established legal system of decision-making in which EIA recently has claimed to have a formal part. So, it is obvious that experiences obtained in the Netherlands cannot be transferred without caution to the socio-economic and legal settings in so many developing countries. If this is kept in mind, some of the lessons learned in the Netherlands so far, may be worthwhile observing in developing countries.

In the following, first some of the most important facts and characteristics of EIA in the Netherlands are outlined. Then, some of the successful and inhibiting aspects in the Dutch context of EIA are discussed.

Some facts and characteristics

History

The introduction of EIA in the Netherlands has an extended history of development. In May 1981, the proposed legislation on EIA was submitted to Parliament. Five years later in May 1986, the regulations on

EIA were written into law through an extension of the Environmental Protection (General Provisions) Act. In September 1987, the legal requirement to carry out EIA in support of decision-making processes was substantiated when an Administrative Executive Order came into force stating which projects, plans or programmes must be subjected to EIA before a decision can be made. From May 1981 until September 1987 an interim policy was carried out, during which, on a voluntary basis, EIA was applied to a limited number of initiatives in conformity with the draft regulations. As a result, at this point in time, more than 70 EIAs have started since 1981, of which 34 were started after September 1987 when EIA became compulsory. Of the more than 70 EIAs a decision has been reached in 10 cases, including for instance the construction of an industrial plant on natural gas desulphurization, a site for the controlled deposition of contaminated dredged sludge from the Rotterdam port area, two coal-fired electricity plants, secure landfills for hazardous wastes and domestic wastes, the construction of motorways, outdoor recreational facilities, etc. Thus, only a small number of EIA-processes have been completed with a decision and the accumulated practical experiences only permit somewhat tentative conclusions.

Characteristics

EIA in the Netherlands is a legal and structured process with time limits in most steps of the process. EIA is fully incorporated in the formal existing decision-making process which applies to the activity or plan concerned. In this way EIA provides only an input in the decision-making and maintains an equilibrium with the other interests represented in each case.

The necessity for carrying out EIA is determined by a positive list of activities and related decisions. The list is outlined in the General Administrative Order. This list will be reviewed periodically for omissions and inclusions. The first time this will take place will be in 1990 and subsequently following each time-span of 5 years.

The following parties are involved in the EIA-process:
1 *Proponent:* a private enterprise or government agency that wishes to undertake an activity and therefore wants a decision on its proposed activity.
2 *Competent authority:* the relevant government agency which must make the decision. The competent authority can be at the national or at the local level, depending on the kind of decision that is required.
3 *Commission for EIA:* an independent commission of experts advising the competent authority on the guidelines for the environmental impact statement (EIS) and following the preparation of the EIS reviews its contents on its scientific quality, completeness and relevance of the presented information for the decision that has to be made; and
4 *The public* can participate in the process to which it has easy access.

The public can present its views and comments both in written form and orally during public hearings in each case.

Procedure

The Act on EIA prescribes a number of steps which must be taken in the course of each decision-making process. Most of these steps are bound by time limits which are set to avoid unnecessary delays due to the application of EIA. The time limits apply to the competent authority, the Commission for EIA and the public. The proponent is exempted from time limits and may determine its own time schedule.

The procedural steps include the following:

1 preparatory work, including matching of the EIA-process with the decision-making procedural steps by the competent authority and the preparation of a starting document by the proponent;
2 announcement of the start of the EIA by the competent authority;
3 scoping for the EIS with inputs from the commission for EIA and the public — the scoping period has a time limit;
4 establishment of the guidelines for the EIS by the competent authority at the end of the scoping period;
5 preparation of the EIS by the proponent (no time limit);
6 submission of the EIS to the competent authority and preliminary review of the EIS by the competent authority with regard to its acceptability;
7 announcement of the EIS together with the application for the licence or the draft plan by the competent authority (the announcement must be made within a certain limit);
8 review of the EIS and the licence application or draft plan by the competent authority with inputs from the Commission for EIA and the public (the review has a time limit);
9 decision on the activity with consideration of environmental aspects and motivation by the competent authority (the decision must be made within a time limit);
10 possible appeal against the decision by persons or agencies concerned; and
11 in case of execution of the activity: monitoring and post-development auditing by the proponent with possible application of mitigating measures to be decided upon by the competent authority.

Experiences with EIA: facilitating and inhibiting aspects and factors

The more than 70 EIAs that were started since the introduction of EIA and the 10 decisions which have been made so far have brought along much valuable experience. It is thought that of these the following aspects and factors could be of importance for consideration by EIA-practitioners in developing countries:

1   If there is a legal framework for decision-making about plans, programmes and activities, then the EIA should be incorporated in existing decision-making procedures. Only in doing this a replication of procedures in time and effort can be avoided. Also, by incorporating the EIA in the existing decision-making procedures, the interest of the enivironment can be balanced against the other interests at stake. Only, if there is no legal framework available for reaching a decision, the EIA procedure can be used as a substitute.

2   The setting of time limits for the inputs of all parties concerned except the proponent is essential. The proponent cannot be bound by time limits as he must be enabled to determine a time schedule for his own activity. Time limits for the steps to be carried out by the competent authority and for the inputs by advisers, independent experts and the public in the process are necessary in order to guarantee speedy progress. It would be inadmissible if delays would be caused by the application of EIA, for it would deter hopeful investors.

3   A positive list of activities, plans and programmes which details the obligation to carry out EIA, creates instant certainty as to which initiatives must be subjected to EIA and which initiatives need not. This is an advantage to the would-be investor. The use of a positive list however has also drawbacks. First, certain activities which may cause important adverse impacts on the environment, may have been overlooked. If a consensus can be reached, new activities can be added to the list. Another drawback is presented in the problem that in most cases threshold values must be set. For instance, it can be imagined that an EIA is required for a proposed urban expansion with several thousands of houses and buildings but that no EIA would be needed if only a few houses will be built. The positive list and the thresholds values must be handled flexibly and must be adaptable to changing conditions. Therefore, a periodical review is mandatory.

4   The process of scoping the proposed activity resulting in the establishment of guidelines is able to highlight possible bottlenecks and friction points in a very early stage of the decision making. The setting of guidelines creates clarity for the proponent as to how he should go about the development of his activity. Also scoping can help proponents to develop alternative solutions to their problem and avoid an early fixation on a certain solution which may be unfavourable to the environment.

5   Independent inputs in the EIA-process through public participation and the role of independent advisers and experts contribute towards the prevention of 'sweetheart-impact statements' with preconceived conclusions. Independent advisers and experts should be truly

independent and be impartial to the activity and to the decision-making. Public participation can increase the public acceptance of proposed activities and thus decrease the opposition (and the number of appeals) against decisions. In this manner, the decision-making process can actually be accelerated. If public participation cannot be arranged for whatever reason possible, the organization of work-shops can be considered as a substitute with invited participants from the community concerned.

6   The development of alternative solutions is an essential part of the EIA process. One of the alternatives should be the alternative which offers the best protection of the environment. This alternative can be formed in either the site-selection, or in the implementation of the activity or in its management or in combination of all three aspects. The alternative which offers the best protection of the environment should not make unreasonable demands in terms of costs and inputs. It must be of equal depth and detail as the preferred design in order to be able to compete with it.

7   If available EIAs should refer to a higher-level planning framework as a matter of reference to planning goals and standards. If such a framework is absent, a project-to-project approach can be the result with standards and targets changing from one project to another. On the other hand a higher-level planning framework should not set too rigid standards. In that case EIA will be left with little flexibility and can become meaningless to such an extent that it only will require to fill out the necessary forms.

8   Once a project is decided upon and implementation will begin, monitoring the activity should start, if possible. Only then, can be learned to what extent the prediction of impacts appears to be accurate. This entails a learning effect for future activities of a similar nature. In addition, monitoring and post-development auditing can expose developments which are more unfavourable to the environ-ment than originally thought. This in turn would enable the application of mitigating measures. It is important that a monitoring programme covering the essential elements of the activity, be set up at the same time as the decision is made. The proponent and the competent authority must look together into the problem of finding the funds to cover the cost of monitoring.

13

Environmental impact assessment of development projects: experience from Nordic Aid

Per Wramner

Many developing countries face serious environmental problems (including exhaustion of natural resources) which are increasing both in extent and intensity. The environmental deterioration makes it more and more difficult to provide for basic human needs (food, water, fuelwood, etc,), affects the health situation negatively and constitutes an obvious obstacle to development. Pollution and poisoning from industrial sources constitute a substantial part of the environmental degradation in many areas.

The environmental problems of the developing countries have to be attacked in several ways. One of these ways is to see that development projects pay greater heed to the environment. This has to be done both by avoiding or minimizing negative side effects, and by carrying out specific activities in the field of conservation and rehabilitation.

One major element in the endeavours to get development projects to pay greater attention to the environment is to carry out a proper environmental impacts assessment (EIA). This means that all programmes and projects which may affect the environment are assessed at the earliest stages of project formulation.

EIA is a procedure for encouraging decision-makers to take account of the possible effects of development investments on environmental quality and natural resources productivity, and a tool for collecting and assembling the data which planners need in order to make development projects more sustainable and environmentally sound. EIA is usually applied in support of policies for the sustainable and equitable use of natural resources and the prevention of environmental degradation (Wramner, 1987).

The concept of environmental impact assessment (EIA)

EIA is a wide concept that has been given various definitions. EIA has also been utilized for various purposes in various situations. Common to all definitions is that EIA is a measure which aims at finding out environmental effects of proposed projects, programmes and other activities which affect, or may affect, the environment (including the natural resources base). Usually, EIA also aims at finding out what can be done to avoid or minimize negative environmental effects (Wramner, 1987).

EIA is usually part of a process. The EIA process refers to a wide range of activities preceding and following the assessment itself. The process might begin, for example, with an initial screening exercise to determine whether a full EIA is required or not. After the assessment has been prepared and a decision taken, the process can continue through programmes of monitoring and evaluating the environmental effects of the activity during and after implementation.

EIA is typically both a tool for analysing environmental effects and a procedure for bringing this analysis to bear on decisions. The overall objective is to ensure that development does not cause non-acceptable environmental damage and reduction of the productivity of natural systems. EIA, in itself, does not solve problems or substitute for the formulation and implementation of appropriate policies.

It has to be stressed that EIA is not enough to bring about environmentally sound development projects. Unless it is incorporated early enough in the project cycle to influence planning and design, and unless its results play a part in decision-making, the effort is in vain. Therefore, EIA as such, does not solve the typical environmental problems associated with certain types of development projects. It just provides systematic predictions and assessments of effects (Wramner, 1987).

EIA aims at ensuring that the necessary questions are asked, and providing a technique for receiving the relevant data and analysing the information for solving environmental problems. Regardless of the overall institutional context, there is often a bias toward engineering and economic analysis of a project. EIA counteracts this bias. It is rarely easy to introduce EIA early enough in the process of identifying options and identifying the feasibility of proposed projects so that it can be comfortably incorporated in design and implementation decisions.

As a result, EIA is often geared to influencing the various decision points in the project cycle and providing technical guidance for project preparation, giving criteria for project design, an action plan for environmental management to be included in the project agreement, or a basis for evaluating the environmental consequences of a completed project.

The United Nations Environment Programme has decided on goals and principles for EIA. It is defined as 'an examination, analysis and assessment of planned activities with a view to ensuring environmentally sound and sustainable development' (UNEP, 1987).

The goals and principles (3 and 13 in number respectively) are necessarily general in nature, but lay down the importance of EIA as a tool for environmentally sound projects and programmes. A basic goal is to establish that, before decisions are taken on activities which are likely to significantly affect the environment, the environmental effects of these activities are taken fully into account. The principles cover various aspects of EIA and stress, *inter alia*, the necessity for rules deciding when and how to carry out EIA.

One principle is that EIA should include, as a minimum:

1   a description of the proposed activity;
2   a description of the potentially-affected environment, including specific information necessary for identifying and assessing the environmental effects of the proposed activity;
3   a description of practical alternatives as appropriate;
4   an assessment of the likely or potential environmental impacts of the proposed activity and alternatives, including the direct, indirect, cumulative, short-term and long-term effects;
5   an identification and description of measures available to mitigate adverse environmental impacts of the proposed activity, alternatives, and an assessment of those measures;
6   an indication of gaps in knowledge and uncertainties which may be encountered in compiling the required information;
7   an indication of whether the environment of any other State or area beyond national jurisdiction is likely to be affected by the proposed activity and alternatives;
8   a brief, non-technical summary of the information provided under the above headings.

General application of EIA in development assistance programmes and projects

EIA has become widely applied around the world in recent years. A majority of developed countries have taken various steps in carrying out EIA of their domestic programmes and projects. An increasing number of developing countries are also initiating EIA procedures, particularly in Southeast Asia, where about half the countries have legal requirements and three-quarters have conducted EIAs. South Asia, the Middle East and Latin America are also making progress, while EIA is less developed in Africa.

The approaches to EIA taken by various countries differ widely in terms of their legal/institutional base, focus, scope and procedures. Generally speaking, however, one can distinguish between an informal-implicit and a formal-explicit approach. There is a tendency to move from the former to the latter aproach (Wramner, 1987).

The application of EIA to development assistance activities is much less advanced than for domestic development, but considerable progress has been made recently and the process continues rapidly. However, EIA is, for the most part, done on an *ad hoc* basis. In most donor countries, aid agencies use discretion in deciding whether or not to perform such an assessment.

The organization for Economic Co-operation and Development (OECD) has made a study on EIA of development programmes and projects. OECD has also recommended its member countries to incorporate an EIA-procedure in the planning of its development assistance programmes and projects (OECD, 1986).

The importance of EIA as a tool to bring about development activities that are compatible with environmental requirements is underlined by OECD. There is a need for EIA in a wide range of programmes and projects which are outlined in a check list. It includes industrial activities (e.g. metallurgical plants, wood processing plants, chemical plants, power plants, cement plants, refinery and petrochemical plants, agro-industries), extractive industries (e.g. mining, quarrying, extraction of peat, oil and gas), waste management and disposal (e.g. sewerage systems and treatment plants, waste landfills, treatment plants for household waste and for hazardous waste), infrastructure and exploitation of hydraulic resources.

Constraints to carrying out EIA in developing countries have also been identified by OECD (1986) and are as follows;

1 insufficient political awareness of the need for environmental assessment;
2 insufficient public participation;
3 lacking or inadequate legislative frameworks;
4 lack of an institutional base;
5 insufficient skilled manpower;
6 lack of scientific data and information;
7 insufficient financial resources.

The OECD member countries are recommended to assist recipient countries to overcome these constraints.

Application of EIA in Nordic development assistance programmes and projects

In a report by a Nordic working group set up by the Nordic Council, which was presented in 1982 (Wramner *et al.*, 1983), the interrelation between the environment of developing countries and the development assistance of the Nordic countries is discussed. It is noted that all the Nordic countries have declared that they aspire to pay more attention to the environmental aspects of their development assistance. However, it is also noted that all the countries are finding it hard to live up to these stated aspirations in the practical implementation of development co-operation. EIA is generally not used as an instrument to bring about an integration of environment and development.

In the report it is strongly recommended that the Nordic countries, together with the recipient countries, should incorporate the environmental aspects at as early a stage as possible into the planning of development assistance programmes and projects. When doing so, use should be made of, *inter alia*, EIA.

The situation in Nordic countries as regards EIA of aid programmes and projects in 1985 is described by OECD (1986).

In *Denmark*, EIA is an essential component in the appraisal and evaluation of many DANIDA (Danish International Development Agency) financed projects. However, DANIDA has not yet participated in the preparation of environmental profiles or financed any major environmental impact statements in developing countries. A working group of DANIDA and the Ministry of the Environment has identified six main types of project for which an EIA should be prepared.

In *Finland*, EIA is being introduced as an element of the preparation of development assistance projects, financed by Finnish aid agency FINNIDA. The Ministry for Foreign Affairs has set up a permanent working group in co-operation with the Ministry of the Environment. The aim of the working group is to improve the procedures and methods for incorporating environmental aspects into development co-operation projects and programmes.

In *Norway*, decisions on projects which require an EIA are taken on a case-by-case basis by the responsible project officer in NORAD (Norwegian Agency for International Development). No decision has yet been taken on how to identify which projects are most in need of environmental assessment. A joint body of the Ministry of Development and of the Ministry of Environment is presently dealing with the issue of introducing a screening procedure for projects requiring an environmental assessment.

In *Sweden*, SIDA (Swedish International Development Agency) has no formal procedures for EIA. Environmental considerations are instead given on an *ad hoc* basis to a growing number of aid projects both in the planning process and in the follow-up and evaluation of the projects. SIDA's capacity to take care of environmental aspects in development assistance has been increased by the recruitment of an environmental adviser in the central office.

OECD's examination showed that EIA of aid programmes and projects was not a regular procedure in any of the Nordic countries in 1986. This means that the countries had not implemented the EIA-recommendation of the Nordic working group which was made in 1982 (Wramner *et al.*, 1983).

A Nordic workshop on EIA in development assistance was held in Finland in 1988 (Johansson, 1988). The current situation in the Nordic countries was presented and discussed. It can be summarized as follows:

In *Denmark*, a plan of action for strengthening the consideration of environmental aspects in official development assistance is being drawn up. It will include guidelines for planning aid projects. The issue of ensuring appropriate environmental screening of all projects is being considered, but this work is still in progress (Richter, 1988).

In *Finland*, a set of draft guidelines for EIA of development assistance projects have been worked out. The use of them proceeds in steps depending on which phase of the project cycle is in question. In the initial fact-finding and negotiating stages, OECD's check-list may be used for making a rough environmental assessment. When working out the Terms of Reference for the preparation of a project document, a matrix may be used as a check-list of potential environmental effects of the project. During the preparation of a project document the identified risks may be scrutinized against screening tables. The guidelines were discussed at the Nordic workshop and are now being revised with regard to the outcome of the discussion. They turned out to be too static, technical and general for industrial projects (Haldin, 1988; Wramner, 1988).

In *Norway*, an EIA-system is being worked out. It is designed for use in the routine planning and administration of development aid projects and consists of three stages, namely initial screening of projects, initial environmental evaluation and full assessment (Kristoffersen, 1988). One booklet for the initial screening of projects, consisting of check-lists for each project category, has been produced (Norwegian Ministry of Development Co-operation NORAD, 1988). Booklets for each project category consisting of general information and guidelines for the initial environmental evaluation as well as a booklet consisting of guidelines for the full assessment will be produced.

In *Sweden*, the environmental aspects of development assistance have recently been given increased weight. The Parliament has decided to add environmental considerations to the main objectives of Swedish development assistance. However, no work aiming at incorporating EIA as a compulsory component in the preparation of programmes and projects, which may affect the environment negatively, has yet started.

The conclusion is that the situation has improved somewhat since 1985 but is still not satisfactory. The decisive importance of the environment is generally recognized but the real progress is slow. The long discussed idea of a compulsory EIA of aid programmes and projects, which may affect the environment negatively, is far from being realized. In all the countries, such programmes and projects may still be approved without having been subject to an EIA.

Consequences of the lack of EIA

The consequences of the lack of EIA of Nordic aid programmes and projects have not been studied systematically. However, available information from all the Nordic countries indicates that negative environmental consequences, which could have been avoided or reduced with the help of an EIA, have occurred in a number of cases.

One example, which has been studied scientifically, is the establishment of a large integrated pulp and paper mill in the Mufindi District of Tanzania. SIDA was one of the donors and the Nordic Investment Bank one of the lenders to the project. The environmental effects are summarized by, *inter alia*, Christiansson and Ashuvud (1985).

The Tanzanian Government formally authorized the construction of the mill in 1977. The decision was based on a very limited knowledge of the environmental effects. The feasibility study did not take up any potential ecological effects. Uncertainty regarding these external effects did not, however, delay the authorization of the project and support by donors.

Some environmental investigations were made later on, but a proper EIA was never carried out. Most of the environmental effects remain to be seen. Not until the mill has been in production for some time, which is not yet the case, will the total impacts on the environment be discerned.

The establishment of the mill strongly influences the natural environment. Four types of impacts can be discerned:

1   Immigration and urbanization cause increased pressure on and competition for land, water, building material, energy, etc.
2   Unavoidable air and water pollutants affect the natural and agricultural ecosystems. These effects include acidification of soils and possible damage of tea plantations caused by sulphur dioxide and other emissions into the atmosphere and reduced fish catch and deteriorated domestic water supply caused by effluents of wastewater containing oxygen demanding and toxic substances.
3   Increased food requirements cause intensification of agriculture (including animal husbandry) and clearance for cultivation of areas covered by grass, bush or woodland which results in land degradation.
4   The establishment of mill presupposes forestry operations which affect the environment in several ways. The sustainable supply of wood is an issue of crucial importance which is closely linked to the environment.

The negative environmental consequences of the mill may be far-reaching and may cover vast areas. Production, human life etc. may be drastically affected. At least some of these consequences could have been avoided or reduced if they had been known and taken into consideration in the planning phase of the project. Others are inevitable but a better picture of them, when it was decided to establish the mill, could have contributed to a better decision (Christiansson and Ashuvud, 1985).

Discussion

It is evident that the Nordic countries aspire to pay greater heed to the environmental aspects of their development assistance. The aid authorities have got clear political directives to improve the integration of environment and development and have decided to take a series of steps to bring this about. However, this new policy has only had a limited impact on the concrete actions at the programme and project levels. The Nordic aid authorities are encountering manifest difficulties in their efforts to convert their environmental aspirations into practical action. One reason for this is the lack of a compulsory EIA-procedure. It is remarkable that such a procedure has not been introduced in any of the Nordic countries up to now. Several other circumstances also contribute to the current situation.

When analysing the difficulties in the Nordic countries it is essential to remember that the corresponding difficulties – often considerably aggravated – exist on the recipient side. It is the interrelation between donor and recipient that ultimately determines the outcome in practice (Wramner *et al.*, 1983).

Many of the problems which are faced in the attempts to introduce EIA are common to the whole environmental sector. One such problem of basic importance is that environmental questions have only been to the fore in development assistance context for a short time. Not until the last decade did we obtain more detailed knowledge (nevertheless far from comprehensive) on the interrelation between the environment and development. A more general awareness of this interrelation has not become manifest until recently and is still frequently missing, especially in the development sphere. Many of the problems that have arisen must be seen in the light of this circumstance. (Wramner *et al.*, 1983).

The recipient-oriented development assistance policy of the Nordic countries has also been an obstacle in this context. The recipient countries have up to now only rarely asked for assistance in the environmental field or for commitments in which special heed would be paid to environmental considerations. However, this attitude seems now to be changing rapidly.

The lack of sufficient knowledge of ecological conditions and the environmental situation in many developing countries does not facilitate an integration of environment and development. There is also a lack of know-how and experience in the various bodies which are involved in development assistance activities. Environmental conservation spans many sectors and a large number of people with widely varying background are affected by its issues.

Over and above the problem of the general level of knowledge, there are problems caused by the fact that there are not enough environmental experts in the development assistance administrations. Nor are these bodies generally organized in such a way that they make it easy for environmental aspects to be brought to the fore.

Many problems also arise because the perception of environmental questioning is too narrow. Especially in the practical work, people are often not entirely clear about the importance of an integrated approach and about the interrelation between population, natural resources, environment and development. Environmental issues are regarded more or less as purely technical questions having no relation to the social, cultural, political, etc. conditions which on many occasions are extremely decisive. In these cases purely environmental measures are not sufficient but the social and other problems must also be grappled with if the intended outcome is to be obtained. Here collaboration between those representing environmental considerations and other sectors is required (Wramner *et al.*, 1983).

In addition to the general obstacles to a better integration of environment and development in the foreign aid of the Nordic countries, which do not facilitate the introduction of EIA, some specific problems regarding EIA will be discussed.

The EIA-procedures have largely been developed in the industrialized countries and for large-scale projects (e.g. industrial and infrastructural development). This creates a risk of implying importance to wrong issues when applying EIA to development assistance. The ecological and socio-economic conditions in developing countries differ considerably from those in industrialized countries. The emphasis of Nordic foreign aid lies within the sector of agricultural and rural development. In this sector the concept of EIA is less developed and more difficult to apply than in the industrial sector (Wramner, 1987). These circumstances have contributed to the slow progress of EIA in Nordic development assistance (including programmes and projects in the industrial field).

The Nordic aid authorities have met with technical problems in their endeavours to develop EIA-procedures. The standardized, static approach to EIA, which predominates in many countries, has proved to be of limited value to Nordic aid programmes and projects, also in the industrial field (Haldin, 1988, Wramner, 1988). The Nordic experiences indicate that an EIA-procedure should be more descriptive, flexible and informal than some of the procedures which have been developed recently. This applies specifically to programmes and projects in the field of agriculture and rural development but also to industrial and infrastructural activities.

Check-lists , manuals, etc. may facilitate the accomplishment of EIA. The preparation of such means may contribute considerably to the introduction of EIA as an integral part of the planning of aid programmes and projects. However, too rigid and detailed forms, matrices, etc. may have the opposite effect and should be avoided in EIA-procedures (Wramner, 1987).

Finally, it has to be underlined that the slow introduction of EIA in Nordic development assistance also is due to insufficient priority given to this issue both at governmental level and at aid agency level. Strong directives, sufficient budgetary allocations and involvement of qualified expertise would certainly have resulted in a much faster progress than has now been the case.

References

Christiansson, C. and Ashuvud, J. (1985) Heavy Industry in a Rural Tropical Ecosystem. *Ambio*, **14** (3)

Haldin, G. (1988) Summary of the Experiences of the Working Groups in the Application of the FINNIDA Guidelines for EIA, *Nordic Workshop on EIA in Development Assistance*, FINNIDA, Helsinki

Johansson, D. 1988, Opening Statement, *Nordic Workshop on EIA in Development Assistance*, FINNIDA, Helsinki

Kristofferson, H. (1988) NORAD's Draft for EIA of Development Aid Projects, *Nordic Workshop on EIA in Development Assistance*, FINNIDA, Helsinki

Norwegian Ministry of Development Co-operation, NORAD (1988) *Environmental Impact Assessment (EIA) of Development Aid Projects*, NORAD, Oslo

OECD (1986) Environmental Assessment and Development Assistance, *Environment Monographs* No. 4, OECD, Paris

Richter, N. (1988) DANIDA's procedures for Incorporating Environmental Considerations into Development Assistance In *Nordic Workshop on EIA in Development Asssistance*, FINNIDA, Helsinki

UNEP (1987) *Goals and Principles for EIA*, Decision 14/25 of the Governing Council, UNEP, Nairobi

Wramner, P. (1987) *Procedures for EIA of FAO's Field Projects: A Preliminary Study*, Report to AGRE, FAO, Rome

Wramner, P, (1988) Report of Working Group II: Xeset Hydropower Project, Laos, *Nordic Workshop on EIA in Development Assistance*, FINNIDA, Helsinki

Wramner, P. *et al.* (1983) Environment and Development Assistance, *Nordisk Utredningsserie 1982:9*, Stockholm

14

Environmental assessment and review during the project cycle: the Asian Development Bank's approach

Bindu N. Lohani

A systematic and comprehensive environmental assessment and review (EAR) throughout the project cycle is one of the policies of the Asian Development Bank (ADB). The EAR is unique and provides a pragmatic approach to incorporating environmental considerations in project planning. This chapter, based on ADB's publication *Environmental Planning and Management and the Project Cycle*, will be described by engaging the project cycle — project identification, fact-finding/preparation, pre-appraisal/appraisal, negotiations, implementation and supervision, completion and post-evaluation (Figure 14.1). The ADS's EAR procedure was also recently presented in the POLMET 88 in Hongkong.

Environmental assessment and review during the project cycle

The initial step in the project cycle is the identification of projects that may be financed by the Bank. This is achieved by sending missions on a regular basis to developing member countries (DMCs) to review their overall social and economic circumstances. The product of such reviews — 'Country Programme Papers' — permits sector work, programme and projects financed by the Bank to be considered in the perspective of existing and projected environmental and natural resources conditions. To assist in this task, Briefing Profiles for Country Programming Missions: Environmental and Natural Resources Development Projects are being established for each DMC. These attempt to identify major environmental and natural resources concerns in the DMCs, list environmental or relevant line agencies in the DMCs to be consulted, and provide examples of environmental resources development projects for possible funding by the Bank.

Parallel with these profiles, country strategy studies, sector reports (e.g. forestry, fisheries, and agricultural and rural development), surveys (e.g. energy and irrigation) and regional studies are subject to environmental

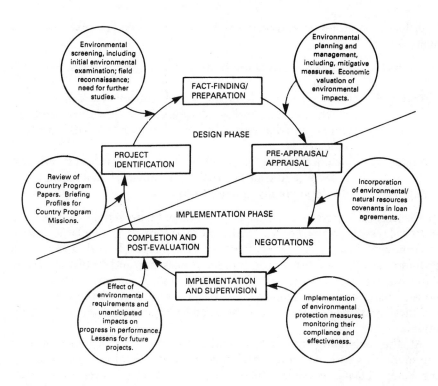

Figure 14.1 *The project cycle: environmental and natural resources planning and management*

review. The aim is to ensure that management strategies are designed for sustained productivity of the resource base. To encourage the longer-term view of development, the environment specialists are preparing environmental and natural resources profiles for each DMC. The profiles attempt to identify major environmental and natural resources constraints and opportunities likely to affect economic development and to delineate planning and management needs, development programmes, and potential projects with which to correct critical cases of loss or degradation of environmental and natural resources.

To initiate their project review activities, the environment specialists liaise with Project Managers and their staff to prepare a series of reports on those projects stipulated in country programme papers as project profiles – a portfolio covering a 3-year pipeline. In the first report – preliminary environmental screening of loans and technical assistance projects – potentially significant environmental impacts associated with the proposed development projects are identified and the appropriate budgetary provision for the necessary services of environment specialists and/or staff consultants is agreed. This is achieved, in part, by dividing the proposed Bank projects into four broad impact categories, reflecting the severity of their likely environmental impacts and thus their need for environmental analysis:

Category A: includes projects rarely having significant adverse environmental impacts;

Category B: those generally inducing significant adverse impacts, but which can be readily identified and quantified and for which remedial measures can be prescribed without much difficulty;

Category C: includes those invariably having significant adverse impacts requiring detailed environmental analysis; and

Category D: environmentally-oriented projects.

In the second report – secondary environmental screening of loan and technical assistance projects – with more information available, major environmental concerns are specified and the scope of work and a work programme are established for project processing and implementation. After further consultation with the relevant staff, a summary report – in-house liaison and participation of environmental specialists in loan and technical assistance projects – is forwarded to senior management for their review.

At the beginning of each calendar year, the environmental unit communicates with environmental agencies and official contact points in the Bank's DMCs notifying them about incoming projects which may generate significant environmental impacts and necessary remedial measures. Follow-up discussions allow an exchange of information and advice to be given on the handling of difficult problems.

Fact-finding/preparation

Contributing formal and informal environmental reviews at the project preparation stage is crucial because this is the most effective way of avoiding conception and design errors which could prove difficult and costly to rectify at a later stage. Such reviews include comments in project planning and design expressed in project briefs establishing terms of reference for missions, and examining back-to-office reports of project preparation/fact-finding missions. When necessary, the environment specialists attend management review meetings on the Bank's project to review the proposed treatment of environmental and natural resources issues.

For some projects, one of the Bank's environmental specialists or a staff consultant may be engaged to visit the proposed project site(s) to undertake an initial environmental examination. When the Mission returns to headquarters, the significance of the previously identified impacts is subjected to additional screening and the need for a more detailed assessment is determined. If a potential problem is confirmed, more detailed studies may be required to establish mitigation measures and to incorporate them in project planning and design. When necessary the specialists help determine the objectives, scope of work programme and implementation schedule for consulting services to conduct such studies as part of a loan or technical assistance project.

To support their review function, the environment specialists deploy especially developed environmental guidelines to help staff determine whether or not a proposed project is likely to generate significant environmental impacts − adverse or beneficial. They also enable staff to prepare an initial environmental examination as a means to confirm the nature and extent of the impacts and, where such impacts are considered adverse, to specify the need for more detailed study. To date the following guidelines have been prepared: environmental guidelines for selected infrastructure projects, environmental guidelines for selected industry and power development projects, environmental guidelines for agricultural and natural resources projects, and guidelines for integrated regional economic-cum-environmental development planning. Advisory notes have also been furnished, including: health and safety implications of development projects, assessing socio-cultural impacts of development projects, and environmental assessment in natural resources planning.

Pre-appraisal/appraisal

This is the comprehensive review stage of the project cycle at which environmental issues are merged with technical, institutional, socio-economic and financial parameters and the foundation laid for implementing the project and evaluating it upon completion. To ensure representation of the environmental dimension, assessment is conducted and a statement on the significant impacts of the project and the detailing of measures adopted to reduce adverse impacts.

The use of the Bank's environmental guidelines is often stipulated in the consultant's terms of reference for both technical assistance and appraisal reports.

Negotiations

After appraisal, environmental planning and management requirements may be discussed during loan negotiations between the Bank and the borrower. Agreements reached on environmental practices are incorporated in loan covenants.

To assist Bank's staff to accommodate environmental statutes and administrative considerations during project processing and implementation, the environment unit has produced a document entitled 'Environmental legislation and administration: briefing profiles of selected developing member countries of the Asian Development Bank'. A compilation of loan agreements covering 1982 to 1988 − Bank loan agreements: environmental protection measures — has also been made available.

Implementation and supervision

Supervision missions during the implementation and supervision stage review progress with the borrower to ensure that environmental control measures are implemented during the construction and operation of the project. This is particularly important at the construction phase since the associated activities often produce the most significant adverse impacts upon the environment.

Completion and post-evaluation

After disbursements have terminated, a project completion report is prepared as a factual, historical record. The Bank requires the inclusion of a 'general assessment of the significant environmental impacts (where possible, this should include sociocultural impacts) generated during the project implementation, particularly with reference to those issues considered at the time of project appraisal. If the project included environmental control measures, evaluate their implementation and effectiveness.' Post-evaluation includes a final analysis as to whether the project met proposed environmental requirements and whether any unanticipated effects were induced as a result of project activities. Attempts are made to review and assess: beneficial and detrimental environmental impacts of the project; siting and design/operational alternatives considered and reasons for final choice; environmental protection measures adopted and the effect of such measures upon project costs and on the economic evaluation of the project; and the environmental aspects of the project in relation to overall cost-benefit analysis. Such determinations are conducted both in terms of standards existing at the time of project approval and by current standards. Lessons drawn from these evaluations are useful for improving the planning and design of future projects.

Project monitoring information system

A project monitoring information system operated by the environment unit keeps track of all loan and technical assistance projects throughout the project processing. Project officers and the Bank's management are regularly informed of the status of projects with respect to their environmental impacts and necessary control measures. Through this system, project officers are also advised on the need for follow-up action during and after project implementation. In future, the project monitoring information system will be available for on-line access by the Bank's project staff.

Conclusion

The Bank has established a systematic and comprehensive environmental assessment and review procedure to ensure that environmental and natural resources considerations are adequately incorporated in the planning, design and implementation of development projects.

Reference

Asian Development Bank (1988) *Environmental Planning and Management and the Project Cycle*, paper No. 1, May, Manila.

15

Application of the environmental impact assessment in the appraisal of major development projects in Tanzania

G. L. Kamukala

It is now becoming clear in many developing countries, that environmental protection measures should be incorporated into development planning in order to sustain development. In the past, development strategies did not take into consideration the complexity of the environmental problems as a result of development. Environmental issues in the development planning were only considered when there was an 'environmental crisis', thus considering the symptoms and not the disease.

Now greater attention in Tanzania National Development Planning is being paid to environmental considerations — interrelationship between resources, environment and development. In a few projects environmental protection measures have been considered as an integral component of the development planning. The undue emphasis accorded to economic planning at the expense of environmental planning which has led to a number of negative environmental impacts is now being examined.

Early 1984 the Government started a study concerning the extent to which environmental impacts of development projects have been considered. This study looked into both the existing planning procedure of the incorporation of environmental protection measures in new development projects and the present pollution situation at major existing installations e.g. industries, dam and reservoir construction etc. In most of these cases, very few projects had incorporated any mitigation measures in their design. As a result these activities pose a threat to the environment. The study also realized that there was no government routine procedure to be followed in incoporating environmental protection measures in the projects.

Although Tanzania, has had several laws with a bearing on the environment for a number of years Environmental Impact Assessment (EIA) of proposed development projects had never been undertaken. From the foregoing it was imperative to undertake Environmental Impact Assessment to planned or new development projects as a means to evaluate the impact resulting from the projects. The National Environmental Management council (NEMC) undertook the task of preparing guidelines and procedure to be followed in any new major development project.

Environmental protection measures.

The study revealed that most major development projects have an impact on the environment as a consequence of discharges of pollution into the atmosphere, water and handling of solid wastes products or changing of water regimes through damming; irrigation etc.

Thus, as a long-term measure the need for a strong environmental protection legislation, which could embrace all aspects of environmental impact from development projects was underlined. The law should spell out clearly the necessity of undertaking:

1   An environmental impact assessment at the planning stage of major development projects.
2   Address itself to the question of existing major developments, that already show negative impacts to the environment.
3   Have provision for an environmental monitoring programme for such developments. As a short-term measure efforts were made to incorporate environmental protection measures in the existing institutional set up, particularly the Licensing Board (Licensing and Registration Act, 1967). Every new development with a possible environmental impact should at the planning stage be scrutinized by authorized agencies so as to incorporate economically and technically feasible environmental protection measures at the early stage of the project.

There are some signs of success towards the realization of this short-term measure.

The national institutional mechanism (NEMC)

In October 1983 the Act of Parliament No. 19 was passed that established the National Environment Management Council to deal with all environmental matters. The Council became operational in September, 1986.

It is recommended by the Council that environmental considerations should be viewed as an integral part of the project planning process beginning with an early identification of the project alternatives and the potentially significant environmental impacts associated with them and continuing through the planning cycle.

Section 4 (c) of Act No. 9 which provides for the formation of the Council, states that one of the functions of the Council is 'to evaluate existing and proposed policies and activities of the government directed to control pollution and enhancement of the environment and to the accomplishment of other objectives which affect the quality of the environment and on the basis of that formulate policies and programmes which will achieve more effective management and enhancement of environmental quality'.

Furthermore section 4 (d) provides that the council has to 'recommend measures to ensure the government policies, including those for the development and conservation of natural resources, take adequate account of environmental effects'. To this end, among its functions; the Council therefore pays much attention to the environmental impacts likely to be caused by development projects. This is done through a comprehensive scrutiny of the project proposals which are supposed to be submitted to the Council.

The Council has to ensure that environmental considerations are taken immediately at the planning stages of these projects. Currently strict methods or procedures of EIA have been undertaken, only in two major development projects, and a monitoring programme for one of these projects has been instituted.

The National Environment Management Council is trying to devise a procedure which compulsorily requires the feasibility study of a major project to include Environmental Impact Assessment. At the same time the Council is examining the possibility of including EIA in the overall development planning process.

EIA in two major development projects

Two major development projects in the country successfully included EIA in the planning stage. These are:

1   The Southern Pulp and Paper Mill (SPM).
2   The Stiegler's Gorge Project.
    The former has succeeded in taking off.

The Southern Pulp and Paper Mill (SPM)

Pulp and paper mills are among the most polluting industries if environmental considerations are not incorporated right from the planning stage. Such industries have pollution from air emissions, (e.g. sulphur dioxide, dust, hydrogen sulphide) and wastewater.

EIA methodologies differ in different countries but what was done in this case was the examination, analysis and assessment of the planned activity with a view to ensuring environmentally sound and sustainable development. The parameters of study were dictated after scoping likely impacts.

Before the start-up of this project different studies on planning processes, environmental and socio-economic impacts were carried out. The results of such studies contributed to the improvement of methods and techniques for industrial development planning, especially the evaluation of socio-economic and ecological effects.

Monitoring of socio-economic and environmental effects over an extended period during construction and operation of the pulp and paper mill is one of the factors that made the project successful.

Direct environmental problems which were likely to occur as a consequence of emissions to air and water, partly have been eliminated through appropriate technical design. Mitigation measures were incorporated in the orginal mill design.

These include treatment facilities for wastewater from the mill, i.e. use of oxidation ponds. In addition recycling of processed water was applied. For air emissions basic equipments like electrostatic precipitators have been installed in order to adsorb and control the amount of emissions into the air. In collaboration with NEMC, an environmental monitoring programme for wastewater has been instituted. This programme is to be complemented with air emissions monitoring this year.

The mill is located about 600 km from the coast − Dar es Salaam. At the planning stage as already mentioned EIA was undertaken. The Impact evaluation was based on the following problems.

1   Wastewater discharge
2   Emission from the recovery boiler
3   Emission from the lime kiln
4   Emission from the power boiler.

Wastewater treatment
All wastewater is treated in a wastewater treatment plant which includes the following steps:

1   Pretreatment − wastewater is mixed, neutralized and screened.
2   Primary clarification − removal of total suspended solids (80 per cent efficiency), mainly fibres removed.
3   Treatment in an aerated lagoon − it is a biological treatment for dissolved organic substances. There are eight aerators which supply air to allow for aerobic decomposition. The retention time of the ponds is 7 days. Measurement of BOD is done regularly.
4   Post-settling − post-settling ponds remove more solids before allowing the water to be discharged to the spillway.
5   Sludge treatment − dried for use as landfill. From the investigations so far done, the mill has been able to meet the emission guidelines for wastewater treatment issued by NEMC. It should also be noted that the monitoring of the river where the wastewater is discharged is a continuous process in order to ensure that NEMC guidelines are met.

Gas emissions

The stack gases from the recovery boiler contain mainly dust, sulphur dioxide and reduced sulphur compounds. These pollutants are removed by the following means:

1   The gases are treated in an electrostatic precipitator which removes dust.
2   The mill has also installed a black liquor oxidation tank in which the hydrogen sulphide in the liquor partly is oxidized before the evaporation.
3   The gases from the lime kiln contain dust, sulphur dioxide and reduced sulphur compounds. These are treated in a scrubber which mainly reduces dust. A proper operation of the lime kiln is essential for controlling the discharge of hydrogen sulphide. The lime scrubber is also used to control the pH of mill effluent.

However, during different stages of the SPM project serious concern was expressed regarding environmental effects of the air pollution. The most serious concern was from the tea growers — Brooke Bond; which is located north-west of the SPM mills on the Mufindi Plateau, about 600 m above the mill at a distance of 9 km from the factory. The worries mainly concerned the emission of sulphur dioxide, which was feared to affect the tea leaves.

Luckily, so far no detrimental effects have been reported by the tea growers, despite that the factory has been in operation for 4 years. The air emission monitoring, which shortly will start at the mill upon the request by NEMC, will follow in particular the sulphur dioxide emissions.

Environmental monitoring
In 1985 the National Environmental Management Council in collaboration with SPM established the environmental monitoring programme for the water effluent and its effect on the receiving water body.

To ensure that the monitoring was carried out smoothly, the Mill established an environmental function closely linked to the process, a chemical laboratory with special staff for the current environmental protection work. At the initiative of NEMC a comprehensive environmental survey was made of the mill by a consultant in 1987 during which a detailed monitoring was made of all air and water emissions in order to assess the performance in relation to the design criteria of the plant.

Stiegler's gorge project

Stiegler's gorge multipurpose project is within the Rufiji River Basin. The basin covers about 170 000 km^2 which is approximetely 20 per cent of the total area supporting a population of about 10 per cent of the country. It is estimated that over 60 per cent of the hydropower potential of the country is within the River Basin. Thus, in 1975 the Government established the Rufiji River Basin Development Authority (RUBADA) to plan and manage the River Basin as a single dynamic system. The rationale of creating a central authority lies, *inter alia*, in the need for co-ordination of development in the river with the primary objective of ensuring sustained resource use for development. The Stiegler's Gorge project involves the construction of a 134 m high dam at the gorge 230 km upstream from the Indian Ocean.

The objective mainly was the production of hydro-electricity. The energy produced would be over 200 MW at full capacity. Coupled with this, was to develop fisheries in the reservoir, irrigate agriculture, control floods and promote tourism. However, such developments, it was envisaged, would influence the water quality in the reservoir and downstream, affecting to some degree the aquatic ecology and the biology of the flora and fauna of the area.

The river impoundment was to be undertaken in the Selous Game Reserve (an uninhabited reserve of 46 000 km²) of very high ecological interest. As such, it was imperative for RUBADA to carry out studies on the impacts of the dam and associated developments to the area.

In 1978 RUBADA embarked upon an EIA study of the multipurpose project. The study included:

1   The economics of power production – including demand for electricity and cost production of electricity compared with other alternatives.
2   The benefits and costs of the project to:
    – fisheries
    – agriculture
    – forestry
    – wildlife conservation
    – tourism
    – communication.
3   Impacts of the project and associated developments:
    – physical environment
    – biological environment
    – socio-cultural and economic impact.
4   Mitigation measures of the impacts.

After the EIA multidisciplinary study, the project was shelved because of several environmental 'bottlenecks'. The degree of disruption to the environment, particularly ecological e.g. wildlife conservation and physical environment, was too great to allow the construction of the dam. The cost of the mitigation measures were considered to be too high as compared with other beneficial effects. There was some fear that by undertaking the project there was a danger of compromising the future needs. At the same time some uncertainties remained unsolved even after the completion of the study.

Conclusion

The country now advocates the rational utilization of its resources to avoid over-exploitation or devastation of the natural resources and the environment for sustainable development. Every new development project with a possible environmental impact must at the planning stage undertake an EIA which should be part of the feasibility study. Such a study would enable the authority concerned to incorporate economically and technically feasible environmental protection measures at the early stage of the project. In the long-run we hope the EIA concept would be incorporated in the overall development planning process.

16

Canada's environmental assessment procedure for a water-related development

Peter J. Reynolds

This chapter presents a descriptive analysis of the environmental assessment and review process in Canada, with a discussion of the underlying policy rationale, its strengths and drawbacks, and how it has been improved.

To illustrate the working of the full process as applied to a water-related development of interest to developing nations, a case study has been selected for discussion. This was the Lower Churchill Hydroelectric Project, which is located in the Atlantic province of Newfoundland/Labrador, downstream of the giant Churchill Falls power plant. The proposal was submitted for public review under the guidance of an environmental panel in 1980, and presently is 'on hold' due to instabilities in the energy economy.

In Canada, the review of project proposals to ascertain environmental effects can be regulated by either the provincial or the federal level of government, since environmental responsibilities fall in both areas of jurisdiction. This chapter refers to the federal environmental review process, and will look at a case example within the purview of federal responsibility.

The federal Environmental Assessment and Review Process, or 'EARP', came into effect in 1974. Adjustments were made in 1977, and in 1984 EARP guidelines were issued. Presently, federal environmental assessment is implemented by reference to these comprehensive guidelines. Some 14 years after conception, the programme still is evolving; a recent review examined a number of weaknesses, and recommended improvements.

The process, which has several stages is applied to any undertaking for which the federal government has a decision-making role. The onus and authority for making the assessment rests with the government department that is undertaking the proposal or initiative, and the departmental minister is called the initiating minister. However, the Department of Environment also becomes involved, because it has the Environmental Assessment and Review Office which oversees the process.

The Office provides advice, procedural guidelines, secretariats for detailed public reviews (carried out by panels appointed by the Minister of Environment) and arranges for co-operative efforts – such as federal–provincial or territorial participation in reviews. The Office also advises the Minister of Environment, acts as a federal voice internationally on environmental assessment, and provides funding and technical support for research.

Designated crown corporations also are expected to implement the EARP, if it is within their authority and policy reach to do so. Boards and regulatory bodies who can regulate in regard to the proposed project also are expected to implement the process if they legally can.

EARP also would apply to federal agencies providing aid in other countries – like Canadian International Development Agency (CIDA), but the publishing of results depends on the consent of recipient countries. Detailed assessment, called a panel review, may well be inappropriate, due to difficulties in some cases.

To summarize, the EARP guidelines are followed by a federal department if it undertakes a proposed project; can make decisions about a proposal of another organization; has an effect on a federal area of responsibility; uses federal government funds; and/or is located on federal government lands, including offshore. The project's initiator conducts environmental assessment but the Department of Environment oversees the process.

The process

The Canadian federal government's environmental assessment procedure has two main phases, an initial assessment and a public review.

Initial assessments are a screening process to determine potential environmental impacts and directly-related social impacts that a project could create. It is carried out by the initiating department early in the planning process. During initial assessment, specialized departments like Environment Canada, Health and Welfare, Fisheries and Oceans etc. may provide advice to the initiating department. The assessments are documented and made available to all interested parties at the Federal Environmental Assessment and Review Office (FEARO). Actions that could allay or avoid important environmental impacts identified in the initial assessment must be incorporated in any proposal that proceeds to the next step.

After initial assessment, four courses of action become possible, depending on the potential effects identified. If insignificant potential environmental damage is discerned, or if effects can be allayed by known means, the proposal may proceed to implementation. However, if significant potentially adverse effects are identified or if public concern is high enough, the Initiating Minister must refer the proposal to the Minister of Environment for an independent panel review. In the third case, if adverse environmental impacts are unknown, the initiating department must undertake an in-depth study, or initial environmental evaluation, and then decide if the proposal needs a public review. If yes, the Minister of Environment arranges for a panel review.

In the final alternative, where potential adverse environmental effects identified by the initial assessment are not acceptable, the initiating department must either modify and reassess, or abandon the project proposal.

A public review entails a detailed examination of potential environmental and direct social effects for those proposals with identified significant environmental effects.

It is carried out by an independent, temporary panel appointed by the Minister of Environment, and composed of mainly non-government people. Terms of reference can include general socio-economic and technological assessments but the main responsibility is to investigate potentially adverse environmental effects of a proposal, the scope and weight of issues, and public views.

Each panel undertakes public information programmes, and holds informal public hearings to get comments on the issue. The proponent (planner) of the proposal presents an environmental impacts statement which becomes publicly available and which describes the undertaking in detail, relating it to the present state of the environment, and identifying potential impacts as well as explaining how adverse effects can be reduced. After the hearing the panel writes a report for the Ministers of Environment and the initiating department which describes the project, the site, the potential impacts and issues, and which makes recommendations.

Role of panel review

Public reviews are very important because they provide a neutral forum for consultation and, eventually lead to improved co-ordination and delivery of government services. Public participation in environmental proposals also plumbs public opinion, establishes the major issues involved, and helps ensure that environmental and socio-economic concerns are factored in to industrial decision-making.

Unfortunately, involvement by affected individuals and groups in forums is unequal because of financial costs, lack of access to expert advice, isolation, lack of time to analyse data, language and cultural differences and limited time to organize a response. How the government should organize and administer an equitable public participation programme thus becomes an issue.

Panel reviews are complex and lengthy. A proposal may involve different environmental assessment and regulatory processes, various federal departments and their mandates, different levels of governments, etc. It requires great effort to be fair, comprehensive and efficient. It is also important to find ways to avoid waste of resources, and to avoid duplication of processes.

The term 'comprehensive' — as in 'comprehensive assessment' – means addressing scientific and biophysical effects, as well as human related concerns — social, health, economic, cultural, etc. of a project. This involves obtaining specialized knowledge in narrow areas of expertise. It is also important that government agencies involved be seen to carry out the assessment in a consistent, accountable manner. It takes several years to 'debug' and strengthen the procedures. There is still ample room for improvement in the Canadian method.

It would be beneficial, for example, to improve public accessibility to federal environmental decision-making. This could be done by strengthening openness of the self-assessment approach, and also by improving the public review phase. There is also a need to integrate more evenly the modern environmental values with traditional economic decisions in some federal jurisdictions. For example, crown corporations do not necessarily need to apply environmental assessment to new projects. Only a small number of crown corporations disturb the environment through their activities. However, unless it is corporate policy these companies do not neccessarily need to apply environmental reviews to their projects — nor need they comply with provincial regulations — and so escape the environmental safety nets.

Regulatory agencies still are inconsistent in considering environmental values, because of varying legal capacity to do so. They may have rigorous qualifications for reviews — like the National Energy Board; no legal basis for them — like the Canadian Transport Commission; or a more open mandate to look at the environment — as in the case of the Atomic Energy Control Board.

EARP guidelines

It is important to know what exactly is meant in Canada by the 'guidelines' which underwrite the Environmental Assessment and Review Process.

The updated, procedural guidelines are documented in great detail in a 37 page Initial Assessment Guide from the Federal Environmental Assessment Review Office of Environment Canada in Ottawa. This provides an overview of all aspects of EARP including how to conduct assessments, with the nine steps taken, elements to be covered by departments with special expertise, etc.

Briefly, the Guide covers onus, documentation, instructions how to do, duties of initiating departments, proponents, panels and reviews; initial assessment categories, technical methods, information required, definitions of effects, format considerations; public consultations; quantifying effects criteria (magnitude, risk, prevalence, etc.), thresholds of concerns, mitigation measures, monitoring and follow-up. Items such as types of activities which may warrant a referral to the Public Panel Review stage, and what goes into the Report to the Minister also are included.

This is quite a bit to chew, but the skeleton of what the guidelines accomplish is contained in Figure 16.1.

In regard to both phases of EARP, there is always room for improvement in a programme, to bring it nearer to the ideal of delivering comprehensive and open review at least cost. There are a number of mainly procedural changes that would enhance the programme, especially by improving public access to studies.

Openness, for example, needs to be strengthened in the self-assessment approach. The initial evaluation made by initiating departments could be published and made available in the area affected, and residents could be notified.

The self-assessment phase could also be required to identify alternatives to the project proposal early.

Also, the screening process could be enhanced by adding a new criterion. The present initial assessment mechanism permits 'exclusion lists' for projects which excuse identified 'benign project' types from assessment. A corresponding list of kinds of projects which require mandatory initial environmental evaluation could be developed through interdepartmental consultation with the Federal Environmental Assessment Review Office.

In addition, comprehensiveness of self-evaluation could be ensured by specifying in a guideline or regulation that assessment must include – but not be limited to – rationale, possible alternatives, biophysical and related social, health, economic and cultural effects of development, mitigation, and implementation and post-implementation monitoring plans.

The public review by panel phase of EARP has resulted in significant adjustments to projects assessed, but there is room for improvement of the procedure, such as by avoiding duplication of hearings. This would mean clarifying the roles of other regulatory agencies on a project to avoid serial hearings on the same issue. Instead, a regulatory agency could hold a single hearing for all aspects of the proposal – including environmental implications – provided this was effectively handled.

Other problems include unequal access by the affected public to environmental hearings. Specified groups, e.g. some aboriginal groups or community organizations, receive support to attend meetings, but others are excluded for financial reasons. Strengthened scope of the EARP would result if it could be applied to crown corporations and regulatory agencies; the quality of environmental assessment among these government agencies presently is uneven. They could be asked to comply with EARP by amending their charter legislation. Another possible change is expansion of the role of the Department of Environment in initiating environmental reviews under EARP.

Finally, there is need for a system of periodically evaluating EARP itself, in terms of implementation and effectiveness. The Canadian Government is sensitive to the possibility of imposing planning requirements and extra

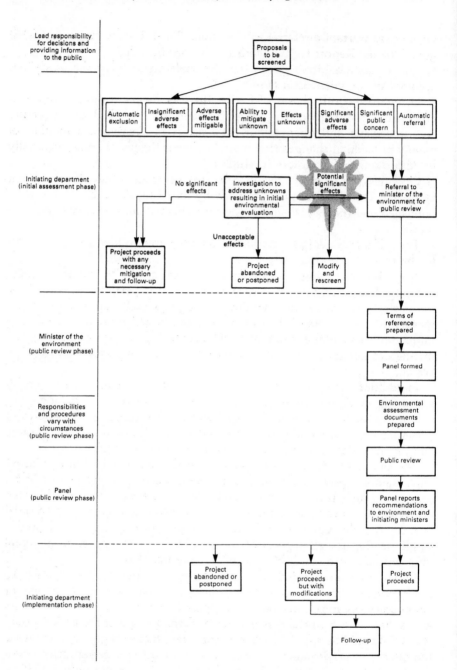

Figure 16.1   *Environmental assessment and review process*

costs on private and government agencies through environmental assessment. Therefore, the resource implications of the provisions of the EARP and any change there to need to be imputed and balanced against benefits which accrue.

Case study: hydro proposal

The Churchill River is located in the Atlantic province of Newfoundland, in the semi-wilderness but hydro-rich mainland area of Labrador. Most of the populatiom is settled on the triangular island portion of the province, all of which lies south of Labrador.

Island Newfoundland lacks coal and hydro resources for electric power – although it has undeveloped off-shore oil resources under deep water – and is anxious to develop Labrador. Following completion of the 5225 MW hydroelectric Station at Churchill Falls in the 1960s the lower river reaches were studied. Some 1700 MW was found available at a site Gull Island, and another 600 MW of developable capacity was assessed at Muskrat Falls. A subsequent proposal envisioned a full power development on the Lower Churchill, with transmission lines tied to the existing station at Churchill Falls.

An Environmental Assessment Panel was appointed to conduct a review of the proposal, and it reported in December, 1980. The proponent of the project (Lower Churchill Development Corporation or LCDC) is a crown corporation with shares jointly owned by the Government of Canada and the Province of Newfoundland and Labrador. A federal department involved in project funding, Energy, Mines and Resources, had asked for a public review under the Federal Environmental Assessment and Review Process.

The review covered potential power generating sites at Muskrat Falls and Gull Island, and transmission facilities. Environmental impact statements were completed by LCDC in 1980. The panel requested comments from concerned government agencies and the public, then organized public meetings in seven centres of the province. The panel then reviewed all information received and reached conclusions, which were duly reported to the federal Minister of Environment.

Project description

The hydroelectric sites being assessed are isolated (see Figure 16.2). The nearest communities are 40 km and 90 km, respectively, from Muskrat and Gull Island. A proposed 400 kV direct current single-circuit transmission line would cross southern Labrador areas and the Strait of Belle Isle, passing near coastal settlements. The line then would cross Newfoundland

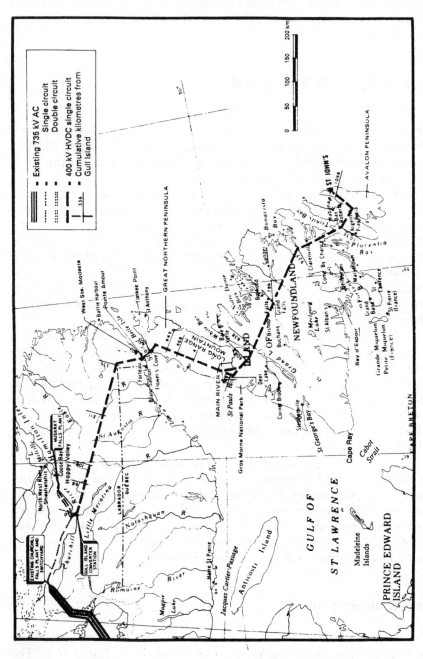

Figure 16.2 *Proposed transmission lines route*

Island from north to south-east, terminating at Grand Falls on the southern peninsula of Avalon. Overall length would be 1088 km. The transmission route avoids population centres except for Grand Falls and St. John's.

The Muskrat Falls project involves dams, spillway, and flanking dykes. The powerhouse would be located north of the falls at the bottom of a rock knoll, and intake tunnels through the knoll would feed four generating units. A natural dam between the rock knoll and the north shore of the river would be stabilized during construction. The reservoir's normal elevation would be 39 m above sea-level, and discharge would be into the Churchill River near sea-level.

The Gull Island plan called for a rockfill dam located at the head of Grizzle Rapids, with diversion tunnels and a flip bucket spillway and powerhouse. Water intakes from the approach channel via penstocks would drive six generating units. Normal reservoir level would be the same as at Muskrat Falls. Both stations would be remote-controlled from the existing Churchill Falls generating station. An 188 km alternating-current (AC) transmission intertie would integrate Churchill Falls and the Lower Churchill stations, following the road from Churchill Falls to Happy Valley and Gull Island, to a converter station beside the river. Other AC lines would link Muskrat Falls to Gull Island.

If both Gull and Muskrat were developed, two ± 400 kV direct current transmission lines would be required to Island Newfoundland. It would include 400 km of line in Labrador and 18 km with four seabed cables in two trenches across Belle Isle Strait. On Island Newfoundland, the line would run from Yankee Point on the north shore to Gros Morne National Park and down Great North Peninsula. A double line would cross the Long Range Mountains, join and run south-east to an inverter station at Grand Falls. From Grand Falls, a 314 km $\pm$ DC line would continue to Avalon. Construction cost was estimated at $4.3 billion (1980 $), with 6.5 years' construction time for Gull Island, and for Muskrat Falls at $3.2 billion and 5.5 years.

Process in action

The Federal Environmental Assessment and Review Process is intended to cover all projects within the sphere of federal interest which may have adverse effects on the environment, and to ensure that the results are incorporated into planning and implementation.

In the case of the Lower Churchill Project, an Environmental Assessment Panel was appointed to review environmental and socioeconomic consequences of the undertaking, and to make recommendations to the Minister of the Environment. The Panel included a chairman from the federal assessment office, two private-sector members, and three government members — from the initiating department, from Fisheries and Oceans, and from the provincial government. Public information and participation were arranged for the interested public, and 133 presentations were heard. A native Indian to English translation service was provided.

Based on proponent and public verbal and written statements and other data, the Panel arrived at conclusions regarding the various project impacts. These included effects on geological, hydrological and water quality, fisheries, wildlife and land use, forestry, local community and general environment sectors of the affected social economy.

Native Indian land claims also were raised, although the sympathetic Panel had no mandate to touch this area. The Naskapi-Montagnais-Innu people stated their homeland was affected by the project, and they would contest it by legal means. The proponent LCDC then pointed out that it needed assurance that it could proceed with the project. A disappointing feature of the project was revealed at the hearings, that communities could not tap into the project's energy transmitted past their doors for local use. Hardware to stop and step down DC transmission to usable voltage is too costly.

The assessment

The geological impacts were a major issue with the hydraulic power development because 45% of Muskrat Falls site and 75% of Gull Island site had steep shorelines where slumping and bank erosion were likely events – particularly downstream of Muskrat Falls. The rocky knoll at Muskrat, which formed a natural dam, would need stabilizing to prevent failure. Post-construction erosion monitoring for bank slumps was felt necessary.

Hydrological and water quality impacts of the Lower Churchill projects were expected to be small, with no major flow or water quality changes resulting. Preparation and flooding would create short-term damage only, but the topic was raised at public hearings. Reduced ice jams below Muskrat Falls due to the project also were noted.

The Churchill River drops 126 km from tailrace of the upper, existing plant to sea level. Since main flow already is controlled by upstream storage, and flows from tributaries are unregulated, water regimes are little changed by the project. Because of narrowness of the lower valley, both Gull Island and Muskrat Falls would be developed as run of river, with small storage. The increased water surface would be 36 km^2 and 86 km^2 only, with drawdowns of 1 m and 6 m respectively. Main water quality impacts would be sediment collecting in reservoirs. Flooding impacts would be small, but still could create some conflict between land and water uses. There was fear of temporary mercury pick-up from flooded area. Long-term reservoir water quality monitoring related to fish development was recommended by the panel.

Compensation was requested for expected damages to fisheries and wildlife habitats, and to commercial forestry. Sixteen species of fish, including salmon, trout and whitefish support angling and native subsistence. Trap lines would be flooded and serious damage suffered by animal habitats; and timber operators rights-of-way would be submerged. The wood resource was unsurveyed and had no attached value, but flooded stands below the new reservoir shoreline were recommended for clearing and salvage. The proponent LCDC raised a problem in reaching sites to be cleared, since no cutting equipment was available to boat access. Possible damage to moose habitat and migration patterns was foreseen and needed study.

The Federal Fisheries representative pinpointed fish kills related to dewatering of their habitat during the 11-day reservoir filling period. Migration through flow releases from the Upper Churchill would be difficult, but fish refuges were available in deeper river-bed reaches. The marine crossing had limited possible impacts on fish and fishing income. Entrainment of fish in the penstock control at the downstream end of the dam was possible; some fish could die due to nitrogen supersaturation. However, to mitigate impacts, a new fishery would be established in the Upper Churchill reservoir. The proponent also had proposals to stock ouananiche to compensate for lost brook trout; and to design generating plant to allow for waste heat utilization from generator cooling water for warm water fish cultivation.

In regards to environmental protection, the Panel requested adequate measures during construction. The proponent, Lower Churchill Development Corporation, responded with a plan to incorporate standard provincial environmental protection clauses in all contracts, with specific environmental requirements listed, to be enforced by a company environmental officer. This was very close to the Panel's views. The LCDC also aired a proposal to train local people to direct remedial action by contractors.

General environmental impact issues raised at hearings included water-related and other impacts of transmission lines, such as plans for herbicide use near water bodies (which involves the Federal Pesticide Review Board), contingency plans for containing contaminant spills; borrow pits, design of the submarine cable crossing; and limited electric field effects near residences. One issue was, herbicide use would multiply where split transmission routes were planned, or where existing corridors were rejected (because of greater mileage or hazards). The marine crossing involved two trenches with cables each and trenching was judged satisfactory to avoid iceberg grounding. Borrow pits were to be according to provincial maintenance standards.

The socio-economic effects of the hydroelectric project on the wilderness native culture involved federal government responsibilities. The influx of workers stressed community and undeveloped areas, disturbed Indian life-style and incited land claim issues. The Indians wanted a share in the project's economic benefits, through some of the 2600 jobs created. The white communities had suffered an economic decline, and briefs mentiond opportunities for jobs, related training, chances to bid on small contracts. and local preference purchasing.

Recommendations

The panel eventually concluded after review that the project was a rational choice to meet a demonstrated need; that it fulfilled national energy self-sufficiency goals; that the methods of surveillance and enforcement were adequate if vigorously applied; and that it could be acceptable provided certain environmental and socio-economic conditions were met. In all, the panel made 20 recommendations, which were reported to the Minister of the Environment. Briefly, in addition to the above, the findings were:

1   adequate staff should be provided by LCDC to survey and enforce environmental aims during construction;
2   seismic and riverbank stability problems were under control with current technology at design and construction stage;
3   erosion monitoring was necessary below Muskrat Falls for bank slumping;
4   long-term post impoundment monitoring was required in regard to fish development options, possible mercury concentrations;
5   land and wildlife use by Indians were viable during and after construction;
6   compensatory payments should be made to cover economic fishery losses due to reservoir construction and submarine crossing, for lost trapping income, and for blockage of existing forest use;
7   financial benefits of salvaging drowned forest should be assessed;
8   study moose migration and develop mitigation for any damage to moose habitat;
9   clear woods along reservoir perimeter for other uses and have plan to delineate clearings;
10 avoid opening new transmission rights of way from Grand Falls to Avalon (Island); but use old corridors;
11 organize employment locally with advance notices, training to the job;
12 constrain community disruption by giving time to plan for influx, exchange information;
13 industrial spin-offs from the project, if any, should be fully assessed beforehand by appropriate authorities, with attention directed to impacts on Indians.

The Lower Churchill project was put 'on ice' during the 1980s, due to uncertainties in the financial and energy outlook. It will very likely proceed during the 1990s, when economic conditions are riper for development, and all export-related agreements are in place. When the project does proceed, environmental safeguards will be an integral element of the plan, due in good part to the exhaustive review procedure just described.

17
Proposed EIA methodology for India

Radha Gopalan, Kalpana Sekaran and Maitreyee Banerjee

Environmental Impact Assessment (EIA) involves analyses and evaluation of adverse and/or beneficial effects of human actions on the environment. The assessment is carried out by identifying the changes that may occur in the environment following the introduction of development plans or projects in any inhabited locale. The qualitative and quantitative results obtained from such evaluations are thereafter used for selecting a suitable or perhaps the best alternative modus of development (Rau and Wooten, 1980; Westman, 1985; Bisset, 1987).

Environment refers to interactions of living organisms or the biotic community with physical or abiotic surroundings which comprises light, air, temperature, humidity etc. Impact analyses of extraneous developmental projects in the environment measures the extent of alterations occurring in the normal interactive processes of abiotic and biotic components (Dasmann, 1984). Such a study is made simplistic and implementable by limiting the environmental domain in smaller quantifiable units consisting of the three basic components viz., the organisms or the biotic species, the environmental factors or the abiotic surroundings and the environmental processes involved in the interactions of the biotic and abiotic components. These units are conventionally defined as ecosystems and the environmental processes governing the interactions of biotic and abiotic components as ecological processes (Westman, 1985).

The importance of environmental protection was formally recognized in the late sixties. It was observed by the developed countries that all the social, technical, and economic planning and developments at the national levels resulted in continous alterations of the environment. Consequently EIA was adopted as a tool systematically to assess the qualitative and quantitative impacts of these alterations on the ecosystems. In 1970 EIA was accepted as a mandatory requirement for all economic developments by the United States National Environmental Policy Act (Rau and Wooten, 1980).

Current methodologies

Conventionally, the EIA studies have been based on analyses of the effects of new projects on a number of human activity parameters, Such as:

1   change in employment status of the individuals;
2   change in land values in terms of wealth;
3   alterations of health due to change in the air quality, water quality and also due to noise pollution of the environment;
4   change in wildlife and vegetation due to alteration of the human activities;
5   prevalence of natural disasters like flood, earthquakes, famine, land-slides, epidemics;
6   effects on fisheries;
7   effects of siltation and alteration in land use patterns, agriculture, housing and
8   socio-economic conditions.

The final data are expressed in different forms depending on the nature of the methodologies used. In one of the most popularly used methods called the matrix method, the impacts on the human activities are expressed in the form of rows and columns of a matrix. In the checklist method, the impacts are drawn in a tabular form. Some of the other less popular methods still in vogue (mostly in the developed coutries like USA, UK and Canada) include the network method and mapping overlays. The network method focuses both on the direct/immediate and indirect/long-term effects of development on human activities. For example, the impacts of deforestation of an area to install a project is studied by this method both in regards to immediate effects viz., soil erosion on human lives, as well as indirect or long-term effects such as silting of water bodies resulting in disturbances in benthic life and consequently the human life. Mapping overlays provide a cartographic representation of land use patterns and subsequent changes due to the project (Bisset, 1987). Despite the many advancements in EIA methodologies since 1970, the ecosystems continue to exhibit the destabilization effects as aftermaths of implementation of the national development plans. The environmental degenerations are noted to be more severe in populous developing countries such as India, its neighbouring countries and African nations (Kedarnath, 1987). Careful analyses of the causes of failure however, reveal a number of lacunae in the current EIA practices.

Major drawbacks

The major drawbacks of the current methodologies are their inability to predict the environmental disturbances that may harm or benefit all the living species of an ecosystem including the human being. As a result, these studies are valid only for assessing the impacts after the initiation of the projects. The second drawback is that none of the methodologies are sensitive to the continuous time dependent changes occurring in the environmental parameters viz, temperature, humidity, salinity of water, pH, wind velocity, metabolic rate etc. For instance, the data in the checklist and matrix method are obtained following the study of environmental parameters of the concerned locale for a time period ranging from, a few months to a couple of years. These discrete time dependent data are not suitable for relating the changes which occur in the environment as continuous functions of time and hence have little implementable significance. Other disadvantages of the existing EIA practices are:

1   These assess the human activities in qualitative terms and thus cannot reflect quantitatively the rate of degeneration or change in the environment. Both the checklist and the matrix methods qualitatively assess various physico-chemical and environmental parameters and the effects of these changes on human activities. The human activity parameters which are accounted for in these studies are such that precise and quantatitive measures cannot be adopted to prevent ill effects on human lives. For instance, effects of alterations in air quality, water quality and noise on general health of the individuals cannot be expressed in precise measurable terms (Westman, 1985).
2   These are not sensitive to human errors in the assessment of facts. The magnitude of human errors may be variable since the ultimate stress on human life by the developmental activities are assessed by different groups of technical experts who are bound to deliver highly subjective reports.
3   These incorporate lengthy and unwieldy volumes of environmental data.

Simulation model

Attempts have been made to overcome some of the drawbacks of the currently used EIA methods by the animal ecologists group formerly known as Adaptive Environmental Assessment and Management (AEAM) from the University of British Columbia, Canada (Bisset, 1987). They have proposed an EIA model known as the simulation model which incorporates chains of impacts covering huge areas and for a longer time in the future. The time dependent variables identified in this model were broadly classified as social, economic and ecological variables. Unlike the other EIA methods where the usefulness declines once a decision on the project has been made, the simulation model has functioned as a management tool even after the project has become operational. However, the model has not been applicable so far for long-term predictions and judgements of the environmental impacts, even though it can provide more information on time related parameters than the matrix and the checklist methods. The main disadvantage of this method is its cost intensiveness and lack of appropriate data regarding its application for projects like oil refineries, power stations, paper mills etc. (Bisset, 1987).

Focus on India

The EIA practices in India have yet to be recognized as a routine practice in association with all developmental projects. This is primarily due to the fact that until recently, development in India, has been viewed only in terms of the economic returns. Moreover, there has been a lack of technical expertise, for the EIA studies in many major projects related to irrigation, thermal and hydroelectric power projects and as a result these projects could not be effectively implemented. However since 1980, EIA has been made obligatory for all developmental projects by the Environmental Appraisal Committees of India. The objective of the EIA act is to achieve sustained development with minimal environmental degradation and prevention of long-term adverse effects by incorporating suitable prevention and control measures (Ministry of Environment and Forestry, 1986-87).

The checklist method is commonly used in India for EIA studies. Owing to the inherent drawbacks of this method as outlined above it serves to provide only a guideline to the qualitative effects of the project at a particular site, and does not reflect or predict the impacts before the installation. As a result, the EIA practices in India have not been able to fulfil the required objectives for environmental protection *vis-à-vis* the economic development, (Kedarnath, 1987).

Proposed methodology

Principle

In view of the lapses of the current EIA practices it is now essential to re-examine the structures and functions of the environment so that better methods can be developed to control and prevent its degeneration. Environment may be viewed as a multidimensional entity which remains undisturbed as long as its dynamic steady state equilibrium is maintained by continuous exchange of energy between the biotic and abiotic components. (Figure 17.1.). The energy exchange is carried out by a number of metabolic and non-metabolic energy transfer processes *viz.,* radiation, convection, conduction, transpiration, respiration and metabolism. All the non-metabolic transfer processes participate to exchange heat energy whereas the metabolic energy is always exchanged as the chemical energy of food. The exchange of chemical energy is therefore carried out by the food chain or food web.

The energy transfer in the environment is primarily controlled by two principal parameters: (1) physical composition of the environment which regulates the transfer of heat energy and (2) biological composition regulating the transfer of chemical energy. Accordingly, the extent of perturbations in the equilibrium dynamics of ecological processes may be quantitatively measured by continuous time dependent change and the physical and biological components of environment. The time dependent changes of the physical environment are controlled by the biogeochemical cycles of elements viz., C, N, S, P, metals etc. whereas continuous changes of the biotic components are governed primarily by two factors: (1) availability of resources or chemical energy and (2) the diversity or genotypic variations among the living organisms, both of which are also indirectly related to the physico-chemical composition of the environment. The essence of the proposed methodology is the identification of some of the time dependent continuum parameters which constitute the physico-chemical and biological components of the environment and which participate in the energy exchange processes to maintain the dynamic equilibrium of the ecological processes. The continuum parameters which may be evaluated are temperature, humidity, metabolic processes, population density, elemental composition of air and water, soil fertility and primary productivity.

Methodology

The proposed methodology is designed with the objectives of:

1   predicting the long-term deviations of the physico-biological compo-
    nents of the environment before initiation of the project;
2   predicting the changes occurring in the environment as continuous
    time dependent functions; and
3   expressing the environmental variations (both biotic and abiotic in
    quantitative figures so that precise and appropriate pictures can be
    taken to control the problems.

A schematic diagram of the proposed new methodology is given in figure 17.1.

Discussion

The three continuum parameters which are thought to be critical in the proposed method for assessing the impacts of new developments on the ecodynamicity are:

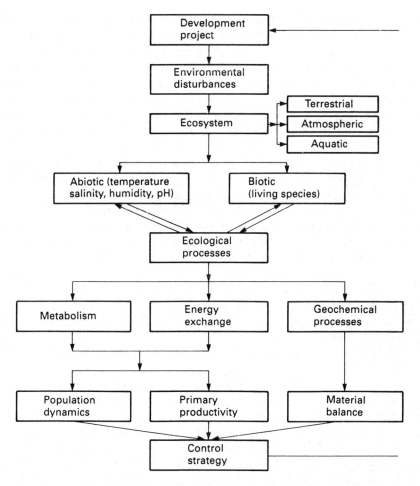

Figure 17.1 *Schematic diagram of proposed EIA methodology (for details, see text)*

1 population dynamics of animals, plants and human beings,
2 primary productivity of the photosynthetic plants,
3 mass balance of oxygen and nitrogen which are essential elements for the living species in the ecosystem

Population dynamics of the living species is considered to be the most appropriate mode of quantitative assessments of impacts in the environment. Since population is a direct function of the physical environment (i.e., the climate) and the available chemical resources, it has the inherent ability to represent the overall dynamicity of energy exchanges. Study of population dynamics for EIA is therefore more suitable and appropriate for all environmental conditions especially for a populous country such as India. Such a study would not only be comprehensive with respect to assessing the overall dynamic changes in the ecosystem equilibrium but would also relate the structural and functional parameters like age mortality, natality, spatial distribution, immigration, migration etc. of the population of all living species with the surrounding physical environment. With the aid of appropriate mathematical models for population dynamics of living species in the specific ecosystems, it would be possible to extrapolate and predict the impacts of a project even before its initiation. The dynamics of the population can be studied with the help of censorship data as well as laboratory and field experimentation data. The EIA of population dynamics is also sensitive to the wide spectrum of geographical and climatic variations, which so far have not been explicitly considered in any of the current practices in India. The population dynamics as an EIA tool can further be made exhaustive and intensive by incorporating the dynamics of food webs existing in the ecosystem. For this a crucial trophic unit or a keystone species will have to be identified in the food web, which upon removal from the food web would cause structural and functional changes in the overall populations. For instance, alteration in the feeding habitats of the prey, owing to environmental changes would be reflected in subsequent changes in dynamics of the population of the entire food chain or food web. (Westman, 1985).

The primary productivity of all phototrophic plants in the ecosystem may be a more suitable parameter for EIA practices in India. Primary productivity reflects the rate of metabolic conversion of carbon dioxide in the environment to organic carbon in plants. Measurement of primary productivity as a function of time therefore relates the energy exchange between the plants and the surrounding environment. Disturbance in the chemical composition of the environment due to the unsteady state of elemental cycles would ultimately alter the carbon dioxide concentration of the atmosphere and hence the primary productivity. Since the primary producers constitute the basic supporting nutrients in the food chains of all populations, its quantitative estimation in an ecosystem would provide an assessment of the overall impact on both the biological and abiological part of the environment.

Elemental mass balance of oxygen and nitrogen in the ecosystem is another equally suitable measure for the EIA study. Since these elements are essential for supporting all life, material balance of different species of oxygen and nitrogen in the ecosystem is more appropriate for establishing the interrelation between the environment and the living species of the locale.

It needs to be emphasized that the perspective of the present methodology is different from the current EIA practices. The methodologies presently in vogue view the environment as a one dimensional entity exhibiting a uniform and limited range of physico-chemical changes such as rainfall, diurnal and nocturnal temperatures, etc. in response to various human activities. For instance, the current practices are focused on evaluating the effects of climatic changes on the migration of human

Table 17.1 Comparison of the proposed new EIA methodology with the existing methodologies

Methods used	Mode of data expression	Abiological (temperature, humidity, pH, salinity)			Biological (animal activities, human activities)			References
		Qual.	Quan.	Pred.	Qual.	Quan.	Pred.	
Existing								
Check list	Tables	+	–	–	+	–	–	Bisset (1987)
Matrix	Matrix representation	+	–/+(?)	–	+	–	–	Bisset (1987)
Network	Flow chart	+	–/+(?)	–/+ (?)	+	–/+(?)	–/+(?)	Westman (1985)
Mapping overlays	Topographic representation	+	–	–	+	–	–	Bisset (1987)
Proposed	Continuum parameters of ecological processes	+	+	+	+	+	+	

Notes: Qual., qualitative; Quan., quantitative; Pred., predictability; +, parameter detected by the method; –, parameter not detected by the method; –/+(?), sensitivity of the method to detection is doubtful

beings from the locale. These environmental changes do not explicitly relate to the human activity parameters with the effects of variations in climate geography, cultural and social ethics of the living species. The new methodology on the contrary estimates the deviations in the environment with respect to its biological and physico-chemical components and hence is specific in terms of climate, geography, physical locale as well as cultural habitats of animals and human beings. The sensitivity of this method depends on the selection of the critical ecosystems of a locale and the time dependent parameters which quantify the disturbances in the environment of the selected ecosytems. For instance the impact of installation of a chemical fertilizer factory in a locale can be best assessed quantitatively by identifying the impacts on the continuum parameters of the adjacent terrestrial and aquatic ecosystems. Thus this methodology reflects the precise magnitude of environmental disturbances as functions of diurnal and seasonal variations of the climate of the ecosystem as well as geographical and social variations of all biotic species. EIA study by these parameters has a number of advantages over the currently used methodologies. Table 17.1 presents a comparison of the proposed methodology with the existing ones. An additional advantage of the new approach is that it can be easily implemented in practice.

Conclusion

It has been shown in this paper that the EIA methodologies for each country should be specifically based on climatic, social and cultural characteristics. The methodologies adopted must be able to reflect the impact on the environment in quantitative terms, and should also enable a long-term forecasting of the environmental changes before the commencement of a project in a locale. The existing methodologies in this regard are unsuitable due to their qualitative and generalized approach towards analyses of environmental impact. Besides, they are inherently incapable of forecasting long-term changes. The new methodology overcomes all the shortcomings of existing methods of EIA. In addition the proposed method is expected to be much less cost intensive and exhaustive as it entails the measurements of a few continuum parameters.

Acknowledgements

The authors thank Professor C. Natarajan for his encouragement. One of the authors (Radha Gopalan) acknowledges the financial assistance provided by the CSIR.

References

Bisset, R. (1987) In *Environmental Impact Assessment for developing countries* (eds. A. K. Biswas and Qu. Geping), Tycooly International Publishers, London.

Dasmann, R. F. (1984) *Environmental Conservation.* John Wiley and Sons, New York.

Kedarnath, S. (1987) In *Environmental Impact Assessment for developing countries* (eds. A. K. Biswas and Qu. Geping), Tycooly International Publishers, London.

Ministry of Environment and Forestry, Annual Report 1986–87, Government of India Publication.

Rau, J. G. and Wooten, D. C. (1980) *Environmental Impact Analysis Handbook*, McGraw Hill, New York.

Westman, W. E. (1985) *Ecology, Impact Assessment and Environmental Planning*, Tycooly International Publishers, London.

18

Devising an effective environmental impact assessment system for a developing country: the case of the Turks and Caicos Islands*

Ron Bisset

Since 1970, when the National Environmental Policy Act became law in the USA, environmental impact analysis (EIA) has spread widely throughout the world. Many developing countries now have laws which require EIAs for major projects. In other countries EIAs are undertaken, but on an *ad hoc* informal basis or in response to administrative measures (which may lack the force of law) issued by national governments. The formal, legalistic approach is probably the preferred option by most countries. In recent years, the problems of utilizing, successfully, EIA as a decision-making aid and means of environmental protection have received considerable attention (for example, Monosowski, 1984; Sammy and Ahmad, 1985; Biswas and Geping, 1987; United Nations Environment Programme, 1987; Marshall, 1988).

In this chapter these problems are discussed and reference is made to particular issues relevant to small island developing nations. Specifically, attention is focused on the Turks and Caicos Islands, a small archipelago in the Caribbean. In early 1988, Cobham Resource Consultants (CRC) undertook a mission, on behalf of UNCHS (HABITAT), to the Islands to provide the following:

1 description of the main habitat types (known as natural resource units);
2 environmental policies to be utilized in conjunction with the national physical development plan;
3 guidelines on the environmental consequences of selected project types (such as marinas and solid wastes disposal) and resource management actions (such as groundwater extraction and protection and salina management) to assist government decision-making;

*Much of this paper is based on a report *Turks and Caicos Islands: Ecological Survey and Environmental Policies* (1988) prepared by Cobham Resource Consultants for UNCHS (HABITAT). The author acknowledges the assistance of Dr J. F. Wagner and Dr. Bacon in preparation of this paper.

4   advice on institutional strengthening to implement environmental policies; and
5   a workable EIA system.

The EIA system devised will be described in detail and its particular features related to the problems faced by developing countries. It will be argued that the EIA procedure will be of interest to other developing countries either about to introduce EIA procedures or in the process of altering existing procedures to make them more effective.

Problems of EIA in developing countries

Most commentators on EIA in developing countries agree on the main problems which hinder effective use of EIA. These are summarized below:

Lack of trained human resources

Developing countries lack trained human resources in many fields, but this is particularly true of EIA. This leads to inadequate preparation of EIAs and review of completed reports. These consequences cause frustration among the few trained personnel who are responsible for EIA procedures and also leads to decision-makers/project proponents and the public becoming disillusioned with the utility of EIA. This occurs because the EIA reports are, often, not suitable as decision-making aids (being too long, too descriptive and insufficiently analytical, and failing to address the main issues pertinent to decision-making).

Lack of financial resources

This factor relates closely to lack of trained human resources and contributes to and reinforces the consequences described above.

Lack of information on environmental and social systems (baseline data)

There is no doubt that this is an important constraint − in many developing nations very little is known on the structure and functioning of important ecosystems. Generally, more is known in developed countries about the nature of their environments, thus making preparation of EIA reports easier. However, lack of baseline data is sometimes considered to be a bigger constraint than it need be. Strategies exist to assist EIAs, involving little-known environments, to ensure that *only* the most relevant baseline data are collected (for example, Beanlands and Duinker, 1983).

There is no doubt, however, that if the baseline data do not exist they have to be obtained and this is expensive in terms of scarce human and other resources.

Low status of environmental departments or agencies

In many developing countries environmental departments/agencies have been established only since 1972 (year of Stockholm Conference on the Human Environment). Usually, these bodies are responsible for EIA procedures. Unfortunately, because of their recent origin and the traditional importance attached to development and economic growth, these organizations have a relatively low status in the governmental bureaucratic hierarchy. This factor reduces, significantly, their ability to enforce, effectively, both the EIA procedures and any quality criteria they may have regarding content of EIA reports.

Limited public knowledge of EIA/public participation

In most developing countries there are only a few individuals and/or non-governmental organizations with knowledge of EIA. Also, there is rarely a tradition of public participation in developmental decision-making. Those two factors mean that there is no effective external political impetus which pushes governments to implement EIA effectively. Also, local people can assist with provision of baseline data, but only if consulted. Such consultation is not undertaken in many cases.

Lack of co-ordination between agencies at national/local levels

As Monosowski (1984) has pointed out, particularly with reference to Brazil, there is often a strict demarcation of responsibilities and struggles for resources and power between government sectoral agencies. This inhibits co-operative work, particularly in EIA, when consultation and information exchange is important.

Lack of willingness of proponent agencies to internalize EIA requirements

Lim (1985) in a review of EIA procedures in the Republic of Korea, the Philippines and in Brazil found such agencies to have a low awareness of EIA and its objectives and were unwilling to alter, significantly, their decision-making process to take account of the results of EIA.

Lack of precise role definition for the various participants in EIA procedures

Should there be vagueness or ambiguity regarding the precise nature of institutional relationships then accountability declines and confusion results. The situation characterizes a number of different countries.

Lack of information exchange

Despite the above problems, good, relevant EIA reports *are* produced in developing countries. In some cases they are the product of innovative conceptual/methodological work, in one country, which might be applied, usefully, elsewhere. Unfortunately, EIA reports are often confidential and very few copies are printed. Only a fortunate few are aware of their existence and even less have read them. The results are not synthesized and produced in more widely accessible form such as international environment/development journals. The outcome of this state of affairs is a 'reinvention of the wheel', in which work done in one EIA is duplicated for another because the opportunity for learning from past experience is absent. In the context of developing countries where scarce resources are being devoted to EIA this is an undesirable and wasteful situation.

The combined results of all these factors have been identified as contributing to the following consequences which, probably, apply to nearly all developing countries (Lim, 1985):

1   Fewer EIAs are undertaken than legal or other requirements would seem to indicate.
2   Most EIAs seem to have been a function of justifying a decision (usually to develop) which has been made and are concerned only with remedial measures. Rarely do they consider alternative courses of action at an early stage of the project planning cycle, in order to choose the most environmentally favourable.

These problems typify many developing countries regardless of size. Small island developing countries, it might be thought, would exhibit some of them, but not others. Experience of the Turks and Caicos Islands, indicated that most if not all of these problems were present, accompanied by a few specific difficulties. Before proceeding to these issues and to the proposed EIA system it will be useful to review, briefly, the main environmental characteristics of the Turks and Caicos Islands.

Turks and Caicos Islands: environmental background

The Turks and Caicos Islands are a small group of low-lying islands to the south of the Bahamas. The climate is dry, almost semi-arid and the vegetation is, therefore, typical of this type of climatic regime. The soil is sandy and there are some areas where limestone predominates. Due to these conditions rainwater sinks quickly into a limited number of underground lenses (areas of fresh groundwater) or moves rapidly through the Islands and out into the sea. There are no permanent sources of surface freshwater in the Islands and the supply of freshwater is a constant problem for the inhabitants, particularly with regard to economic development. The lack of freshwater, coupled with poor soil conditions has had a harmful effect on agriculture, contributing to its decline. At present, nearly all foodstuffs for local people and tourists are imported from either the Dominican Republic or from Miami, USA.

The population of the Turks and Caicos Islands is approximately 13 000 and the economic development of the Islands to improve the standard of living of the local people is, perhaps, the highest political priority. There has been a continual out-migration of active and ambitious Islanders to the USA and to the Bahamas, and this, in turn, has had a harmful effect on the ability to achieve economic growth. Unfortunately, also, past events have reduced the number of options available. Until the 1960s the production of salt for export was an important source of income and employment, but economic pressures made salt from the Islands uneconomic and resulted in the present situation in which no salt is produced. Similarly, the production of sisal and cotton has ceased. Of the 'traditional' industries, fishing alone has remained important as a source of income and employment. However the fishing industry, particularly that based on lobster (crawfish) and conch, is under pressure. Should present, uncontrolled overfishing continue then it is almost certain that fisheries based on these species will decline, and perhaps, disappear.

These economic activities, particularly salt production and 'plantation' style agriculture, were 'non-sustainable', that is, certain acceptable levels of production (in terms of income/employment) could not be kept at desired levels. Sustainable development, on the other hand, is development which can be maintained at the desired levels, other matters being equal, because the natural resource base upon which development depends is being managed to ensure that economic benefits remain at these levels.

Many economic activities are based on natural resources such as soil, freshwater or fish species. If these resources are not managed wisely then their usefulness for various types of economic activity can be harmed and the production of wealth ceases. If groundwater is used for irrigation then it should not be polluted with chemicals that might damage the crops being irrigated. Similarly, overfishing reduces the population of valued fish species to the point where very few individuals are left. The fishermen find them harder to catch and, thus catches decline. This, in turn, means less income.

Although many economic activities are dependent on natural resources, the link is sometimes not appreciated. The relationship between fisheries and the fish species upon which they depend is fairly well understood. The threats are overfishing, destruction of nursery areas and pollution. In the case of salt production in salinas, this was dependent on sea-water relatively free of pollutants. 'Over-production' was not a problem, but had the sea-water become contaminated difficulties would have occurred.

A recognition of the dependency between economic activities and natural resources enables management to be practised to maintain the resources, and hence, the economic activities. The thriving tourism industry is a good case in point. The main reasons why tourists visit the Islands are well known: beaches, climate, clear sea-water and reefs. Should all or any of these features of the environment 'disappear' then the attractiveness of the Islands to tourists will have been reduced, possibly significantly. The climate is unlikely to change, but beaches, sea-water quality (clarity and cleanliness) and reefs are all very sensitive to changes in their surroundings and the uses made of them. They can be affected by tourism-related developments themselves (for example, too much recreation pressure on reefs causing damage) and by developments having nothing to do with tourism (for example, offshore mining/dredging causing beach erosion). So, there is a need for careful analysis of proposed developments to ensure that they do not cause unforeseen damage to natural resources, which may be somewhat distant, upon which other economic activities depend.

The inhabited Islands are of widely differing size, but all are small. This means that the Islands have large areas of coastline, including beaches, compared with the total area of land. A consequence of this is that nowhere is far from the coast and the sea. The coast and seas are of prime importance for tourism development and possible expansion of fisheries. Inland development, if not assessed properly and appropriate actions (if needed) taken, can easily affect coastal and marine resources in a harmful way.

In many respects the Turks and Caicos Islands conform to a 'classic' description of a small island country and its economy. The characteristics are relevant to any discussion of the role of the EIA in development planning. Cocossis (1987) has listed these features as:

1 *Fragile ecosystems* – resulting from great genetic diversity, survival of archaic forms and reduced interspecies competition. If disturbed these ecosystems can behave with great volatility and vulnerability.
2 *Homogenous indigenous sociocultural systems* – isolation leads to closer knit communities. Lack of social diversity leads to lack of adaptability in the face of extraneous change-inducing factors, for example, tourism.
3 *Economic limitations* – islands possess a relatively narrow economic base due, in part, to limited local availability of natural resources. The local market is small and transport costs for both imports and exports are high. Economies are typical of marginal, peripheral locations. Dependence on vital imports such as foodstuffs and machinery is common. Again vulnerability is a characteristic feature of this segment of small island life.
4 *Close, strong interdependencies between environmental, sociocultural and*

economic systems − small islands do not possess some of the buffer mechanisms which intervene and reduce the transmission of effects along such linkages in large countries with greater diversity in environmental, sociocultural and economic systems. The margin for error is less in small island countries.

Development policies have often ignored these linkages, particularly those to and from environmental systems, with unfortunate adverse consequences, not only for the environment but also for the attainment of economic and social well-being goals. The need for environmentally conscious decision-making in small island economies is great and EIA can make an important contribution, but not if it is applied only at the project level and in a policy/planning context which does not take a systems or holistic approach to development/environment interactions, either through a commitment to a national conservation strategy, a policy of achieving sustainable development or to socially and environmentally aware land use or developmental planning. A policy planning framework of some kind is needed to produce goals/objectives against which the consequences (adverse and beneficial) of project or plan specific changes can be judged.

Within an established policy − planning system EIA can be used in a number of ways to assess:

1   single projects;
2   regional development proposals (project clusters);
3   alternative means of achieving national or regional plan and/or policy goals/objectives;
4   completed national or regional policies, programmes and plans.

All are useful, but a mix, for example of 1 and 3 or 2 and 3 would make a significant contribution to successful economic development planning. (Sadler, 1988.)

EIA and the Turks and Caicos Islands

The Islands do not possess an EIA system, but exhibit the main problems faced by developing countries which have introduced such procedures. Unfortunately, they show other characteristics which can act to make successful EIA implementation difficult.

The government department dealing with natural resources and control of development has extremely limited financial and human resources to implement existing legislation, policies, programmes. Great strain would be imposed if new activities were to be delegated to the department. It was found to be dependent, heavily, on expatriate personnel (on short-term contracts) who had no long-term commitment to the Islands. Further, few local people were available to replace expatriates. For example, in the section dealing with planning there was no local qualified planner. One Islander, only, was in the UK studying planning. The result of this turnover of expatriate middle to senior ranking staff and lack of local skilled personnel is a reduction of long-term continuity.

In small communities the personal factor takes on more significance. In all countries an influential senior individual with drive/enthusiasm and commitment can affect the management of affairs. However, in smaller communities with more informal, face-to-face interaction between senior staff and between government and leaders of business/industry, the scope for individual influence on the direction of affairs is greater. This effect was particularly noticeable in the environment/planning field in the Islands. Should any such influence be negative, as regards EIA, then the consequences can be damaging and long lasting.

Although the Islands have a more restricted range of ecosystems than a large country, there remained a significant range of types about which very little was known. Baseline data collection would still be an important task. Additionally, despite the fact that government departments were small and face-to-face interaction both socially and in work terms was more prevalent than in larger countries, co-operation and information exchange did not appear to be any easier. Size of bureaucracy does not appear a relevant factor in affecting certain types of bureaucratic behaviour (such as boundary maintenance, secrecy and struggle for prestige).

In early 1988 a national physical development plan for the Turks and Caicos Islands was produced. This plan considered environmental matters in a general manner. At the same time a draft Physical Planning Ordinance was being considered by the Islands' government. This Ordinance contained a requirement for EIAs for certain project categories but did not specify how the EIA procedure should be implemented nor give advice on the EIA approach(es) to be used and on the nature and contents of Environmental Impact Statements (EISs).

The EIA system which was devised for the Islands attempted to take into account the special characteristics of the Islands both as a developing country and as a small island nation. It was devised also to complement the environmental policies which were produced to assist the government of the Islands, achieve sustainable development and to increase the effectiveness of the national physical development plan.

A number of prior government decisions/viewpoints had to be taken into account before formulating the EIA system. First, it has been recommended that an environmental adviser be appointed to assist the government in implementation of its developmental and environmental policies. This adviser was to be given an important role in the proposed EIA procedure as both a co-ordinator of the procedure and adviser on individual EIAs. Second, the government had decided, already, that Environmental Impact Statements (EISs) would be prepared by independent experts chosen by the government, but employed by development proponents. Third, to overcome a lack of indigenous expertise it was suggested that a firm of consultants familiar with the Caribbean be retained for a period of 3 years to prepare all EISs. Full use of Caribbean experts was considered essential and counterpart 'on-the-job' training of Island personnel should be undertaken to build up a resource of expertise which could, in the future, reduce reliance on external consultants. Since this recommendation was made IUCN has begun a study to investigate the feasibility of establishing a regional Caribbean 'task force' to prepare EISs in small island nations throughout the Caribbean (Sadler, 1988). Should a regional 'task force' be established it could be the successor to the consultants especially as, after the 3 year period, a small 'pool' of island expertise would have been established and some relevant baseline and other data gathered.

The main features of the proposed EIA system focus on the role of the Department of Planning (part of the Ministry of Natural Resources and Manpower). The steps are:

1   Planning Department establishes, by reference to the list of 'Development activities which may require preparation of an Environmental Impact Statement (EIS)' (Table 18.1), whether an EIS is required. The decision is made by the Director of Planning on the basis of whether the applicant can satisfy the Director that, because of the location/ characteristics of the proposal, no significant adverse impacts will occur.

2   Notification of decision to applicant.

3   Department of Planning initiates scoping meetings to assist preparation of 'Terms of Reference' (TOR).

4   Consultants selected by Department of Planning (possibly in conjunction with applicant).

5   Applicant receives TOR.

6   Draft EIS presented by the applicant to Department of Planning.

7   Review of Draft EIS by Department of Planning in relation to TOR.

8   Final EIS presented by the Applicant before or with planning application (incorporating any amendments and/or additions arising from the review of the draft EIS).

9   Review of the final EIS by government agencies and other relevant organizations.

10   Public review of final EIS (may involve display in public libraries, schools, church halls and public meetings).

11.   Director of Planning prepares report for Physical Planning Board/ Member/Governor (various governmental decision makers) summarizing and incorporating the findings of the final EIS.

12   Decision of Physical Planning Board/Member/Governor.

13   The period between receipt of a planning application accompanied by an EIS and decision by Physical Planning Board/Member/ Governor shall not exceed 60 days.

This proposed procedure covers both private and public sector projects and is based on centralized government control over selection of consultants, formulation of TOR and review of EISs. Also, public

Table 18.1 *Development activities which may require preparation of an environmental impact statement*

1   Marinas.
2   Hotels.
3   Leisure complexes (e.g. a self-contained mix of accommodation, hotels, villas, condominiums and recreation facilities).
4   Residential developments of 10 or more units
5   Commercial and retail centres.
6   Inshore/offshore mineral and aggregate extraction.
7   Onshore mineral and aggregate extraction occupying an area of 0.5 ha (1.25 acres) or more unless occurring in a site already designated for this activity.
8   Land reclamation from the sea.
9   Alterations to wetlands or salinas including cutting mangroves, dredging and/or reclamation.
10 Engineering work modifying coral reefs.
11 Desalination installations.
12 Power stations.
13 Incinerators.
14 Ports/harbours.
15 Coastal erosion control measures involving engineering works.
16 Navigational dredging.
17 Road construction.
18 Causeways.
19 Sanitary landfill operations.
20 Centralized sewage treatment installations and sludge disposal.
21 Anaerobic digestors.
22 Intensive cultivation of vegetables and/or fruit using hydroponic techniques and/or shade houses.
23 Agricultural improvement schemes of 5 ha or more.
24 Residential development in conservation areas designated under the Physical Planning Ordinance, 1988.
25 Development proposals that will generate gaseous emissions, aqueous effluents, solid wastes, noise/vibration and radioactive discharges which might:
    ● seriously degrade water or air quality;
    ● cause serious ecological damage;
    ● cause serious structural damage;
    ● impair the health of human beings.
26 Developments that might cause significant adverse social and economic impacts.
27 Developments involving the storage and use of hazardous materials.

All additions or extensions to such developments shall be accompanied by an EIS, unless specifically exempted by the Director of Planning, or an update of an EIS prepared previously.

involvement is at the discretion of government. 'Scoping' is the main means of ensuring that the procedure is cost-effective and deals only with pertinent impacts. A list of candidate project types, likely to need EIA, is provided. Again, whether or not an EIS will be prepared is made at the discretion of the government. Scoping has a central importance and deserves some detailed attention.

There is no standard or generally accepted list of impacts which must always be investigated in an EIS. The relevant impacts to be investigated depend on the location of the project and the matters considered important in the local decision-making process. For example, one development proposal might entail investigation of five or six impacts while a similar proposal in another location might require examination of only two or three impacts. The contents of one EIS should be regarded as a useful, but not necessarily infallible, guide to the impacts to be discussed in another EIS. Whether or not the impacts discussed in one specific EIS will be investigated in another EIS will depend on the outcome of scoping meetings.

In essence, scoping involves a meeting or a number of meetings between representatives of the main parties having an interest in the proposal and/or its location and environs. The number and type of meetings (whether formal or informal; in public or 'behind closed doors') is at the discretion of the agency co-ordinating the EIS procedure for specific proposals (in the Turks and Caicos Islands this will be the Department of Planning). As one might expect the aim of scoping is to determine the scope of the EIS. The scoping meetings should be led by the Director of Planning assisted by the Environment Adviser. On occasions and at the discretion of the Director of Planning the Environmental Adviser may act in his stead.

In the Turks and Caicos Islands, a suitable forum for scoping would be the present Project Review Group which meets to discuss possible development projects. Representatives of other government ministries, voluntary organizations/public interest groups such as the Chamber of Commerce, could be invited to attend. Similarly, the holding of public meetings to obtain views might occur on occasions. A representative of the applicant must be included in the 'scoping' process. The output of 'scoping' is a consensus (as far as possible) on the impacts to be investigated in the EIA and described/discussed in the EIS.

Impacts identified as requiring assessment should be included in the TOR for the EIS and issued to the applicant, by the Director of Planning, accompanied by the *Regulations on the Preparation and Review of Environmental Impact Statements* (see below).

Once EIA work begins it may be that investigation shows that one or more of the impacts being assessed are of little or no signifiicance or that they can be mitigated. In that case, assessment of these impacts need progress no further and the EIS only contains a short account of the investigation undertaken of the impact(s), the conclusion(s) reached and the reason(s) why further work was abandoned.

Methods to guide scoping

To assist the process of scoping it is important to identify the range of likely significant impacts. The impacts of any project depend on the activities involved (for example, dredging of an access channel) and the characteristics of the proposed site and its environs. Past experience of similar projects is a useful guide, but is insufficient because the impacts of a specific proposal depend on the particular combination of project and site/ surroundings in any one situation.

Assistance is available to guide the initial identification of significant impacts. During the course of the work in the Turks and Caicos Islands a sensitivity index was prepared. This index, in the form of a simple matrix (see Table 18.2), can act as a guide in the 'scoping' process. When an EIS is required the first step would be to identify the project activities expected to occur (for example, channel cutting, water sports). Using knowledge of the natural resource units present at or nearby the proposed site (for example salina or fringing reef), each activity can be checked against each natural resource unit and subsidiary aspects (for example, productivity of each resource unit. From this it is possible to identify natural resource units likely to be highly sensitive to specific project activities (for example, forest/scrub system integrity is highly sensitive to access road construction). Similarly, natural resource units exhibiting moderate to low sensitivities to specific project actions can be identified. Once the likely linkages (impacts) have been determined a decision needs to be made concerning whether investigations and assessments of the interactions between specific project activities and natural resource units are needed. The scaling of sensitivities assists the identification of likely impacts to be referred to in the TOR. It should be noted that sensitivity does not necessarily mean that adverse impacts are to be expected. Sensitivity refers to change(s) which may be adverse or beneficial.

A useful supplementary method to assist scoping is the use of a checklist of impact types. Table 18.3 contains such a list which can be used to guide discussion and focus attention on impacts which *may* require investigation in preparation of an EIS. All of the impacts listed are unlikely to warrant examination in a single EIS.

Another important feature of the proposed EIA Procedure is EIS 'Review'. EISs will be received by the Director of Planning from the project proponent. They will have been prepared by consultants, chosen by the Government to a TOR issued by the Department of Planning. Initially a 'draft' will be submitted to the Director of Planning and the 'draft' EIS will be reviewed to determine that the TOR has been met and that the requirements of the *Regulations on Preparation and Review of Environmental Impact Statements* have been fulfilled. If it is considered that amendments are required or additional work is needed then such work must be undertaken. A 'final' EIS will be prepared and submitted also, to the Director of Planning. The 'final' EIS will be reviewed by the Director of Planning, the Environmental Advisor and representatives of government

Table 18.2   *Interactions between development activities and natural resource units of the Turks and Caicos Islands (accompanied by descriptions of Natural Resource Units sensitivity)*

	Access roads	Boat operations	Canal dredging	Channel cutting	Desalination effluent	Diving operations	Landfill	Sewage disposal	Vegetation clearance	Water sports
Natural Resource Units										
1 Forest/scrub										
System integrity	3		2	1			1		3	
Productivity	3		2	1			1		3	
Component flora	3		2	1			1		3	
Component fauna	2		1	1			1		1	
2 Strand/dune										
System integrity				2						1
Productivity				1						1
Sand stability		1								1
Component flora		1								1
Component fauna										
3 Rock/cave										
System integrity										
Component flora	1			1					2	
Component fauna									1	
4 Freshwater marsh										
System integrity	3		3	3			3			
Productivity	1		3	3			3		2	
Freshwater retention	2		3	3			3			
Component flora	1		2	2			3		2	
Component fauna	1		2	2			3		1	
5 Mangrove/mangal										
System integrity	3		3	3			3		3	
Productivity	2		3	3			3		2	
Water circulation	3		3	3			3			
Component flora	2		2	2	1		3	2	3	
Component fauna	2		3	3	1		3	2	2	
6 Intertidal flat										
System integrity							3			
Productivity					2		3	3		
Component flora		1			1		2	2		1
Component fauna		1			1		2	1		1

Table 18.2 *continued*

	Development activity									
	Access roads	*Boat operations*	*Canal dredging*	*Channel cutting*	*Desalination effluent*	*Diving operations*	*Landfill*	*Sewage disposal*	*Vegetation clearance*	*Water sports*
7 *Salt marsh*										
System integrity	2		3	3			3		2	
Productivity	2		3	3			3		2	
Component flora	2		3	3			3		3	
Component fauna	2		3	3			3		2	
8 *Saltpond/salina*										
System integrity	3	2	3	3			3			
Productivity	2	1	3	3	1		3	2	2	
Water retention	2		3	3			3			
Component flora	1	1	3	3	1		3	2		
Component fauna	1	1	3	3	1		3	2		
9 *Beach*										
System integrity		1		3						
Sand dynamics		1		3		1				1
10 *Sandbank*										
System integrity										
Productivity								2		
Component flora								2		
Component fauna								1		
11 *Seagrass bed*										
System integrity										
Productivity		1			1	1	1	2		1
Sediment Stability		2				2				3
Component flora		1			1	1		2		2
Component fauna		1			1	1		1		2
12 *Fringing reef*										
System integrity		2		2		2				
Physical structure		1		2		2				
Productivity								3		
Component flora		1			1	1	2	2		1
Component fauna		1			1	1	3	2		2
13 *Barrier reef*										
System integrity								1		
Productivity								1		
Component flora						1		1		1
Component fauna						2		1		1

Table 18.2 *continued*

					Development activity					
	Access roads	Boat operations	Canal dredging	Channel cutting	Desalination effluent	Diving operations	Landfill	Sewage disposal	Vegetation clearance	Water sports
14 Patch reef										
System integrity										
Physical structure	1			3		2				
Productivity	1			2				1		
Component flora	1			1		2		1		
Component fauna	1			1		2		1		1
15 Deep reef										
System integrity										
Physical structure						2				
Productivity										
Component flora								1		
Component fauna						2				
16 Underwater cave										
System integrity										
Productivity										
Component flora						2				

Key to symbols: index of sensitivity (that is, potential for damage or alteration to occur).
High = 3
Moderate = 2
Low = 1
Blank space = interaction unlikely to occur

departments (including those involved in a scoping meeting or meetings) and, possibly others, to assist the formulation of advice to be presented to the Physical Planning Board/Member/Governor by the Director of Planning. Guidance on factors to be considered in a review are contained in the '*Regulations*'. Public opinion may be sought at this stage.

One of the most difficult tasks in EIA is to produce a TOR which will assist in production of an EIS which is useful for decision making. To ensure that the EISs will not be too long, too descriptive, full of jargon or unnecessary scientific terms and to ensure they concentrate on analysis and prediction, specific guidance has been given on the preparation and contents of EISs. The guidance was formulated as proposed 'Regulations'

Table 18.3   *Check-list of potential environmental impacts*

The Terms of Reference for a project EIS may cover any or all of, and need not be restricted, to the following impacts of the construction, operational and, where relevant, the decommissioning phases:

1   air, water and land pollutant concentrations at various locations from a source or sources;
2   direct ecological changes resulting from these pollutant concentrations both singly and, where appropriate, in combination covering species of concern (economically, aesthetically and/or because of their rarity), communities and habitats;
3   alterations in ecological processes such as transfer of energy through food chains, decomposition and bioaccumulation which might affect, indirectly, species, communities and habitats;
4   ecological consequences of direct destruction of existing habitat(s) (from actions such as dumping, vegetation clearance and filling);
5   changes in existing sedimentation processes and sand budgets and potential for erosion;
6   ecological consequences of changes in sedimentation processes;
7   noise/vibration levels;
8   odour;
9   induced traffic generation and resulting pollution, ecological impacts, and potential for increase in accidents;
10   changes in sociocultural and socio-economic patterns covering:
   ● decline in valued resources, for example, fish and social/economic consequences;
   ● direct/indirect employment generation;
   ● in-migration and resulting demographic changes;
   ● infrastructure provision (roads, school places, health facilities);
   ● fiscal matters;
   ● cultural changes (including possible conflict) arising from foreign immigrants and/or tourists;
11   health consequences of any or all of the above.

---

to accompany the Physical Planning Ordinance, thus having the force of law. The proposed 'Regulations' are presented below. They will be useful at two stages. First, in preparation of TOR, along with the outcome of scoping and second, in the review of draft/final EISs. It will, of course, be used by those preparing the EISs to ensure that the EISs comply with the law.

Proposed regulations on preparation and review of Environmental Impacts Statements (EISs)

Regulations on the preparation and review of EISs are required to implement the EIA procedures. This section contains the draft contents for regulations to be prepared by the legal officers to the Government.

Definitions

Environmental Impact Statement (EIS)
Report presenting the results of an Environmental Impact Assessment (EIA) implemented for a proposed development activity.

Environmental Impact Assessment (EIA)
Work undertaken to predict, describe and evaluate the expected impacts of a proposed development activity.

Construction phase
Period in which a project, installation or development is being built.

Operational phase
Period in which a project, installation or development is working and generating income through production of goods or provision of services.

Decommissioning phase
Period in which a project, installation or development is abandoned, dismantled, sealed, rendered harmless and/or rehabilitated. Occurs, but not necessarily immediately, after production of goods or provision of services ceases.

Form of an Environmental Impact Statement

1 No EIS shall be more than 100 pages in length (excluding appendices) except those prepared for 'exceptional' proposed projects likely to cause a wide range of significant impacts. Authorization for an EIS to be longer than the 100 page limit may only be obtained from the Director of Planning.
2 An executive summary of no more than five pages must be included at the beginning of the EIS. This summary is to present and highlight the main impact issues pertinent to a decision regarding the proposed project.
3 A glossary of technical terms and units must be provided and use of technical terms should be the minimum consistent with clarity of expression.
4 Cross-referencing must be clear and simple to follow.

5   A full reference list of publications, reports and other documents studied, quoted or otherwise utilized must be provided using the Harvard system of citation as given in the British Standard *Recommendations for Citing Publications by Bibliographical References* (BS 5605) published in 1978 by the British Standards Institute of London.
6   Maximum use must be made of visual aids (maps, drawings, photographs, tables and diagrams) to minimize need for written description in the text.
7   All visual aids must be well-labelled and legible.
8   All units must be given in SI (Système Internationale) and Imperial nomenclature.
9   Twenty copies (20) of the draft and final EISs must be provided to the Director of Planning.

Content of an Environmental Impact Statement

Notwithstanding the requirements of any specific 'Terms of Reference' issued by the Department of Planning all EISs must contain the following:

1   Brief description of local environmental and socio-economic conditions (including health) summarizing the essential elements of the environmental/socio-economic systems in the locality and the trends (if known) occurring. Those aspects to be described must relate to the requirements of the Terms of Reference. This section must not exceed 10 per cent of the number of pages in the final EIS.
2   Brief description of the proposed development activity covering:
   ● need
   ● objectives
   ● technical details
3   Brief description of the time period for which impacts are predicted and the geographic boundaries selected to define the study area, including the reasons for the selection of the time/space boundaries.
4   An account of the prediction and assessment of each impact from the construction, operational and, where relevant, the decommissioning phases.

   Prediction
   Wherever possible, impact predictions should be expressed quantitatively. If models are used to predict impacts (for example a hydraulic model of a tidal regime), a description of the model (its assumptions, strengths and weaknesses), reasons for the choice and data outputs must be provided. This information must be presented in a technical appendix.

   Assessment
   For each impact the magnitude of the predicted change must be calculated, wherever possible, against the predicted state of the

environmental/socio-economic factors at the same future point in time, but on the assumption that the proposed development does not occur.

For each impact, information must be supplied on:
- whether it is reversible/irreversible,
- whether it is adverse/beneficial,
- likelihood of its occurrence,
- spatial boundaries,
- time period within which it will occur if different from overall time period for all impact predictions identified in 3 above.

5   A discussion of the distribution of these impacts in time/space to identify the mix of these impacts on people/communities and species/habitats to identify, in particular, localities likely to be stressed by a number of adverse impacts. An assessment of the overall significance of such cumulative impacts must be provided.

6   Measures to prevent or reduce significant adverse impacts/enhance beneficial effects and an assessment of their likely success.

7   Description of residual adverse impacts which cannot be mitigated.

8   Description of monitoring schemes.

9   Discussion of potential uses of the environment which will be prevented or rendered less productive due to adverse impacts.

10 Discussion of possible effects of the environmental impacts of a project on the ability of the project to achieve its objectives.

Conclusions

There is a growing realization and agreement that EIA procedures in developing countries should be cost-effective and that this basic requirement means that EIA practice, as found in many 'developed' countires, is perhaps too slow, cumbersome and expensive for most developing countries. There appears to be a need for a streamlined and simplified approach to utilize EIA more quickly and efficiently; in EIA jargon this has been described as a 'fast-track' system (Sadler, 1988).

This viewpoint is based on a pragmatic concept of EIA as being, primarily, a decision-making aid. As such EISs have to meet certain 'requirements', for example, they have to assist decision makers to consider environmental aspects in conjunction (sometimes, perhaps, in competition!) with technical, economic and political factors. This means EISs should only cover the main issues relevant to a decision, be short, easy to read and give clear statements of findings. Seen from this perspective, they are not scientific analyses of all impacts from a project which only produce conclusions once all relevant data have been collected and interpreted. This does not mean, however, that scientific method and scientists need not be used – they are a necessity – but their input/role needs to be controlled carefully to ensure that they are applied to answer the needs of the decision makers, not the requirements of their scientific peers and the 'academic' criteria of published papers. The 'Regulations' have been devised to ensure that the EISs produced are pertinent to decision-making. In addition, the strong, central control of the Department of Planning and the reliance on a single consultancy should ensure that, after an initial familiarization process, all participants in the EIA procedures know their role and the needs/requirements/activities of others taking part in the EIA system.

The use of 'scoping' and production of 'draft' EISs are significant. 'Scoping' aims to ensure that the EIA only addresses the main impacts/issues, *thus saving valuable scarce resources*, and 'draft' EISs allow the opportunity for government and others to determine that the work has been done according to the TOR and the 'Regulations'. This enables alterations and additions to be made before submission of the final EIS. This should ensure that the final EIS is a useful document and avoid the need to make changes at such a late stage in the EIA process.

The problems faced by developing countries were outlined above. Many challenges confront those responsible for introducing EIA procedures and those involved in managing and adapting existing procedures. It is believed that the main features of the proposed system are relevant outside small island developing economies because such countries share most of the problems faced by all developing countries. Experience of the system proposed for the Turks and Caicos Islands can only be evaluated after a few years' implementation. Such an evaluation would be essential, but we must await the passage of time to find out if the system is able to cope successfully with the context in which it must operate.

References

Biswas, A. and Geping, Qu. (eds.) (1987) *Environmental Impact Analysis for Developing Countries*, Tycooly International, London.

Beanlands, G. E. and Duinker, P. N. (1983) *An Ecological Framework for Environmental Assessment in Canada*, Federal Environmental Assessment Review Office, Hull, Quebec.

Cocossis, H. (1987) Planning for Islands. *Ekistics* **54** (323/324), 84–87.

Lim, G.-C. (1985) Theory and practice of EIA implementation: a comparative study of three developing countries. *Environmental Impact Assessment Review* **5**(2), 133–153.

Marshall, D. *et al.* (1988) *Final statement on impact assessment for international development*, Federal Environmental Assessment Review Office, Vancouver.

Monosowski, E. (1984) *EIA in Developing Countries: Problems/Possibilities of Application.* Paper presented at International Seminar on Environment Impact Assessment, 8–21 July, 1984, University of Aberdeen, Scotland, UK.

Sadler, B. (1988) *Impact Assessment, Development Planning and International Assistance in Post-Brundtland Perspective*, Institute of the North American West, Victoria, Canada.

Sammy, G. and Ahmad, Y. (1985) *Guidelines to Environmental Impact Assessment in Developing Countries*, Hodder and Stoughton, London.

United Nations Environment Programme (1987) Principles of environmental impact assessment. *Environmental Policy and Law*, **17**, 36–37.

Part IV

Summary and Recommendations

19
Summary and recommendations.
Asit K. Biswas

An International Conference on Environmental Impact Analysis for Developing Countries was held in Hyatt Regency Hotel, New Delhi, India, during 28th November to 2nd December 1988. The Conference was organized by the Pollution Control Research Institute, Hardwar, India, with the support and co-operation of the Government of India through Bharat Heavy Electricals Ltd (BHEL), United Nations Development Programme, United Nations Environment Programme, United Nations Industrial Development Organization, International Association for Clean Technology, International Society for Ecological Modelling and International Water Resources Association.

While welcoming the distinguished guests and experts, Mr P. S. Gupta, Chairman and Managing Director, BHEL highlighted that over the years, mankind has rather ruthlessly neglected the environmental protection aspects in the name of industrial development, which has resulted in large-scale pollution of air, water and soil and has contributed to major deforestation. All this is seriously telling upon the living conditions on our planet and threatens to raise the earth's temperature through the green-house effect.

In his address Mr Gamil M. Hamdy, Resident Representative, UNDP, New Delhi, brought out that through fuller knowledge and wiser action we can achieve for ourselves and posterity a better life in an environment more in keeping with the human needs and hopes.

In the keynote address, H E Mr Z. R. Ansari, Minister of Environment and Forests, pointed out that the procedures have been laid down to ensure environmental considerations are taken into account while selecting technology and sites. While assessing the impact for a certain industry, all the necessary parameters including social costs are also to be taken into consideration.

Inaugurating the Conference, H E Mr J. Vengala Rao, Minister of Industry, emphasized that environmental protection is as important in developing countries as in developed countries. However, developing countries like India, on their way to industrialization, could usefully adopt the experience of developed countries. India has been giving utmost importance to economic and industrial growth that is consistent with environmental preservation.

As the Minister of Industry, H E Mr Vengala Rao, had to endeavour always to strike a balance between industrial growth and environmental protection. Industry has environmental impacts in terms of consumption of raw maerials and discharge of waste products. There is often conflict between environmentalists and people interested in growth and industrial expansion. He pointed out that the advocates of industry argue that industrial growth will be hampered if environmental regulations are applied too rigidly but the environmentalists maintain that unless there is a certain rigidity in the enforcement of anti-pollution regulations, the long-term environmental impact due to unregulated industry is injurious to society at large. In India, legal requirements for environmental clearance of projects have been made quite strict. While these environmental measures will require additional capital costs as well as extra time for project clearance, the Government considers these costs worthwhle for the long-term interest of the country as a whole.

The Minister further said that developing countries must strike a reasonable balance between industrial growth and environmental preservation. The underlying concept has to be that human beings must approach nature with reverence. The bounty of nature in all its aspects should be used with caution and restraint. Development must avoid over-exploitation and abuse of nature and resources. Ultimately human happiness will depend upon our ability to live in harmony and peace with nature.

In addition to the opening and valedictory sessions, the Conference was organized into 13 major technical sessions: EIA Methodology, EIA for Developing Countries, Water Pollution Impacts, Environmental Impact of Water Systems, Noise Impacts and Case Studies, Waste Management and Land Use Impacts, Air Pollution Impacts, EIA Case Studies, Biological Impacts, Environmental Impact of Industry, Environmental Impact of Thermal Power Plants, EIA Case Studies from Industry, and Education and Training for EIA.

A total of 109 papers were presented during the 13 sessions over a period of $4\frac{1}{2}$ days. These papers were selected by an international panel of experts from 362 abstracts initially received by the Pollution Control Research Institute. As to be expected for a Conference with such a comprehensive scope, discussions were wide ranging and covered practically all aspects of environmental impact assessment.

Since it will not be useful to review all the issues that were raised during the Conference, the present summary covers primarily the main issues raised by the participants.

1 Issues complementary between environment and development

There was complete unanimity among the participants about the need for a proper balance between environmental conservation and the overall development. N. C. Thanh (Thailand) and D. C. Tam (Canada) summed up this view that environment must not be ignored and development must not be impeded. Most of the debates so far on environment and development issues have often involved considerable amount of emotion from all sides but not enough reasoning and facts. Ideally, every environment–development issue should be analysed objectively and dispassionately so that decisions can be made which will enable development to proceed without destroying the resource base and the environment on which the very process of development depends. For this to occur, it would be necessary to create rational and sensible environmental awareness in all people concerned: planners, environmentalists, engineers, economists and other related professionals, politicians and the general public.

2 EIA must be made mandatory

It was agreed that all developing countries must strive for a legal framework which would make EIA mandatory for new projects or expansion of existing projects. While the legal basis for carrying out EIA is an essential prerequisite, it was cautioned that it is one of the several other considerations which need to be satisfied concurrently in order that the environment can be protected.

The countries that make EIA mandatory must have the appropriate institutional framework within which such assessments can be objectively carried out. Equally, it is important to ensure that adequate manpower with appropriate expertise is available within the country to carry out the impact assessments and to review them objectively. An example was given of a country, where EIA has been made mandatory for several years, but out of several thousand projects subjected to EIA, not even one was ever denied clearance.

3 Current EIA methodologies and processes are flawed

Current EIA methodologies and processes are seriously flawed, and not surprisingly their application to developing countries leave much to be desired. EIA, as it is practised at present, is an art and not a science. Furthermore, EIA process has been defined in different ways in different developing countries. No two developing countries appear to have defined it in the same way. As the Executive Director of the United Nations Environment Programme, Dr Mostafa K. Tolba, in his message to the Conference, pointed out the linkages of EIA to the 'planning of social and economic developments are still not clear. What is needed most are cost-effective and efficient means of implementing EIA as part of the approaches to achieving sustainable development.'

All development projects have both negative and positive impacts but EIA, as it is currently practised, only concentrates on negative environmental impacts. It is unfortunate that the positive impacts are now completely ignored, as Prof. Asit K. Biswas, President of the International

Society for Ecological Modelling, pointed out during the valedictory session of the Conference. EIA addresses itself to both positive and negative impacts. The overall thrust of EIA must be shifted to maximizing the positive environmental impacts and minimizing the adverse impacts rather than focusing exclusively on negative impacts. Only by taking such a holistic approach, environmental conservation can be practised and enhanced.

Despite numerous EIA handbooks, manuals and guidelines prepared by national organizations and academic institutions, participants felt that the EIA reports are still too academic, bureaucratic, mechanistic and voluminous. Often they do not concentrate on major environmental issues but provide lengthy deliberations on fringe issues that could be counterproductive and consume resources that are more urgently needed for analysis of other important problems.

4 EIA reports are mostly too mechanistic

An objective analysis of EIAs carried out in developing countries indicate that they are often too mechanistic. For example, waste discharges and effluent emissions are generally described in terms of concentration levels in the atmosphere and surface waters. The entire emphasis is on whether the concentration levels are permissible or not. What these discharges and emissions actually mean in terms of human and animal health and the biota are mostly ignored. If indeed there is any discussion, it tends to be somewhat general or superficial.

Analysts often appear to have no clear idea as to what type of information is needed by the decision-makers. Accordingly they may count the number of trees in one area, but may not consider what could be the long-term impacts on the forest due to the increased levels of pollution. It is assumed that as long as concentration levels are within permissible limits, no other problem exists.

Equally, many EIA reports now contain numerous tables of collected data, without any clear idea about their relevance and even necessity. In many developing countries there is now far too much emphasis on data collection but not enough on their analysis, interpretation and their environmental implications.

5 Lack of follow-up monitoring

EIA, as it is practised now, ends immediately after the environmental clearance of a project has been received. Compliance monitoring is seldom carried out, either by the project authorities or by the responsible government agencies. This practice is contributing to several problems, among which are the following:

a) Pseudo-analysis: In the absence of any follow-up monitoring, many pseudo-analyses of EIA, are now being carried out with the main objective of only getting the projects cleared quickly, for implementation irrespective of the environmental costs. The whole purpose of such pseudo-analysis is to justify projects based on 'manufactured' data and/or deliberately skewed analysis. Such pseudo-analysis, whenever carried out, circumvents the whole purpose of EIA.

b) Prediction difficulties: In most EIAs of major development projects, it is impossible to predict with complete reliability all potential environmental impacts, their magnitudes and times of occurrence. Uncertainty is unavoidable in most environmental prediction. Thus, follow-up monitoring must be an essential requirement, if environmental impacts are to be properly managed.

c) Effectiveness of EIA without follow-up monitoring, it is not possible to judge the overall effectiveness of any EIA. Proper monitoring and evaluation are essential to ensure that the recommendations made by the study will actually be implemented. Reliable data on post-project observed impacts and their comparison with the predicted ones can give a clear indication of the accuracy of the earlier EIA predictions. Such results could be successfully used to develop more cost-effective methodology in the future.

6 *Data availability and reliability*

One of the most important constraints for carrying out reliable EIAs in developing countries, within a reasonable timeframe, was identified by the participants to be poor data availability and reliability. It was pointed out that very often much more environmental data exist in a developing country than people generally believe. However, poor or non-existent data retrieval and management system, inter-Ministerial and/or inter-institutional, rivalry, unnecessary classification of data as secret or confidential, and official apathy, often ensure that data are not easily available. Often people who need the information may not even know who is collecting various environmental data, where they are stored and how these can be obtained.

An equally serious problem is the reliability of available data. While much of the data collected are of reasonable quality, equally there are several instances of unreliable data which were collected at wrong places, or with improperly calibrated equipment, incorrectly analysed, or simply 'manufactured'. It is a very difficult, expensive and time-consuming process to separate unreliable data from good data within any given data set.

There is an urgent need to develop proper environmental data management systems, which are easily available to the analysts within reasonable time and cost. Since the availability of computers is not a major problem in most developing countries, it should be possible to develop appropriate environmental data management systems.

7 Cost-effectiveness of EIA

Opponents of EIA have sometimes claimed that the benefits from such assessments are outweighed by the delays in project implementation, which generally tend to increase their cost. While on the basis of the present practice there is partial validity to this claim, many speakers pointed out that the main reason for such delays was that EIA was either not properly conceived or not integrated in the project cycle from the beginning. Often, only after project planning has been completed, people think about EIA. This is why delays sometimes could occur in project implementation. Properly conceived EIAs must be integrated in the project planning right from the initial stage. This would not only improve the overall quality of the project but would also reduce substantially or even eliminate, any delay mainly due to EIA. EIA costs are found to be relatively small, when compared with the total project costs.

An important observation was that even when the quality of EIA predictions were somewhat poor, and they caused cost and time overruns, they did, however, contribute to measurable environmental benefits.

It was argued by Professor Biswas that in developing countries often 'best' is the enemy of 'good'. What one should be aiming for is a good EIA study that could identify, say some 80 per cent of the potential environmental impacts within a reasonable time frame and acceptable cost. If proper follow-up monitoring is ensured, whatever may be the lacunaè in the analysis, these can be identified in time and appropriate remedial actions can be taken.

8 Presentation of EIA results

Many of the participants raised the issue of poor presentation of EIA results. For complex EIAs, the results often are presented in several bulky volumes. Very few people, if any, actually have time to study such reports in depth, let alone understand them. There is an urgent need to present the results of such analyses succinctly and clearly. To the extent it is possible, attempts should be made to present results in graphic forms which could be easily understandable by non-experts. As computers become widely available in developing countries, their costs continue to decline and the technology of computer-graphics improves substantially, computers should play a more and more important role not only for carrying out analysis but also for displaying EIA results graphically.

9 Public Participation

During the entire conference, considerable debate centred on what should be the role of public participation in the EIA process. The overall view of the participants was that the public currently has very little say in the process in nearly all developing countries. It is difficult, often even impossible, to obtain or consult copies of the EIA Reports. The public has an equally limited, if any, role in most developing countries to question or comment on the quality of the reports or conduct of the environmental clearance process.

While an overwhelming number of participants favoured more public involvement, there were a few dissenting voices preaching caution due to such problems as illiteracy and ignorance that currently exist among many who could be involved in the process.

10 Education and Training

Many argued that one of the most important factors that could significantly improve the EIA process is good education and training. Currently very few educational and training courses exist in developing countries that properly consider various EIA methodologies available in depth. Information on the legal and regulatory frameworks and institutional arrangements are also necessary. Education and training processes are important since the fundamental factors behind all EIA predictions are still the best professional judgement and/or experience with similar projects earlier.

Both short-term and long-term courses are necessary. These courses, however, must be multidisciplinary, and the focus should be on the practical and operational aspects of EIA and not on theoretical implications.

In his closing address, H E Madhavsinh Solanki, the Indian Minister of Planning, said the view that the pursuit of environmental and development goals could be combined has now been accepted, and India has endeavoured to incorporate this philosophy in her development planning and also to devise mechanism to operationalize it in practice. India's Seventh Five Year Plan (1985–90) states that 'if the gains in productivity are to be sustained, resources must also continue to be available over time. This requires that, while providing for current needs the resources be so managed as to enable sustainable development.'

The Minister pointed out that a country like India faces many problems due to the enormity of her development needs and the paucity of resources. But in the area of the environment, India has three distinct advantages. First, the country as a comparatively 'late-comer' in the area of the environment, can learn from the experiences of other countries that are ahead of her. Second, India effectively uses the planning mechanism for steering and guiding socio-economic development which provides a balance between the public and the private sectors as well as short-term and long-term interests of the country. Thus a conscious effort can be made to incorporate long-term environmental considerations in the development programmes in a systematic manner. Third, most of the large projects in the area of industry, power and infrastructure are in the public sector, where again it is easier to take care of the environmental considerations in accordance with the public policy and long-term social interest. The fact that the Pollution Control Research Institute of Bharat Heavy Electricals Ltd, a major public sector undertaking, organized a major international EIA Conference is a manifestation of that public concern.

Recommendations

On the basis of papers presented and the ensuing discussions, there was general agreement among the participants on the following recommendations:

1   EIA should be made mandatory in a phased manner. The phasing can be done based on priorities and expansion of infrastructure. Laws and regulations, however, by themselves, are not enough. All efforts should be made to ensure that the legal requirements are actually implemented. UNEP and UNDP should assist those countries that require assistance, to develop appropriate legal frameworks and their implementation.

2   EIA methodologies should incorporate requirement for climatic, social and cultural characteristics. Methodologies that are currently available for EIA are generally not appropriate for developing countries. It is necessary to ensure that the methodologies developed would enable developing countries to carry out EIA within limited cost and expertise available and that it can be completed within a reasonable timeframe. Equally, EIA must consider both positive and negative environmental impacts. National and international organizations should work together to develop operational EIA methodologies.

3   An objective and reliable review of the current status of the effectiveness of using EIA in developing countries, methodologies used, and their relative merits, and constraints, main features of their implementation processes and the emerging trends be carried out. As a first step, it is recommended that UNEP, and the Asian Development Bank (ADB) prepare such a review for the Asian region.

4   For establishing clear and unambiguous guidelines for EIA that are acceptable to relevant Ministries, United Nations Agencies, Asian and other Development Banks and bilateral aid organizations, it is recommended that National Workshops be organized, which would include all the relevant parties.

5   It is recommended that UNEP and International Society for Ecological Modelling collaborate together to prepare a handbook on good EIA case studies from developing countries in the field of air, water and solid wastes. Such a book would be useful to analysts in developing countries.

6   Monitoring and follow-up work is required to see how the forecasts made by the initial EIA studies compare with the actual impacts after the implementation of the projects. It is recommended that national and international organizations collaborate on a series of specific case studies where EIA forecasts made during the project approval phase are compared with the observed impacts after implementation. Results of such intercomparison studies should be made widely available.

7   Risk analysis and social impact analysis should be integrated within the framework of EIA methodologies. UNEP and ADB in collaboration with IACT and ISEM, should sponsor research to develop operational methodologies for risk analysis and social impact analysis.

8   Public participation is an important requirement for EIA, UNEP, UNIDO and UNDP should sponsor studies to review the extent of public participation and their relative effectiveness in conducting EIA studies in various developing countries. Such comparative studies would assist countries to determine the best alternative available to them to ensure public involvement in EIA.

9   Education and training in EIA are essential for all developing countries. All international and national organizations should encourage education and training on EIA to develop adequate expertise in developing countries.

Index